A Quick Index to Twenty Essential Questions

BUILDING TYPE BASICS FOR

senior living

BUILDING TYPE BASICS FOR

senior living

Stephen A. Kliment, Series Founder and Editor

BRADFORD PERKINS
with
J. DAVID HOGLUND, DOUGLAS KING, ERIC COHEN

WILEY

JOHN WILEY & SONS, INC.

For general information on our other products and services or for technical support, please contact our Customer Care Department within the United States at (800) 762-2974, outside the United States at (317) 572-3993 or fax (317) 572-4002.

Wiley also publishes its books in a variety of electronic formats. Some content that appears in print may not be available in electronic books. For more information about Wiley products, visit our web site at www.wiley.com.

Library of Congress Cataloging-in-Publication Data:

Building type basics for senior living / by Perkins Eastman Architects.
    p. cm.—(Building type basics series)
Includes bibliographical references and index.
  ISBN 0-471-22672-6 (Cloth)
  1. Aged—Institutional care—United States—Planning. 2. Old age
homes—United States—Design and construction. 3. Day care centers for
the aged—United States—Design and construction. 4. Nursing
homes—United States—Design and construction. 5. Congregate
housing—United States—Design and construction. 6. Life care
communities—United States—Design and construction. 7. Retirement
communities—United States—Design and construction. I. Perkins Eastman
Architects. II. Series.
  HV1454.2.U6B85 2003
  725'.56'0973--dc21
                                    2003011762

Printed in the United States of America.

10 9 8 7 6 5

For Margery Isabella Blair Perkins, who made writing and research enjoyable for her children, and for Charles Pruitt, Jr., who was a creative pioneer in conceiving and developing sensitive living and care environments for the aging.

CONTENTS

CONTENTS

PREFACE

STEPHEN A. KLIMENT *Series Founder and Editor*

As author Bradford Perkins points out, the over-65 age group makes up the fastest-growing segment of the population. By the year 2000, the number of "old" people (over 65 years) numbered more than 31 million and the "very old" (over 85) in excess of 3 million. By 2030, these figures are expected to reach 71 million and 9 million, respectively. Many of these will need special housing that will fit their needs and preferences.

Until the 1980s, the approach to housing the aged was anything but admirable. Individuals not able to live in their own homes had to fall back on an often unattractive mix of highly institutional nursing homes, personal care homes of inconsistent quality, and a handful of retirement communities. Recent efforts to remedy this state of affairs have yielded some good outcomes, however. Among the most significant is the concept that the needs of the aged are not reducible to a single, limited set of design solutions.

The result has been a surge in the design and construction of different facility types, including adult day-care; long-term care; assisted living; independent/congregate living; special assisted living for persons with dementia and Alzheimer's disease; hospices; continuing care retirement communities (CCRCs); and communities for active adults. Demand for these types of buildings will soar, given the demographic trends cited above. The task of planning and designing these facilities is not simple, and the author's firm Perkins Eastman has emerged as one of the key architectural organizations to meet this growing and changing market.

This volume in Wiley's "Building Types Basics" series provides planning and design guidelines, as well as admonitions and lessons to be learned from completed buildings of a variety of types. It is geared to the informational needs of architects, planners, urban designers, and professional consultants, as well as sponsors and administrators.

Building Type Basics for Senior Living, like the other volumes published in the Wiley series to date, is not a coffee-table book lavish with color photography but meager in usable content. Instead, it contains hands-on information that architects, their clients, and consultants require in their work, especially in the crucial early phases of a project. Students at schools of architecture, planning, urban design, and landscape architecture will also find the volume useful, as a kind of Cliffs Notes to get a head start on a studio problem.

Following the format of the other volumes in the series, *Senior Living* is tightly organized for ease of use. The volume responds to a set of twenty most commonly asked questions about a building type in the early phases of its design. The twenty questions include predesign (programming) guidelines; details of the project delivery process; design concerns unique to the building type; site planning; codes and ADA matters;

energy and environmental challenges; engineering systems; lighting and acoustic pointers; signs and wayfinding; renovation issues; and cost and feasibility factors.

For a listing of the twenty questions, see the endpapers at the front and back of this volume. You may use these endpapers also as an index.

I hope you find this volume inspiring and helpful.

ACKNOWLEDGMENTS

Many more than the four authors listed on the cover made significant contributions to this book.

Perkins Eastman colleagues include:

- Stephanie Danes, AIA, and Laura Nettleton, AIA, provided input to the text related to sustainability issues.

- Susan DiMotta, ASID, contributed to all text on interior materials and design issues, as well as providing a review of images.

- Mitchell Green, AIA, contributed his experience, as an architect and as the general manager, Development Division, Half Century More, Japan's leading developer of facilities for the aging.

- Sarah Mechling provided image coordination, with advisement and oversight by Gretchen Bank.

- Martin Siefering, AIA, provided a review of the text related to technologies.

- Allan Schlossberg, AIA, provided most of the text for the section on programming geriatric medical facilities.

- Diana Sung, AIA, and Daniel Zito, AIA, provided a review of the text on adult day care and skilled nursing settings.

- Mark Weiner, FACHE, contributed his experience in health services administration, program development, marketing, and corporate planning to the review of most sections of the book.

- Charles Williams provided a review of text related to building materials and maintenance.

- And Erica Schwartz and Rebecca Perkins acted as research assistants.

Other consultants include:

- Paul Bello, PE, of AKF Engineers provided review of the text related to mechanical, electrical, plumbing, and fire-safety systems.

- Nancy Cummings, MBA, vice president and director, Marjorie Doyle Rockwell Center, for her review of text related to staffing and care for persons with Alzheimer's.

- Daniel Herman, managing director of Zeigler and Company Senior Living Finance provided a review of the text related to financing issues.

- Georges Jaquemart, PE, AICP, of Buckhurst, Fish, and Jaquemart contributed his experience as a planner to a review of the text related to site issues.

- Keith Loo, PE of Goldstein Associates provided review of the text related to structural issues.

- Nicholas Park and Charles Simko of Prosource Systems provided a review of the text related to low voltage and communications.

CHAPTER 1

PROGRAM (PREDESIGN)

According to the 2000 U.S. census, the 65 and over population now exceeds 35 million and is growing rapidly. Demographic projections for 2025 show the influence of the baby boomers, with the over-65 population growing by more than 80 percent, the over 75 by 52 percent, and over 85 by 42 percent. By 2030 almost 70 million people in the U.S. will be over 65. More people are living longer, and the growth of the over-100 age group is even more startling. In 2000 approximately 100,000 were over 100 years old, and by 2050 this figure is expected to reach a staggering total of almost 1 million. As a result, meeting the housing and care needs of this rapidly growing segment of the population has become a major challenge for public policy, sponsors and operators of facilities for the aging, and the design professions.

The increasing numbers of older people, combined with changes in the way these people want to live their later years and their expectation of a higher quality of life, are creating the need for new care and housing options. Thus, new ideas about senior care and housing have developed that look at these environments not simply as health-care facilities but as seniors' homes.

The fastest-growing part of the older population is also the group that most needs appropriately designed environments.

These demographic trends are not unique to the United States. The world's population aged 65 or over is expected to

> To ensure success in remedying existing problems and to avoid creating new ones, design should start with a clear understanding of the population. *(Hiatt 1991)*

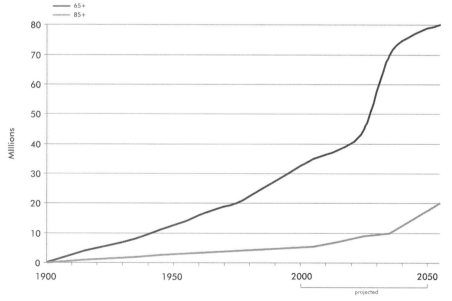

◀ *Total number of persons age 65 or older in the United States, by age group, 1900 to 2050, in millions. U.S. Census Bureau, Decennial Census Data and Population Projections.*

Note: Data for the years 2000 to 2050 are middle-series projections of the population.
Reference population: These data refer to the resident population.
Source: U.S. Census Bureau, Decennial Census Data and Population Projections.

increase from 6.9 percent to 16.4 percent by 2050. European countries have been facing the challenges of a rapidly aging population and low birth rates. The rising cost of care, services, and housing for the aging has led to public policy changes in many countries. Asia is preparing for what many are referring to as the "Aging Tsunami." In Japan, for example, there are already more people over the age of 60 than under the age of 29.

In many countries, these demographic changes are coupled with changes in the makeup of the traditional multigenerational family. Older adults are living alone, using informal support to meet their needs for services or relying on primary-care health services that offer inadequate support for their specialized needs.

The United States is also challenged by demographics that speak of a more diverse population. Ethnic groups, particularly Hispanic and Asian, will present unique cross-cultural requirements, and new affinity groups will rise as "communities" are developed around shared values such as sexual preference.

▶ This couple is part of the fastest growing segment of the population in most developed countries.

The implications of these changes are extensive, because they demand a much more flexible system that combines services with housing. The aging in all countries have unique needs that must be recognized by those who provide them with care and housing. Most older adults will never occupy a residence designed specifically for aging persons of certain abilities; instead most will stay at home and rely on family or community-based services. The environment as a whole—including airports, shopping malls, and urban centers—must be planned and designed to respond to a large growing segment of the population that will, over time, move a little slower, grasp a little weaker, react less responsively, and process information in different ways. The built environment has a greater impact on the quality of life of those who require a more supportive setting than any other major demographic group. If properly designed, the living facility can enhance an older person's independence, dignity, health, and enjoyment of life. If poorly planned and detailed, it can imprison, confuse, and depress.

In recent decades, the direct impact of design on the aging has become more widely recognized by both the general public and design professionals. Prior to this time, the frail elderly who could no longer live in their own homes had few, if any, good alternatives. Most of the very old saw a shared room at an "old folks home" as the only option. For the majority, it was a dreaded choice; tens of thousands of families can tell stories of the trauma of having to place Mom or Dad in an institution. By 1980, there was a growing demand for more attractive options that would meet health and support service needs within more residential settings. Lifestyle options for retirement have had to adapt to a changing clientele who are older with more needs but expect higher-quality housing and activities than even a decade ago.

Older adults are looking for more options. Today's 70-year-olds are better educated, generally have more money than their predecessors, and expect to be physically and intellectually stimulated. Baby boomers are upsetting the spectrum once again as they look for options for their parents as well as their vision for their own later life. Products of postwar consumerism, they have quality, service, and delivery expectations that do not fit with traditional patterns of health-care and aging service delivery. This book provides an overview of the major issues involved in the planning, design, and development of specialized environments for this new group of aging Americans. Specifically, this book describes the issues associated with each of the eight major building types within the general framework of design for aging. The following are general definitions of these eight types. Please see the following sections for more detailed descriptions, as well as distinctions among the types.

Geriatric Outpatient Clinic: A specialized medical clinic that focuses on the wide range of physical, psychological, social, and medical needs related primarily to aging

Adult Day Care/Adult Day Health: A daily program that provides a varying blend of social and medical support during daytime hours for those still residing in their own homes or with their families

Nursing Homes/Long-Term Care: Traditionally, a medically based model of care for very frail seniors requiring 24-hour care

Assisted Living Residences: A catchall name for a wide variety of programs that balance housing with support of "activities of daily living" (ADLs), such as bathing, dressing, and so on

Dementia/Alzheimer's Care: A specialized program and setting crafted to meet the special needs of people with cognitive impairment, that is, impairment of abilities related to thought, perception, and memory

Independent/Residential Living Apartments/Congregate Housing: Housing with services designed for the elderly such as one meal per day, housekeeping, and activities

Continuing Care Retirement Community (CCRC): A model of retirement living that provides a full spectrum of services and living accommodations, from independent living through assisted living and nursing care

Active Adult Communities: A variety of lifestyle choice models of living that may simply provide more carefree living with an appropriately designed residence linked to active recreation, entertainment, and continuing education options as well as proximity to healthcare fitness and other community services

THE AGING PROCESS AND DESIGN

Housing for the elderly has not traditionally attracted the level of design inquiry required to transform it from boilerplate solutions based on older or inappropriate models. Unfortunately, many of the existing design criteria are prescriptive, often contained in codes in the

> It is often said that the value and meaning of a civilization can be documented from the record it leaves in the form of architecture, and that the true measure of the compassion and civility of a society lies in how well it treats its frail older people. (Regnier 1994, p. vii)

form of minimum square-footage requirements and standards. Part of the dread experienced by those contemplating the nursing home option is directly attributable to the acute-care hospital model that historically served as the basis for the codes that govern virtually all nursing home design. Social concepts of privacy, independence and personalization were not often viewed as a priority under this model. Accessibility has also been poorly understood, with its singular focus on dimensions based on younger partially paralyzed veterans in wheelchairs. For many older adults, the changes attributed to aging are subtle, often invisible to the observer, and shifting with time.

To begin to understand why the growing volume of senior housing is both necessary and inevitable, it is important to understand some of the basics of the aging process in a human being, with its range of barriers and limitations, and to see how it impacts environmental design. The interaction of social and psychological issues may affect the individual's dignity, impeding participation in a full and complete life in ways not unlike the effects of physical limitations.

Because of their numbers and increased political activity, the expanding over-65 age group has become a distinctive social group with a life expectancy nearing 73 years for males and 79 for females. According to the 2000 U.S. census, women outnumber men by more than 10 to 7 in the 65-and-older age group. (Women over 65 outnumber men by 20.6 million to 14.4 million.) Although statistical data creates a distinctive group called "elderly," it is incorrect to think that there is any "average" or "typical" older person. Like the rest of us,

they have different pasts and expectations of life shaped by divergent ethnic and racial backgrounds, role models, lifestyles, personal experiences, health histories, and familial settings.

Aging is often viewed from two related perspectives: the study of the biological process (geriatrics) and the study of the social passage that occurs over time (gerontology). Biological aging is measured as the decline in the body's ability to maintain a balanced interaction of the organs, muscles, bones, and endocrine systems. The gradualness of this process, unlike a traumatic event, can fill an individual with doubts about their physical and mental capabilities. Like physical changes, social changes require adaptation as family and work-related roles are redefined.

Biological Aging

The body is composed of a variety of interactive systems that maintain its operation. As the individual ages, these systems begin to deteriorate in a relatively predictable way. Thus, to design a facility that suits the needs of the aging, it is important to take into account these physical changes and the implications they have for the designed environment. Well-designed facilities not only accommodate the disabilities that come with aging but also permit residents to exercise their remaining abilities as much as possible.

Communicating systems

Changes in the endocrine system, which controls hormones, can alter the maintenance of body temperature or decrease the body's ability to correctly identify and react suitably to stimuli, thereby increasing the individual's vulnerability. In addition, the nervous system becomes less efficient at coordinating movement: reflexes degrade, and reaction time is slowed. The nervous system's ability to store and recall information also diminishes with age.

Design implications:
There are many ways for a designer to help make the aging individual's environment better suited to the physical disabilities caused by the diminished functioning of the endocrine and nervous systems. They include

- Extending time-operated devices (elevator doors, automatic entrances) to allow more time to complete activities

- Distinguishing repetitive/symmetrical spaces by providing landmarks (objects, views to the outside) and increasing the salience of important directional information, referred to in this book as "wayfinding"

- Avoiding self-locking doors

- Providing electrical appliances with lights that remind people that they are on

- Designing mechanical systems that allow flexible temperature control and avoid significant draft/moving air

Mechanical systems

The muscular system loses strength and bulk after age 30. With lack of movement, muscular atrophy can affect posture, endurance, and joint positions. The skeletal system loses calcium, making bones brittle and increasingly vulnerable to accidents. The skeletal system also loses elasticity, affecting bending, kneeling, turning, and rising.

Design implications
In response to these physical changes, it is recommended that the designer

- Avoid devices that require twisting, pinching, or other precise manipulation

- Provide frequent places to rest in hallways and near elevators

- Provide chairs with arms and straight backs (see Chapter 14)

- Meet accessibility requirements but focus on how the physical needs of older adults vary from younger disabled user groups upon which many standards are based

- Avoid loose rugs, raised thresholds, or slippery surfaces that may affect balance or gait changes

- Provide furniture that has an appropriate seat height (see Chapter 14)

- Provide opportunities for physical fitness

Control systems

The control systems of aging individuals often function less effectively than those of younger people. The digestive system can be affected in many ways, including reduced bladder control, difficulty with digestion, and (without proper diet) malnutrition. Declining efficiency in the respiratory system and in oxygenating blood can lead to curtailed movement and diminished energy reserves. The efficiency of the cardiovascular system generally declines with age and is subject to disease and hereditary conditions that can reduce blood supply to the brain, causing dizziness, blackouts, and blurred vision.

Design implications
To create an environment that assists individuals with these problems, the designer should

- Provide frequent and easily accessible bathrooms
- Provide eat-in kitchens, preferably with windows, that encourage good eating habits
- Minimize walking distances
- Provide dining options that help stimulate appetite and increase social opportunities

Detection senses

All of the five senses are affected by aging, especially those on which we are most dependent: sight and hearing. The senses of taste, smell, and touch change over time, and there is also a diminished ability to detect pain or pressure. Because taste is approximately 90 percent dependent on aroma, some aging persons experience a decreased ability to enjoy food. Most individuals experience hearing problems as they get older. Usually higher frequencies are lost first. In addition, inner-ear changes affect balance, which often leads to falls. Impaired vision has a significant effect on how people perceive and use the environment. While some issues are correctable with surgery, others require different means of support.

- Aging eyes take longer to adjust their focus between objects near and far.
- Glare can cause momentary blindness.
- Higher light levels are needed to compensate for failing eyesight.
- The lens of the eye yellows and thickens, changing the perception of color.
- Depth perception is altered.

▶ *Normal vision. Understanding the deteriorating vision of the aging helps inform design. National Eye Institute, National Institutes of Health.*

▶▶ *Cataract vision*

▶ *Glaucoma vision*
▶▶ *Macular degeneration*

Design implications

The designer has the opportunity to adapt the environment to make up for diminished vision and hearing abilities. He or she can also limit the senior's dependence on certain senses by substituting others. The designer may

- Provide information by using more than one sense, such as visual and auditory alarms

- Encourage dining settings that increase visual and olfactory connections with food

- Avoid shiny surfaces, which reflect light sources and cause glare

- Increase all light levels to provide sufficient lighting for general activities and task-specific needs

- Prevent excessive background noises that limit reception of information (see Chapter 12)

- Use tactile information for orientation, such as handrails, floor and wall textures, and the warmth of the sun (see Chapter 15)

Social Passage

The literature on aging has commonly focused on the physical changes related to advancing age. However, the way older people are viewed by society and the way the older person as an individual finds purpose are affected by the subtle, often invisible changes within the aging individual. Four main theories attempt to explain the changes in the way adults interact with other people and their environment as they age. Any or all of these theories may apply for each individual at different times, as none of us has a static personality and factors such as health, finances and social involvement may affect

▲ A central role for most facilities for the aging is to encourage continued social interaction.

us differently from time to time. These theories should be seen as tools for the designer to begin to understand the mind-set of the aging adult.

Disengagement theory

As they age, some individuals will withdraw from certain roles and responsibilities. This is called the "disengagement theory," because these individuals disengage themselves from some aspects of their place in the societal structure. Of course, satisfactory disengagement can occur only when the individual and the environment or society agree on the pace of withdrawal from certain roles and responsibilities. For example, an aging homemaker might determine that meal preparation is no longer central to her role and thereby have successful disengagement. Conversely, forcing disengagement by providing apartments with no kitchens may inhibit successful aging.

Design implications

In response to those seniors who are seeking to alter their roles, there should be opportunities for participation in a

Today we look back at the 1960s and find it hard to believe that residents were regularly institutionalized because they were incontinent—a muscle-control problem, not a health-care problem. (*Regnier 2002, p. ix*)

larger community with access to community facilities, such as a library or community center, and services, such as stores. In addition, there should be opportunities for individuals to make choices to alter their roles and responsibilities. An example of this would be the provision of apartments with kitchens in addition to meal programs, allowing a homemaker to choose whether or not to disengage from her position as one whose responsibility is to prepare meals.

Activity theory

Some individuals, rather than simply disengaging from previous roles, will seek to replace roles from which they have been displaced. For example, upon retirement a corporate executive might become a volunteer board president.

Design implications

In response to the activity theory, seniors should be provided with opportunities to take on new roles and responsibilities. This might include access to lifelong learning or to spaces that will encourage community connections and promote volunteerism.

▼ *The caregiver is still the most important aspect of any senior care setting. Woodside Place Alzheimer Residence, Oakmont, Pennsylvania. Perkins Eastman Architects PC. Photograph by Martha Rial.*

Continuity theory

Aging individuals often surround themselves with objects and routines that reinforce their self-image. For example, couples who have traditionally hosted family holiday gatherings may select apartments with full kitchens even if they do not continue to prepare meals, or a widower may desire to have a large bed despite the fact that he is the only one using it. As these individuals adapt to changing physical capabilities, new situations, and life experiences, they also develop a strong need to maintain continuity between their old and new lives.

Design implications

In response to this need to maintain a consistent self-image, residents should be allowed to bring their own furniture. The architect should design for large enough spaces and flexible layouts that permit important objects like a large bed or a china closet to be brought in and comfortably situated in the housing environment.

Environmental press and competence

An older individual's ability to adapt and to negotiate the environment is positive if there is a balance between the individual's abilities and the demands of the environment—meaning that the individual is able to physically, mentally, and emotionally cope with his or her surroundings during the activities of daily living. Conversely, it can be negative if the environment is more demanding than the individual's ability. A designer cannot simply expect people to do all of the adapting; spaces must be designed to adapt to their users. For example, walkers or electric carts allow an individual with mobility problems to adapt to various settings. Elevators and widened hallways adapt the milieu to the individual, resulting in a balance of abilities and demands.

Design implications

Because the competence of individuals utilizing these facilities will vary greatly, it is important for the setting to be flexible to allow individuals to adapt. In addition, the environment should provide choice and variety so that individuals can select the settings or services that appropriately adapt the environment to their needs. Providing redundant information for wayfinding through many sources allows individuals to rely on their own innate abilities in combination with the environmental cues, which may involve signage, color, and landmarks. Examples of cues might include the

smell of bread baking, a grandfather clock in the hall, and artwork with a familiar regional scene.

PROGRAMMING & PLANNING GUIDELINES

The following sections of this chapter provide program and planning guidelines for each of the eight building types discussed in this book. These guidelines should be regarded only as a starting point for the project planning or programming effort, because there are a wide variety of successful models within every building type.

Space standards vary. They are a reflection of market preferences and income levels of the target market. Typical net square-foot area ranges for various uses are tabulated below, but these guidelines should not be regarded as absolute

▼ *The combination of new technologies, such as computer entry of medical records and pharmacy prescriptions, combined with the special needs of the aging make it necessary to exceed the code minimum sizes of most exam rooms. Memorial Sloan-Kettering Cancer Center: Laurance S. Rockefeller Outpatient Pavilion, New York City. Perkins Eastman Architects PC. Photograph by Chuck Choi.*

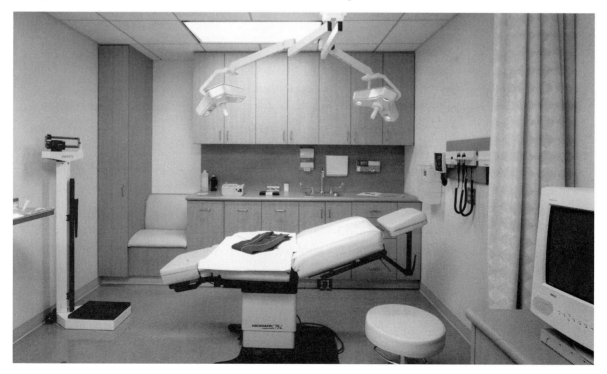

▲ The nurses' station in the Donald W. Reynolds Center on Aging is designed to permit chair-bound patients to converse directly with the nursing staff. University of Arkansas, Donald W. Reynolds Center on Aging, Little Rock, Arkansas. Perkins Eastman Architects PC. Photograph by Tom Conklyn.

models. In addition, when preparing a total program, a grossing factor needs to be accounted for to allow for wall thickness (not included in the net-square foot areas), corridors, stairs, elevators, shafts, mechanical and electrical areas, and the like. Because of the need for wider corridors for maneuvering, and in some senior environment types mandated 8 ft corridors, the grossing factor is typically larger than those used for other building types.

Geriatric Medicine
Introduction/types of users
Geriatric medicine provides health care for older adults with cognitive, emotional, and/or physical challenges. Special expertise within the geriatric field includes psychology, internal medicine, psychiatry, neurology, therapy (physical, occupational, speech, etc.), and social

work. A multidisciplinary team may include services such as assessment for Alzheimer's and dementia, preventive medicine, and clinical services that focus specifically on an older patient group.

Geriatric clinics, as freestanding entities, may include family services, and clinics residing within a nursing home or CCRC often include examination and treatment spaces for general exams as well as dental, ophthalmology, podiatry, and other specialties. These are generally linked to areas for physical, occupational, and speech therapy. Other services that may be provided under the umbrella of geriatric medicine include mobile care (a van equipped to provide medical exams and minor treatments), in-home psychiatric assessment and treatment, agencies that provide coordination of community services for the elderly, and education to caregivers.

Geriatric clinics and outpatient services evolved significantly in the 1990s. Despite the fact that older people represent a high proportion of adults seeking health care, only a small percentage of medical professionals specialize in geriatric medicine. Moreover, there are still many areas without specialized geriatric medicine services. The rapidly aging baby boomer population, medical advances, and the focus on fitness and diet have all led to a healthier, more active older population. Because adults are living longer in their homes or retirement settings, much of the primary care and safety net of senior health services begins with the family practice, or, if available, a specialized geriatric clinic program. Since many general practitioners are not trained in the complexities of geriatric care, specialized clinics can provide a good approach to patient assessment and treatment. Aged care needs range from mostly healthy and active adults to those with general physical impairments, hearing loss, diminished sight, incontinence, cognitive impairments, depression, and the complex influences of one medication upon another. Thus, careful patient treatment often demands numerous specialists.

Geriatric clinic facilities have only begun to explore all of the unique design possibilities for the arrangement of patient and staff spaces, equipment, services, and the supportive environmental needs of older adults, who often spend hours in the clinic. As medical schools continue to refine geriatric training and residency programs, new generations of practitioners will reshape clinical care in geriatrics. Future generations of older adults will continue to demand more services outside of institutional housing environments and seek support to extend their options for living at home. This section outlines emerging trends in geriatric clinic facilities and provides practical planning guidelines to accommodate the needs of older adult patients and their environment. *(Also known as: Geriatric Clinic, Outpatient Geriatric Care, Geriatric Assessment)*

Types of sponsors/settings

Generally, sponsors of geriatric clinical services fall into two broad categories: health-care providers such as hospitals, clinics, primary care centers, skilled nursing centers; and senior housing and community-based service providers. These sponsors can provide services in a number of settings, ranging from formal to informal and small to large, including the following:

- Private community-based practice
- Component of a retirement community
- Part-time presence or affiliation with other sponsors
- Home health service network

Clinic and outpatient settings range from private family practices that are small and personal to major hospital outpatient programs comprising potentially dozens of exam rooms and a home health-care staff for in-home care visits. A suite of exam rooms, which can be used flexibly by community medical practitioners, is common in senior living clinical settings.

Major program elements and design considerations

Most licensed clinics are required to follow minimum area requirements for programs and services set by local and/or state agencies, such as the state depart-

GERIATRIC CLINIC: TYPICAL PROGRAM COMPONENTS		
Clinic Spaces*	**Typical Code Minimum Area (sq ft)**	**Recommended Minimum Area (sq ft)**
Waiting area	20–30 / exam rm.	60–70 /exam rm.
	10–15 /person	20–25 /person + escorts
Clerical/staff work	N/A	200 +
Records/dictation	N/A	10–15 /exam rm
General exam room	90–110	110–130
Procedure room	100–120	140–160
Dental exam/procedure	90–110	140–150
Dental workroom	50–100	50–100
Hearing/speech testing	N/A	110–130
Radiological exam (if provided)	N/A	200–250
Neuro/psych testing	80–90	100–110
Patient consult/staff meeting room	N/A	140–160
Staff office	100–110	110–140
Patient toiletroom (ADA)	50	50
Pharmacy (if provided)	N/A	450 & up
Lab prep/medication supply	50–100	100 & up
Soiled utility room	50–85	50–85
Clean utility room	50–60	50–60
Therapy Spaces**		
PT gym/open equipment area	N/A	1200 & up
Hydrotherapy area (limb tanks only)	N/A	120–150
Equipment storage	N/A	100 & up
OT program area	N/A	250–300
ADL suite (kitchen, bedroom, bath)	N/A	300–400
Training toilet/shower room	80–100	80–100
Staff observation/work area	N/A	200 & up
Staff office	100–110	120–130
Patient consult/staff meeting room	N/A	100–150
Patient toilet room (ADA)	50	50

*Other spaces to consider, depending on the clinic size and program: Family escort education areas; subwaiting areas; patient/family consult rooms; check-in/out rooms; staff interdisciplinary work areas ("bullpens")

**Other spaces to consider, depending on the therapy program and size: hydrotherapy pool or activity pool; audiology/speech therapy; private testing/treatment rooms; locker/changing rooms

ment of health. These requirements must be met when reimbursement for services comes from state or federally funded programs. City or county health departments may also establish minimum standards for outpatient clinic facilities. Regardless of the source, few standards have been developed to support older patient populations, and in some cases, existing standards may even be counterproductive to the end user because they do not reflect the need for greater general accessibility, convenience to toilets, or other special limitations of the frail elderly.

Licensing and other regulatory requirements may also be the result of the selected "occupancy classification" of the clinic facility. It is common for clinics to fall either into a "business" or "health-care" occupancy classification. The health-care classification, used when facilities are affiliated with licensed hospital programs or provide overnight care of any kind, has the strictest standards and the greatest need for monitoring and observation. The business classification, which is often a medical office building setting, typically allows for most outpatient clinic and minor procedure services without significant code restrictions. These two options must be carefully considered as they impact program, services offered, operations and building costs. The table on page 12 provides a summary of typical requirements.

Program/organizational alternatives
There are three commonly used models for clinic design. The basic characteristics of each model are outlined below.

Patient/escort-centered model

- Lower staff efficiency

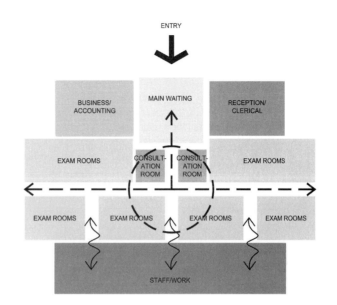

ENTRY

| BUSINESS/ ACCOUNTING | MAIN WAITING | RECEPTION/ CLERICAL |

EXAM ROOMS | CONSULT-ATION ROOM | CONSULT-ATION ROOM | EXAM ROOMS

EXAM ROOMS | EXAM ROOMS | EXAM ROOMS | EXAM ROOMS

STAFF/WORK

- Overlapping use of circulation by staff and patients for access to exam areas
- Shorter circulation for patients
- Public/staff interface functions and private medical staff service functions likely have remote locations
- Staff and patient waiting areas generally positioned for access to natural light

Staff/administration-centered model

- Higher staff efficiency
- Overlapping use of circulation by staff and patients for access to exam areas
- Longer circulation for patients
- Exam rooms and patient waiting areas generally positioned for access to natural light
- Circulation likely to form a "ring," which complicates patient wayfinding

▲ *Patient-centered model. University of Arkansas, Donald W. Reynolds Center on Aging, Little Rock, Arkansas. Perkins Eastman Architects PC.*

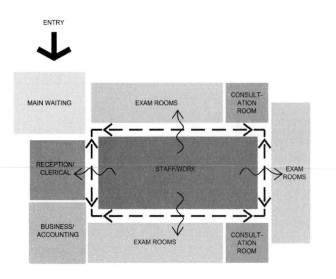

▲ *Staff-centered model. University of Arkansas, Donald W. Reynolds Center on Aging, Little Rock, Arkansas. Perkins Eastman Architects PC.*

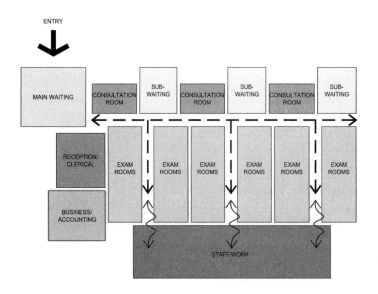

▲ *Hybrid, cluster model. University of Arkansas, Donald W. Reynolds Center on Aging, Little Rock, Arkansas. Perkins Eastman Architects PC.*

Cluster model (hybrid defining parallel subclinic teams)

- Decentralization and repetition of waiting, check-in/out and consult areas
- Moderate to high staff efficiency
- Moderate to low circulation for patients with clear hierarchy of public and semiprivate zones formed by small service clusters
- Staff and patient waiting areas generally positioned for access to natural light

Special design considerations
These are other considerations in designing a geriatric facility, regardless of type or sponsor.

Frailty and limited mobility of many older adults
Geriatric clinics require environments that support frail users. Patients require more time, and in some cases assistance, moving from one area of the clinic to another, reading and preparing needed paperwork, dressing/undressing, and using the toilet. Given the additional time needed to complete physical tasks (dressing, undressing, completing forms, etc.) and the complexity of examinations, testing, and assessments, it is not uncommon for patients to spend between two and four hours in the clinic. This affects the number of exam rooms to be provided, because they cannot be "turned over" as many times as in conventional clinics. While the most supportive clinics attempt to limit the number of transitions/relocations patients will make during their visit, handrails on at least one side of all patient corridors should be provided to assist with mobility. A widened circulation space to allow for

wheelchairs and power-operated vehicles (POVs) as well as other staff/service equipment is recommended. Corridor widths of 6–8 feet are not uncommon, and extreme care should be used to arrange doors that do not swing into corridors, as many patients will be moving along the edges rather than the middle of circulation spaces.

Impact of "escorts" (family caregivers)
Often, a number of family and friends accompany the patient to the outpatient clinic. Given that others often provide transportation to the clinic, it is not uncommon to have between one and three family members or friends for each patient. This places a strain on clinic waiting areas and exam and consult rooms, which must accommodate more people than the clinic is intended to serve directly. Therefore, diversionary activities with a focus on education—such as reading materials, television/video seminars, and direct Internet terminals with established

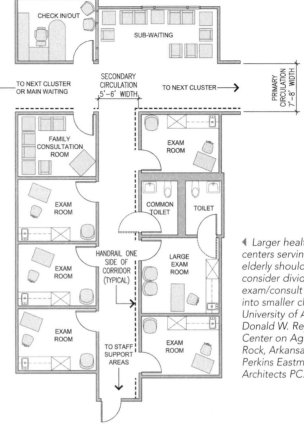

◀ Larger health-care centers serving the elderly should consider dividing the exam/consult areas into smaller clusters. University of Arkansas, Donald W. Reynolds Center on Aging, Little Rock, Arkansas. Perkins Eastman Architects PC.

◀ Patient education with both print- and computer-based materials is becoming a common feature in geriatric medicine centers. Memorial Sloan-Kettering Cancer Center, Laurance S. Rockefeller Outpatient Pavilion, New York City. Perkins Eastman Architects PC. Photograph by Chuck Choi.

links to senior resource sites—can be very helpful. Also, access to snacks and beverages as well as outdoor spaces provides options for lengthy waits.

Access to toilet facilities

In general, public restrooms should be near all clinic waiting areas. They should be single-occupant wheelchair-accessible spaces with wall grab bars or seat-mounted sheltering arm grab bars. Special "break-away" style doors with emergency release hardware should be used to allow reverse operation of the door, should a patient become ill or injured and fall to the floor, blocking the natural in-swing direction of the door. At minimum, each large exam or procedure room should have a connecting accessible toilet room. While it would be preferable to have connecting toilet rooms for all exam rooms, in many cases this is not financially feasible. Instead, it would be helpful to provide a few such rooms, allowing patients to avoid repeatedly dressing and undressing during a long examination or procedure in order to use a common toilet. This does, however, require staff to manage exam-room assignments to partner appropriate spaces with patient needs and intended services.

Large group/family patient consults

With groups including the patient, several family members, and often more than one physician, it becomes impractical to hold open discussions of assessments and treatments in exam rooms. More informal areas such as closed lounges or other conference space can be more appropriate for these consultations and may provide needed privacy for difficult diagnoses.

Need for multiple medical disciplines

A visit to the doctor can be a formidable experience for an anxious, slightly confused, and unsteady older adult. Compounded by complex medical, social, and financial needs, the clinic often needs to be a comprehensive health service center. This allows the physicians and staff to surround the individual with the required disciplines and services needed to assess, treat, and develop a long-term care plan that includes involvement of extended family members. Staff may meet and discuss resident assessments and care plans that involve two or more academic disciplines that are usually considered distinct. For these interdisciplinary sessions, "bullpen" areas must exist where collaborative care planning can occur. These "bullpens" should be isolated from patient areas, convenient to other central staff services such as offices and work cubicles, soiled and clean utility areas, and medication rooms. They should provide for review of charting, X-rays, and other medical records. If teleconferencing technologies are used in the clinic, they should be provided in the "bullpen" areas to allow discussion with off-site specialists or colleagues.

Wayfinding

Many older adults have impaired vision, memory, and/or hearing, so orientation can become a greater challenge, especially in larger clinic facilities. Clustering functions for patient convenience may help reduce walking distances. Use of color, finishes, or lighting to differentiate clinic areas may also be helpful. However, there is no better support system than to allocate highly visible staff areas such as nursing or staff stations throughout the clinic to provide directions. It is important to balance the staff's need for privacy with the patients' need for human contact.

Confidentiality and privacy
The clinic should be zoned to create clear hierarchies between visitor/escort, patient, and staff areas. Due to the high-er than average escort population in the clinic, confidential information such as records, patient consults, and physician discussions must be properly isolated. The interdisciplinary needs of patient assessment often require several professionals to visit a single patient and confer on interrelated assessment and treatment programs.

SAMPLE LARGE OUTPATIENT CLINIC PROGRAM*

SPACE	AREA (sq ft)	SPACE	AREA (sq ft)
Entry/reception		**Staff/support areas**	
Main waiting 20–30 seats	900	Medical records/dictation (high-density filing)	200
Clerical/reception (3–4 person station)	250	Financial counselor office	160
Accessible restrooms (2 @ 50 sq ft)	100	Business manager office	120
Subtotal entry/reception	1,250	Nurse manager office	120
		Neuro/psych office	120
Typical exam cluster		Staff conference room	300
Subwaiting room	150	Open staff work area ("bullpen")	300
Check-in/out room	100	Staff workstations (+/–12 @ 50 sq ft/ea.)	600
Shared toilet room	50	Nurse station (3–4 person station)	250
Standard exam room (5 @ 120 sq ft)	600	Medication/pixus room	80
Large exam room	160	Staff toilet room	50
Toilet room (adjoining large exam)	50	Soiled supply room (2 @ 80 sq ft)	160
Family consult room	150	Clean supply room (2 @ 50 sq ft)	100
Subtotal for 4 exam clusters	5,040	Staff lockers	100
		Janitors' closet	50
Shared patient/specialty exam areas		Equipment storage	80
Blood-drawing room	120	General/supply storage	140
Procedure room	80	Subtotal staff/support areas	2,930
Neuro/psych testing	160		
Radiological exam	240	Total usable square feet	9,920
Subtotal for shared exam areas	700	Multiplier @ 1.4 (for circ., mech., walls, etc.)	3,880
		Total facility program	13,800
*20 exam-room cluster model		(average @ +/-690 sq ft/exam room)	

Lower exam-room turnover

At typical clinic facilities, physicians can manage their patient load by revolving two to three exam rooms per physician. This model assumes 30–40 visits per day. Because geriatric patients usually require longer preparation, need more time to dress and undress, and have more complex medical histories to refresh, it is not uncommon for a single physician to use four to five exam rooms to support a smaller patient load of 20–30 visits/day. To counteract this trend, exam and support areas should be grouped together, reducing time spent between patient exams and helping clinic staff work more effectively.

Environmental comfort

As with other facilities to house or serve older populations, it is good to plan for an increased sensitivity to temperature, drafts, direct sunlight, glare, and artificial illumination levels. HVAC systems should accommodate additional local temperature control for exam rooms, procedure rooms, toilet rooms, and other areas where patients may be undressing. It would not be uncommon to plan for a source of heat during both the summer and winter seasons, as many older adults are cold year-round. Systems should deliver air at the lowest velocity possible to limit the effects of drafts. Exterior windows should be equipped with blinds or shades to help control heat and glare, as well as satisfy any privacy concerns. Artificial lighting should generally be even, and accepted illumination levels should be increased 20–30 percent to accommodate older adults with low-light vision difficulties. Given the length of time many patients may spend in the clinic, select interior finishes that offer variety and color. Residential touches such as window treatments, artwork, and other decorative accessories should be used to add to the visual variety of the clinic.

In some settings the program may be limited to serving the needs of the population of a CCRC or a nursing home. As is discussed later in this chapter, the space program for smaller clinics often ranges from 2,000 to 3,000 NSF. Facilities with a comprehensive rehabilitation program may range from 2,500 to 3,500 NSF for occupational, physical, and related therapy programs

Payment, reimbursement, and regulation

Because of the variety of sponsors, it is hard to generalize on the payment structure. Typically, users will have private insurance or be eligible for Medicare for

SAMPLE CCRC CLINIC PROGRAM	
SPACE	**AREA (sq ft)**
Waiting room (seating for 8–10)	180
Reception/clerical	140
Small exam (2 @ 110 sq ft)	220
Large exam/procedure	140
Dental exam/procedure	140
Dental workroom	65
Lab prep/supply	100
Soiled/clean utility (2 @ 60 sq ft)	120
Patient toilet room (2 @ 50 sq ft)	100
Patient/family consult	120
Staff office (2 @ 135 sq ft)	270
Pharmacy	420
Subtotal usable square feet	**2,015**
Multiplier @ 1.45	907
Total facility program	**2,922**
(average @ +/-730 sq ft/exam room)	

most services. If the clinic is part of a life-care retirement community, the services may be provided at no additional charge as part of the monthly fee or entry fee paid at initial entry to the community. Licensure in most states is typically through the department of health.

Trends/opportunities for innovation

As with all aspects of medical care, geriatric medicine is a rapidly changing field. The funds for multidisciplinary evaluation, more specialized facilities for the aging that conform to the recommendations described above, and greater use of technology (computers in exam rooms for medical records, pharmacy prescriptions, etc.) all point to somewhat larger exam rooms, clinics, and support spaces. The use of teleconferencing technologies in clinics is increasing, allowing access to worldwide specialists and resources for consultations and education. At the same time, the use of technology for home assessment and monitoring has the potential to slow the growing need for specialized geriatric medicine facilities. When linked to a primary-care center, these telemedicine programs can effectively bring the full range of clinic resources to the patient's home. New geriatric clinics must consider the use and impact of these emerging technologies and plan for added space to accommodate the systems and equipment required to support them. Home health-care agencies will also become more integrated with clinic programs as some primary healthcare needs are met in the individual's home.

Adult Day Care

Introduction/types of users

Adult day care is a group program that provides health and social services with-

in a limited daily time frame for frail, physically or cognitively impaired persons over 65 years of age. Features include medical care, preventive and rehabilitative services, and/or Alzheimer's care. Typical hours of operation are 8 A.M. to 5 P.M., but some facilities offer extended hours for their clients and families. Adult day care facilities have evolved as alternatives to assisted living and long-term care for individuals still living at home or with their families. For example, they provide a family caregiver the opportunity to go to work knowing that their aging parent is in a safe active program, and for spouse caregivers it provides much-needed respite.

Day care participants are often cognitively impaired (dementia) and cannot be left alone at home due to safety concerns.

SAMPLE CCRC THERAPY PROGRAM	
SPACE	**AREA (sq ft)**
Waiting room (seating for 6–8)	200
OT/PT directors office (2 @ 120 sq ft)	240
Staff observation/work (for 4 staff)	200
PT gym area	1,070
Open gym area 550 sq ft	
Mat table area 2 @ 140 sq ft	
Weight exercise area 140 sq ft	
Hydro therapy area 100 sq ft	
OT program area (incl. ADL kitchen)	300
Audiology/speech therapy	140
Training toilet/shower	100
Public toilet	50
Equipment storage	100
Subtotal usable square feet	2,400
Multiplier @ 1.25*	600
Total facility program	3,000

*Utilizing open gym areas for access to other program functions can minimize circulation

The National Institute on Adult Daycare, NIAD, in its Standards for Adult Day Care (1984, p. 20) defines adult day care as:
A community-based group program designed to meet the needs of functionally impaired adults through an individual plan of care. It is a structured, comprehensive program that provides a variety of health, social, and related support services in a protective setting during any part of a day but less than 24-hour care. Individuals who participate in adult day care attend on a planned basis during specified hours. Adult day care assists its participants to remain in the community, enabling families and other caregivers to continue caring for an impaired member at home.

Other programs have been developed to meet the needs of very frail/medically compromised individuals who would otherwise be placed in long-term care/nursing homes. While social activities are a significant component of the daily program, these are not "drop-in senior centers." (*Also known as: Adult Day Health-Care Facility, Adult Day Care Center*)

Types of sponsors/owners

It is common to find the same sponsors/owners for both adult day care and geriatric medicine because both provide a community-based network of social and medical services to the aging community. According to the National Council on the Aging (NCOA), of the more than 4,000 programs existing nationwide in 2000, the majority were operated on a nonprofit or public basis, and many were affiliated with larger organizations such as home-care, skilled nursing facilities, medical centers, or multipurpose senior organizations.

Types of settings

The setting for the program can either be within another senior environment (such as a nursing home or retirement community) or as a stand-alone program located in the community. The type of setting in which the adult day-care program is located will determine design and planning decisions that will complement and support the basic philosophy of the service. Also, the location will influence the geographic draw area of the clientele, staff resources, and availablity of adjunct services.

Freestanding models

Community-based programs are typically run as business enterprises and can be found in a variety of locations, from storefront retail-type space to church/synagogue education wings to freestanding buildings. Day-care programs are financially fragile operations, particularly in states where there is little or no public reimbursement program. Adult day care providers are typically well networked with other community-based organizations, social workers, physicians, and hospitals for their client referrals.

Integrated models

Adult day care centers are frequently developed within other residences, such as long-term care, assisted living, or retirement communities. The ability to utilize the resources of a larger parent facility with trained staff increases management, staffing, and purchasing efficiencies and may also produce more creative programming as there are expanded resources. Many senior living providers see adult

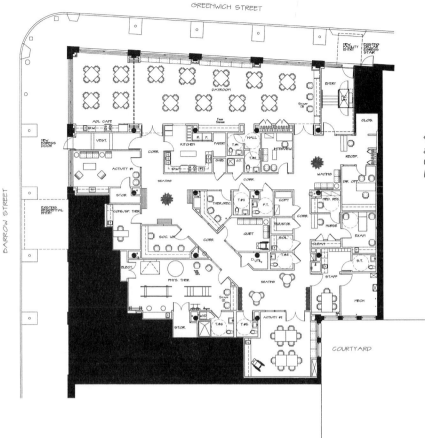

◄ *Plan for a 50-registrant urban adult day care program. Village Center for Care, New York City. Perkins Eastman Architects PC.*

day care as a community service, an expansion of their continuum of services and a natural referral/marketing opportunity for their other residential and care environments

Major program elements and design considerations

It is important to first determine the profile of the participants/clients (range of services and needs) and the number of attendees per day. It is not uncommon to find programs where clients attend on a part-time basis, so that the number of registrants is significantly higher than the actual number of participants on a given day. The type and number of staff will be dependent upon the facility model, and adult day care programs generally follow one or some combination of three models: social, medical, and dementia care.

The definition of the program will help to define the types of activities and services that the facility will offer. Programming meetings with the operator will provide the designer with the space-planning information to accommodate different types of activities and group sizes, equipment, storage requirements, and the extent of nutritional, medical, and rehabilitation services. Typical program components include the following.

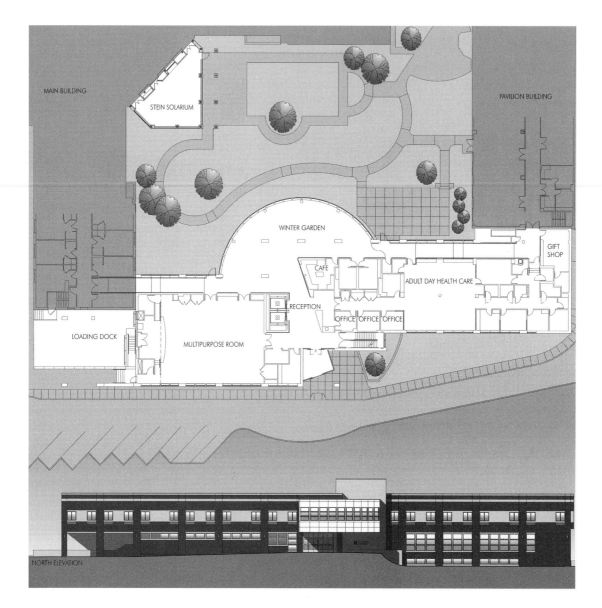

MAIN BUILDING

STEIN SOLARIUM

PAVILION BUILDING

WINTER GARDEN

GIFT SHOP

CAFE

RECEPTION

ADULT DAY HEALTH CARE

OFFICE OFFICE OFFICE

LOADING DOCK

MULTIPURPOSE ROOM

NORTH ELEVATION

▲ Plan for a 30-registrant suburban adult day care program. Sarah R. Neuman Center for Healthcare and Rehabilitation–Weinberg Pavilion, Mamaroneck, New York. Perkins Eastman Architects PC.

Supportive services

Supportive services provided within a program typically include the following. *Transportation.* The provision of transportation for participants is a necessary service and helps guarantee attendance. Whether transportation is publicly or facility provided, it must be reliable, accessible, and attentive to seniors' needs.

Food service. It is good to partner with a food-service provider such as a nursing home or a nutritionist to plan out a meal program that accommodates special dietary needs.

Medical service. For the medical model of adult day care, there are requirements for

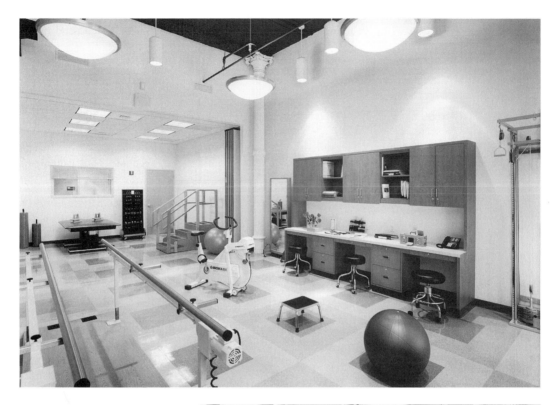

▲ Adult day care may include physical and occupational therapy programs. Village Center for Care, New York City. Perkins Eastman Architects PC.
Photograph by Chuck Choi.

▶ Adult day care typically involves both activities and at least one meal. Village Center for Care, New York City.
Perkins Eastman Architects PC.
Photograph by Chuck Choi.

ADULT DAY CARE: SAMPLE PROGRAM FOR 50 PARTICIPANTS*	
SPACE	**AREA (sq ft)**
Entry/admissions/reception	
Waiting and reception	150
Interview/meeting room	150
Coat/drinking fountain/telephone	80
Wheelchair storage	40
Public toilet	55
Common activities	
Dining/recreation (50 people @ 30 sq ft/person)	1500
General Activities (10 people @ 25 sq ft /person)	250
Activities of daily living (ADLs): kitchen/work area	250
Special Program	
Physical therapy room	400
Exam/treatment room	150
Private counseling room	120
Quiet room (6 persons, 30 sq ft each)	180
Staff area	
Director's office	120
Staff work stations (10 @ 30 sq ft)	300
Staff lounge/multipurpose room	200
Support areas	
Medical records/files	50
Copier/fax station	50
Pantry	200
Storage	100
Toilet rooms	
Single use (4 @ 50 sq ft)	200
Toilet room and shower	100
Staff toilet (1 @ 55 sq ft)	55
Washer/dryer	20
Janitor's closet	40
Mechanical/electrical/telephone	300
Total net area	**5,060**
Total gross area (x 1.3 Gross/Net)	**6,578**

State of New York Department of Health Title 10 Part 713 reference standard. Mechanical spaces, entry, lobby/waiting may not be necessary as part of this program if the day-care space is integrated within a larger building or program, as these would be shared spaces.

the medical assessment of clients. Some sponsors may include other standard check-ups. Dental care and podiatry are two common medical services that can be provided.

Rehabilitation. Rehab services may include:

1. Occupational therapy to help with activities of daily living (ADLs)

   - Small-group activities, such as rehabilitation sessions to help an older person participate in a cooking activity in a kitchen; simple handicraft work or cutting, sewing, knitting, painting, or ceramics in the arts and crafts room; etc.

   - One-on-one activities to help a participant learn how to get in and out of a bathing tub or shower and how to position the body for toileting functions.

2. Physical therapy

   - Ambulation: Most facilities help residents learn to walk using handrails and or aids.

   - Simple modality stations: Some facilities set up a physical therapy room equipped with modality stations for upper and lower body exercise if a physical therapy program is provided. A hand wash sink in the room is necessary, and a single-service toilet room should be provided nearby.

3. Speech therapy. Speech therapy can be provided easily in a private office or small meeting room.

4. Personal hygiene. Providing facilities and staff for bathing clients is important, because many frail seniors using these programs do not have the appropriate facilities or assistance at home.

◀ Newer day care programs often try to create a variety of smaller program areas. North Shore Senior Center, Arthur C. Nielsen, Jr. Campus, Northfield, Illinois. O'Donnell Wicklund Pigozzi and Peterson Architects Inc. Photograph by Steve Hall at Hedrich Blessing.

Adjunct services

Adjunct services are complementary programs that expand the scope of "wellness" programs. They either occur in an adult day care setting or are affiliated with it as part of a service network. They may include medical services (such as audiology, ophthalmology, gynecology, and psychological counseling), exercise programs (such as tai chi, yoga, and dance therapy), a learning center (to teach skills such as computers or languages), etc.

Sample program

A rule of thumb for net area allowance per client or participant is 75–100 net sq ft (NSF), assuming the facility is located all on one level. A program that is located on two contiguous levels requires a larger allowance of GSF per person to allow for stairs, elevators, and corridors.

The program outlined on page 24 is typical of states that are highly regulated and offer significant reimbursement. Space programs, however, vary widely from state to state because of the many differences in codes, regulations, and other variables, and it is not uncommon to find some states permitting the same program outlined above to operate in less than half the space. This may be permitted but is not recommended.

Some facilities may have a small group of Alzheimer's or dementia participants. They have special needs including

History of Adult Day Care:

The concept of adult day care started in 1933 in Moscow as a day hospital program to solve the huge psychiatric bed shortage. Subsequently, in 1943 Great Britain adopted the same idea as a measure to maximize the limited health-care resources for medical and rehabilitation services to war-afflicted veterans. This program became so well received that in the 1950s day hospitals (adult daycare centers) were set up throughout the United Kingdom to attend the needs of frail and physically disabled senior citizens. This system of community-based care-giving had built a direct linkage between the delivery of health-care resources and the national health-care system. Canada and South Africa were the next countries to follow.

The first adult daycare programs in the United States started in the 1960s. The Older Americans Act of 1965 gave support to the development of programs that would provide socialization and recreational services dedicated to seniors.

In 1977, 200 programs were listed in the first directory of adult daycare programs published by the National Council on Aging. There were 600 programs listed in 1980 and 1,200 in 1986 under the National Institute of Adult Day Care Centers. The rapid growth rate demonstrated the need for an alternative to nursing homes for frail seniors who choose to remain in their homes and communities as long as possible.

(National Institute on Adult Daycare 1984)

separate activities and dining space, quiet room, and walking and exercise space to allow for working through occasional periods of agitation. Additional discrete program areas are therefore required.

Payment, reimbursement, and regulations

Some states and other public entities have encouraged day care with Medicaid waiver programs and other forms of reimbursement. The reason for supporting such facilities is that day care helps people stay at home and out of more expensive publicly supported housing or nursing homes. Where reimbursement exists, it is usually accompanied by regulation that leads to larger space requirements.

Licensure of adult day care is required in most states for services provided to three or more individuals. The licensure agencies vary by state and may be part of the department of health, the social service department (public welfare), or a specialized department on aging. Code requirements are usually focused on basic administration, safety, and sanitation standards except in states with reimbursement where stringent space and programmatic standards are often specified.

Broadening and expanding services

As the over-85 population expands in the United States, the demand for health-care resources will become even greater. The advance of medicine has resulted in the increase of the "old-old" census. A community-based health-care system that promotes and supports the concept of wellness for seniors is the future direction for geriatric care. By pooling multiple aspects of medical and social services, a health-care provider can create a network for coordinating and supplying various complex care packages for its clients. These services can include home health care, adult day care, geriatric medicine, and respite care. Although most states only reimburse day care programs through Medicaid, some are beginning to offer Medicare Part B reimbursement if the programs are medically oriented.

PACE

PACE (Program for All-inclusive Care for the Elderly), started by the On Lok senior care group in San Francisco, is a successful model for a comprehensive care system. PACE provides a range of services to clients, including adult day care and primary care, rehabilitation therapy, and home health care. Community-based programs will become more essential as alternatives to costly long-term care. Programs like PACE also offer frail seniors the ability to select the services and programs they need and want.

The real change is that services are brought to the client, rather than the other way around. Frail and physically disabled seniors are able to maintain their independence and choose to stay at home, whether with families or by themselves. The adult day care program of tomorrow will play a major role in realizing the multifaceted community health-care concept.

Integrated dementia care models

Over the past decade there has been a significant increase in the number of specialized assisted living residences for people with dementia. New models are being developed that provide an integrated day care program in which participants with dementia have dedicated program areas and then spend the day in activities with other persons with de-

mentia. These smaller-scale day care programs (usually 10–15 people per day) allow for cost-effective utilization of space and staff resources. These facilities are typically developed with a small social space (sized to meet state licensure requirements) that can be "secured" during arrivals and departures, and used for day care resident dining.

Long-Term Care

Introduction/types of users

In general long-term care and specialized services may fall into the following categories:

- Long-term care: very frail and/or ill residents needing 24-hour nursing
- Hospice/palliative care: residents who are in the last stage of life
- Alzheimer's/dementia care: primarily mid-to late-stage, meaning higher levels of skilled professionals to provide medical care and treatment
- Rehabilitation: short-stay, between hospital and return to home
- Other areas of dedicated programming, staff, and facilities, including respite care or temporary care, and younger adults with brain trauma/injury

Nursing homes provide 24-hour skilled nursing care for the frail elderly and others (individuals with chronic illnesses, traumatic brain injuries, ventilator dependency, etc.) who require a high level of medical care and assistance but do not need the services of an acute-care hospital. Many nursing homes now provide short-term rehabilitative (subacute program with Medicare-licensed beds) stays for those recovering from an injury, operation, or illness; others offer specialized hospice and dementia-specific programs.

Longer-term care residents generally have high care needs and complex medical conditions that require routine skilled-nursing services. This care is provided by licensed nursing staff under the supervision of a family physician or the facility's part- or full-time medical staff.

In the past, many residents were still ambulatory at the time of admission. Now those who are able to walk are typically choosing alternative housing options rather than long-term care facilities. Over the last 20 years the average age and frailty of residents has soared; in some facilities the typical resident is over 85, close to 70 percent use wheelchairs, and over half suffer from Alzheimer's or other forms of dementia.

Residents typically share a room with one to three others, and those who are able to leave their rooms are served meals in a central dining area on the nursing unit or in a central location. At most facilities, activities are also available during the day and evening for these mobile residents. *(Also known as: Nursing Home, Convalescent Care, Nursing Center, Chronic-Care Center, Skilled-Nursing Facility, Skilled-Care Facility, Comprehensive-Care Facility, Intermediate-Care Facility.)*

Types of sponsors/owners

For-profit
For-profit providers accounted for the majority of nursing beds as of 1999. Large national chains such as Beverly Enterprises, Manor Care, Sun Healthcare Group, Mariner Post-Acute Network, and Integrated Health Services own the majority. Smaller privately owned nursing homes still exist in many communities but are not the typical owners of new facilities.

> **1999 Data on Nursing Homes:**
> Proprietary:
> 1,235,800 beds
> Voluntary nonprofit:
> 499,500 beds
> Government & other:
> 144,300 beds

Not-for-profit
Not-for-profit groups, often faith-based organizations, are a common sponsor of long-term care services. A number of facilities are parts of regional organizations or occasionally national networks.

Public
Occasionally local governments, commonly county-based, own and operate nursing beds to serve populations typically underserved due to economic status. The Veterans Administration also has a network of nursing homes.

Types of settings
While most nursing homes are freestanding facilities, some are specialized units in hospitals, continuing-care retirement communities, or other forms of senior housing.

Major program elements and design considerations
Skilled-nursing facilities have four major program components: the resident room, the nursing unit, the common facilities shared by all residents, and the support spaces. All states have codes that establish the minimum square footage of the major spaces, but for a quality facility these minimums are often far too small. There are older facilities where the gross square footage of the entire facility is less than 400 GSF per resident. Today the minimum size for a quality modern facility is over 600 GSF, and the best facilities often exceed 750–800 GSF per resident.

The size, to remain competitive, is likely to grow, since most sponsors now recognize that their facilities are the residents' home, not just a health-care center. Since an extended-stay hotel such as a Marriott Residence Inn or Executive Suites would be programmed to provide at least 700 GSF per guest, it is not surprising that traditional nursing homes are widely disliked in part due to their cramped living spaces and lack of privacy. Nevertheless, they are still a necessary option for almost two million frail aged. With an understanding of the history of long-term care (see sidebar), it is easier to discuss current standards for the major components of a nursing home program.

The resident room

The basic building block of a long-term care facility is the resident room. Most codes establish 100 sq ft as the minimum room size for a single person and 80 sq ft per person in a multibed room. This minimum does not include resident storage or toilet spaces. Other codes establish minimum accessibility and furnishing requirements, which then determine the minimum room size. Most new facilities offer single rooms or shared rooms that improve resident privacy. Most states no longer permit or encourage the building of four-bedded rooms, yet most existing beds are in small shared rooms.

The reality is that a fully wheelchair-accessible room with a bed, side table, dresser, chair, and closet or wardrobe cannot be much smaller than 12' x 12' (144 sq ft). Moreover, sharing a room with a stranger, with nothing but a curtain for privacy, is the single most disliked aspect of nursing homes. Thus, in response to the expectations of residents and their families, a growing number of sponsors have experimented with room designs that offer more resident privacy, and some are now offering private rooms exclusively.

Newer semiprivate room designs are typically "toe-to-toe" or "bi-axial" (with or without a partial dividing wall), L-

---

History of Skilled Care Facility Design

Nursing homes and their programs have evolved for several reasons. Since they were originally thought of as health facilities (as opposed to housing with 24-hour health-care supervision and support), the early models were patterned on acute-care hospitals. As the majority of residents qualified for Medicaid to pay for their stay, states moved to try to contain this rapidly growing part of their budgets. By restricting approval of reimbursement for construction that exceeded often unrealistic limits on maximum allowable costs, they encouraged many sponsors to build code-minimum sized facilities. The older codes in many states did not recognize how old, ill, and cognitively impaired the average resident would become. It is common for many older buildings not to be fully wheelchair-accessible. Moreover, many of the homes do not meet resident needs or expectations for privacy, comfort, and other basic quality-of-life issues. Where newer or renovated centers are being developed, these older homes are becoming obsolete.

---

shaped, or private with a shared toilet. While these room types add square footage, and therefore cost, they are popular with residents, family, and staff. Other specific resident room features in current designs include:

1. Large windows for sunlight with low sills for viewing outside

2. Multiple light sources for reading in bed or chair, observation by staff (especially skin conditions), night lighting (with floor lighting) for easy access to the bathroom

3. Cable TV and telephone conveniently placed based on the most efficient furniture layout

4. Typical furniture provisions:

- Beds with electric or pneumatic controls (dimensions should be checked, as beds vary in size and are significantly larger than standard ones)

- Wardrobe/closets with at least 36" of hanging space

- A dresser

- A nightstand with locking drawer

- A comfortable chair with arms and high back

▲ ▼ *Due to growing resistence to the typical "semiprivate" room (above), sponsors are creating rooms that are more homelike and offer more privacy and dignity. (Below) Copper Ridge, Sykesville, Maryland. Perkins Eastman Architects PC. Photograph by Curtis Martin.*

Each resident room typically has a two-fixture bathroom (except for the one isolation room on each nursing unit, which also has a shower), although some sponsors provide a shower in all bathrooms. The typical features and detailing of the bathroom include:

- A vanity countertop rather than a wall-mounted sink, giving residents space to set grooming devices while using them. An open area below the vanity countertop for use in a seated position and/or maintaining space for mobility devices that frequently have angled fronts, such as a walker, or large space requirements, such as a wheelchair

- A small wall-recessed cabinet or wall-mounted shelf with rounded corners for toiletries placed in a convenient location that does not require reaching over a sink, where visibility and physical ability may be limited

- In shared accommodations, towel bars and a recessed wall cabinet or wall-mounted shelves for each user

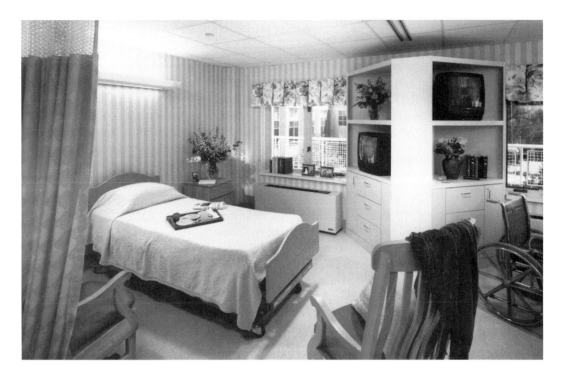

▲ Even greater resident privacy is created by building a wall or a storage unit between the two beds. Sarah R. Neuman Center for Healthcare and Rehabilitation–Weinberg Pavilion, Mamaroneck, New York. Perkins Eastman Architects PC. Photograph by Chuck Choi.

▶ One approach that creates more privacy is to move the beds into a "toe-to-toe" configuration. Joseph L. Morse Geriatric Center, West Palm Beach, Florida. Perkins Eastman Architects PC.

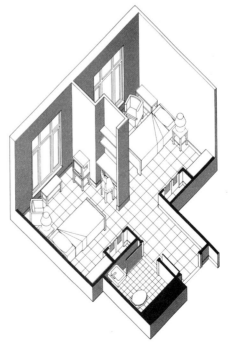

- Multiple lighting sources to illuminate specific tasks and night lighting for accessibility and visual cues
- A nonslip floor surface suitable for a wet area
- A large swinging door or surface-sliding bathroom door (like a barn door) that provides a clear, wide opening (32–42 in.) for maneuverability and eliminates space conflict of a swinging door.
- When required, bedpan washers in each toilet. This will depend on the nursing staff's requirements. Disposable bedpans are now making this institutional plumbing less necessary.
- The proper toilet height, which makes it easier for older people to rise. A handicapped-height toilet or a standard toilet with a raised seat can accomplish this requirement.
- Toilet grab bars. Side (42 in. long) and rear (24 in. long) bars are required by many codes. Alternatively, flip-down grab bars on both sides of the toilet may be mounted on the rear wall, but this option may require a code variance. Some toilet seat manufacturers make products with chairlike arms mounted on both sides, commonly referred to as "sheltering arms." Note that it may be beneficial to specify grab bars that can also function as towel bars, because some residents will use a towel bar for support.

See Chapter 14 for further discussion of finishes and other details.

The bathroom should be residential in appearance but accessible. Residential lighting products, paint-finished grab bars, and conventional tank toilets help to create the appropriate ambience. Most accidents occur in the bathroom, which may present a risk for frail older adults. Easy access from the bed to the toilet room is essential, since frequent use at night is common and particularly risky because older people are more likely to lose their balance or experience disorientation at night.

The nursing unit

A number of resident rooms are typically organized around a nursing station, clean and soiled utility rooms, and bathing, dining, and lounge spaces. The number of residents varies from less than 30 in small specialized units to a maximum of 60 or more permitted in some states. Forty beds is a common size, but there is no universal standard. Moreover, as more nursing units are organized around a series of subnursing stations and decentralized support spaces, the concept of a standard nursing-unit size has decreased in importance.

Designing a unit to maximize staff efficiency is important. The most significant cost of operating a long-term care facility is the staff. A variety of staff, from nursing to dietary to housekeeping, maintains the residents' quality of life and environment. Most nursing units are planned based on licensed nursing and direct-care staff (care attendants or CNAs, certified nursing assistants). Staffing is typically organized in traditional medical-model nursing shifts of 7 A.M.–3 P.M. (morning), 3 P.M.–11 P.M. (afternoon/evening), and 11 P.M.–7 A.M. (night). Staff requirements are based on mandated codes (1 CNA for every 10 residents and a registered nurse (RN) or licensed practical nurse (LPN) for every

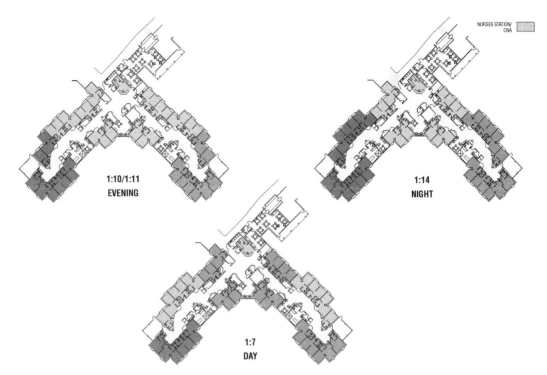

NURSES STATION/
CNA

1:10/1:11
EVENING

1:14
NIGHT

1:7
DAY

Cluster Concepts

40–60 residents is common) and resident care needs. Due to the high physical frailty it is common to find CNA ratios of 1:7 or 1:8 on morning and day shifts and 1:15 to 1:21 on night shifts. Because RN/LPNs are responsible for meeting medical needs, it is typical to find ratios of 1:20 to 1:30 on morning and day shifts and 1:40 to 1:60 on night shifts. Therefore, some nursing units are designed to operate as smaller units in the day that can be combined into a larger unit supervised by a central nurse station at night.

Nursing units have typically been organized in one of the common alphabet shapes L, T, X, V, or Y (see Chapter 3 for further discussion). These shapes emanated from a design/operations philosophy of placing the nurse's station in the center for control, surrounding it with all of the support spaces (utility, bathing, dining, etc.) and locating lounges at the ends of corridors. These plans were also derived from some code requirements mandating a maximum distance (commonly 120 ft) from the nurse's station or utility space to the last resident room. Newer models have explored clustering to decentralize staff and services from the central nurses' station.

"Cluster" design concepts decentralize support areas (bathing, utility, etc.) into multiple locations to minimize walking distances for staff. These design models also distribute the direct-care staff into clusters with workstations (desks) commonly integrated into lounge/living-room spaces. Clusters are

▲ This nursing unit, which incorporates the cluster concept, maximizes staffing efficiency on each shift. New York State Veterans Nursing Home at Montrose, Montrose, New York. Perkins Eastman Architects PC.

typically arranged so that they can change from 7–10 rooms/residents on day shift to 14–21 on night shifts to respond to changing staff needs.

The cluster concept

The cluster concept is a staffing model that utilizes the day, evening, and night shifts to create a "neighborhood"-based nursing unit. A 42-bed nursing unit, for example, can be first subdivided into two "neighborhoods" of 21 beds each and "clusters" of 7.

A sample day, evening, and night shift staffing plan for a 42-bed nursing unit:

Day Shift: 1CNA for every 7 residents/1 RN or LPN for 21 residents

Evening Shift: 1 CNA for every 14 residents/1 RN or LPN for 21 or 42 residents

Night Shift: 1 CNA for every 21 residents/1 RN or LPN for 42 residents

There is one licensed nurse unit manager to supervise and manage the nursing staff for each shift. The number of residents in a cluster varies with the shift. The maximum staffing ratio occurs during the day shift, since residents will require more staff assistance during the active morning and early afternoon hours for meals, bathing, dressing, therapy, and recreation, in addition to medical care. The satellite staff stations for the CNAs need to be located strategically to accommodate the flexible staffing ratios for each shift. Service spaces, such as clean linen and soiled utility, are commonly dispersed throughout the unit into multiple locations to minimize walking distances for staff.

While some older facilities still have only central lounge and dining areas, most facilities now distribute these important functions to each nursing unit. Some of the key considerations in the planning of these spaces include:

Dining. Dining options and space have changed dramatically, shifting away from large-scale rooms for 40–60 residents (or more) served on trays. Newer options promote smaller-scale-dining room experiences coupled with country kitchens and family-style bulk meals served in courses. The quality of the food and the dining experience are important features of any well-run facility. Key design parameters include:

- Provide 25–30 sq ft/person for adequate space to meet the needs of residents in wheelchairs and geriatric chairs.

- When possible, provide multiple dining rooms serving 15–20 residents each.

- Break up large-scale dining rooms into smaller environments for better acoustic control, visual privacy, and a more intimate dining experience.

- Provide an open country kitchen (verify with local department of health) to support the food-service program and other snack/baking activities or provide pantries that allow aromas to stimulate resident appetites.

- Consider additional appropriate space for food-service support that may involve refrigeration (commercial and/or residential style), steam tables, ice machines, microwaves, etc.

- Consider providing a "private dining" room for 8–10 for family visits, birthday parties, and other special meals. This can also be used as a conference room by staff, supportive feeding programs for residents, and recreational activities.

The decentralized stations bring the staff close to the people they serve. New York State Veterans Nursing Home at Montrose, Montrose, New York. Perkins Eastman Architects PC. Photograph by Chuck Choi.

Lounge/activity/living room. A range of social activity spaces within or near nursing units are important to provide:

- Private places for residents and their families/guests
- Informal activity areas for games, cards, or organized activities
- Comfortable places for discussion groups, watching TV, etc.
- Places for small parties (birthday/special occasions) or shared meals ("private dining")

Bathing. Bathing areas have changed from centralized "hygiene machines" to more spalike experiences that afford greater privacy and environmental quality. Facilities tend to view the shower versus tub bathing issue differently, and most states are flexible on which is used. In either case, a private room with a changing/dressing area, access to toilets, and adequate space for bathing makes up a bathing suite. If showers are used they need to be roll-in and large in size for maneuvering residents in shower chairs (48" x 48" minimum). If specialized tubs are used, there needs to be adequate maneuvering space for staff on three sides and for specialized lifts or transfers. Items to consider:

- Nonslip floor services with appropriate drainage
- Storage space for soaps, shampoos, and cleaning products for tubs and showers between uses
- Bathing tub manufacturer product requirements for size, power, water, and access
- Vanity counter for grooming
- Hand-wash sink for staff
- Additional heat source for comfort

- Shower curtains and cubicle curtains to maintain privacy
- Separate external controls for showers so staff don't have to reach into the shower
- Places to put towels, clothes, robes, etc.
- Private, easily-accessed toileting facilities

Clean utility room. A room typically used for storing clean supplies such as IV racks, monitors, adult diapers, medical supplies, etc. Storage cabinets and a hand-wash sink are typically required.

Soiled utility room. A room for temporary storage of soiled linen and clothing until it can be relocated to a central holding or laundry area. As the level of incontinence has increased in long-term care facilities, these spaces have gotten larger and more complex. It is not unusual to find one or two multiple-compartment carts (2' x 4' or so) that sort bed linens, infectious linens, and personal clothing. Limited cabinetry, a hand-wash sink, and bed-pan-washing device are typical features.

Clean linen. Most facilities use some type of a "cart exchange" system, where fully stocked carts are rolled or placed into a closet or room and old carts are taken back for restocking. Depending on the number of beds served, there may be up to two or three carts (24" x 60"or so) and some limited fixed shelving for extra pillows and blankets. This space is, at times, combined with a clean utility room.

Nurses' station. This term is something of a misnomer because there may be up to 10–12 different staff (only 1 or 2 of whom may be nurses) using the records, computer, telephones, and supplies in this location. Providing a reception zone to receive visitors/family and residents is typical, but equally important is a work zone for charting, staffing meetings/care conferences, and private/confidential phone calls about resident care. In many states active medical records are still required to be kept in hard-copy form, but increased use of the computer for ordering, communication with other departments, and record keeping will change as state policies catch up with technology. The need for the nurses' station to act as a central emergency call hub has largely been replaced by pagers and cell phones that route emergency calls to staff wherever they may be.

Common facilities

Additional common areas within a skilled-nursing facility serving all of the nursing units may include:

- Multipurpose room: suitable for large group activities, holiday celebrations, religious services, performances
- Coffee shop/snack bar: often an alternative visitation area for residents and guests
- Gift shop
- Library: often includes computers for resident use as well as a growing choice of reading materials and other media being developed for the aging
- Outdoor terraces and recreation areas
- Art/activity: large centralized space for specialized activities that cannot be accomplished in the nursing unit
- Clinic: space for specialized exams (dental, ophthalmology) and treatment
- Rehabilitation: restorative therapies and rehabilitation, including physical, occupational and speech therapy

Support areas

Away from resident, family, and visitor areas is a large infrastructure that supports the typical long-term care facility. A commercial kitchen, laundry, central receiving and storage, resident storage, housekeeping, facility maintenance and mechanical rooms are typical elements. Office suites for administrative support and areas for staff break, dining, and training are important.

The program on page 39 represents typical (neither minimum nor generous) net space allocations for the most frequently used common and support spaces in a 120–200 bed facility. The specific allocations differ widely for a variety of reasons:

- Special dietary requirements (kosher, etc.), support of other food programs (meals on wheels, day care, etc.), type of food service (tray or bulk delivery to the dining rooms, cook/chill, etc.), and other factors can significantly alter the kitchen area required (see also Chapter 10).

- A special program emphasis—such as a large subacute rehab program—can increase therapy areas.

- A strong activity or faith-based program can significantly increase the need for multipurpose and chapel spaces.

Moreover, there are variations in net-to-gross ratios. The normal ratio used to con-

▼ *Many facilities have renovated and added spaces to create attractive common areas including such features as a coffee shop or snack bar for resident and family interaction. Sarah R. Neuman Center for Healthcare and Rehabilitation-Weinberg Pavilion, Mamaroneck, New York. Perkins Eastman Architects PC. Photograph by Chuck Choi.*

SAMPLE PROGRAM FOR A LONG-TERM RESIDENT NEIGHBORHOOD		
SPACE	**TYPICAL CODE OR MINIMUM AREA (sq ft)**	**RECOMMENDED MINIMUM AREA (sq ft)**
Dining	15 /resident	25–35 /resident
Lounge/activity/living room	10–15 /resident	20–35 /resident
Bathing (fixture= tub or shower)	150; 1 fixture per 15 residents	250; 1 fixture per 15 residents not individually served
Clean utility	40–60; 1 per unit	50–75; 1 per 15–20 residents
Soiled utility	40–60; 1 per unit	60–100; 1 per 15 residents
Clean linen	15–25; 1 per unit	15–25; 1 per 15 residents
Nurses' station and wall work area	150–250	250–500
Medication room	25–40; 1 per unit	50–75; 1 per 15 residents
Resident toilet near dining	Not required	Recommended
Public / visitor toilet	Not required	Recommended
Staff toilet	Required	Required
Resident toilet with bathing	Required	1 per bathing suite
Staff office	Not required	1–2 per unit for nursing supervisor and/or social worker

vert net to gross in a nursing home is 1.45 to 1.65. This relatively high grossing factor is due in part to the typical code requirements for eight-foot corridors.

Payment/reimbursement and regulation

Nursing homes are the most regulated form of senior living due to the concern for protecting the well-being of frail seniors, their historical connection to hospital codes/regulation and the desire to control the quality and cost of nursing-home care. Long-term care facilities are licensed and regulated by the state department of health (DOH) with space and construction standards. The local DOH may also cite federal or national standards, such as the American Institute of Architects' Guidelines for Design and Construction of Hospitals and Health

Care Facilities, American National Standards Institute (ANSI) standards, and the life-safety codes of the National Fire Protection Association (NFPA) and the Americans with Disabilities Act (ADA). State codes that have not been updated recently may not have adopted the most recent versions of the national standards. The cost of nursing-home care (which commonly exceeds $50,000 per year) is typically covered by the resident and his or her family through private financial resources, health insurance, and long-term care insurance, or by Medicaid for financially qualified individuals.

Because of the increasing need and explosive growth of publicly funded reimbursement, local and federal governments have been working to contain costs by reducing reimbursement and changing the services and eligibility for

SAMPLE SUPPORT SPACE PROGRAM FOR A 120–200 BED LONG-TERM CARE FACILITY

SPACE	AREA (sq ft)	SPACE	AREA (sq ft)
Administration		**Facilities/environmental services**	
Reception	150	Housekeeping office	120
Admissions	200	Maintenance shop	240
Administrator	140	Central supply	2000
Assistant administrator	120	Engineering director's office	120
Human resources director	120	Receiving/staging area	500
Finance director	120	Oxygen storage	100
Business office suite	500	Soiled holding room	300
Administrative assistants (2 @ 100 sq ft)	200	Sterilization room	100
Conference room	240	Housekeeping equipment and supplies	120
Work-room, copier, supplies	120	Trash room/compactor	240
Subtotal	1,910	Equipment storage	240
		Central laundry (personal items)	350
Health services administration		Morgue	120
Director of nursing	120	Mail room	100
Assistant director of nursing	100	Cart wash	100
Family conference room	120	Subtotal	4,750
Nursing secretary	100		
In-service director	100	**Clinical/health-care support**	
Social worker office/workstation (may be located on nursing units)	200	Exam room	120
		Consultation room	100
Subtotal	740	Dental and ophthalmology exam rooms	160
		Medical records	200
Common facilities		Medical workstation /charting	100
Physical therapy	800	Subtotal	680
Occupational therapy	500		
OT/PT office	120	**Staff support**	
Barber/beauty shop	250	Staff dining/lounge	400
Arts and activities	300	Locker rooms 2 @ 350 each	700
Meditation/quiet area	500	Training room	400
Volunteers homeroom	200	Subtotal	1,500
Recreation director's office	120		
Gift shop	250	**Optional programs**	
Snack bar	350	Pharmacy for cart exchange	300
Multipurpose room	500	Laundry room (full-service)	1500
Subtotal	3,890	**Total sq ft required (including optional programs)**	14,770
Food service			
Kitchen (food prep, storage, office(s), dish/pot washing, cart wash, etc.)	2,500		

▲ *A growing number of specialized facilities such as hospice and palliative care are being built for individuals in the last days of life and their families. Hospice settings range from small homelike structures to larger specialized facilities. Hospice LaGrange, West Georgia Medical Center, LaGrange, Georgia. Perkins & Will. Photograph by William Nelson.*

reimbursement. Many states have a certificate of need (CON) process, which regulates the construction of new facilities or replacement/renovation of older ones. Some states, such as Pennsylvania, have made it difficult to build or replace existing facilities by declining applications and providing minimal reimbursement for the capital costs.

Trends/opportunities for innovation

The building of new nursing homes has been severely curtailed by state controls, but replacement facilities, major modernizations, and skilled nursing wings in CCRCs and other settings continue.

In the new or renovated settings, the trends have included:

- More private rooms or rooms designed with greater privacy as well as in-room features such as window seats, showers in the bathroom, and space to permit more personal items, such as a favorite chair from home

- Decentralization of the staff away from central bunkerlike nursing stations into smaller resident clusters

- Decentralization of activities, dining, therapy, and other programs into the nursing units and away from single central locations

- Design of less compartmentalized, more homelike common spaces

- More specialized nursing units to meet the needs and/or expectations of the residents

- Special features, such as spalike bathing, to increase the dignity, comfort, and satisfaction of the residents
- Residential-looking finishes, furniture, and lighting to create a more homelike, less medical appearance
- Nursing units to serve specialized needs and populations:

    Dementia (specialized program)

    Dementia (end stage)

    Hospice/palliative

    Rehabilitation/short-term stay

    Ventilator

- Culture change—programs based on concepts that alter the design and operation of long-term care (for more information, see Chapter 3)

    Eden alternative

    Household model

    Pioneer movement

Assisted Living Residences

Introduction/types of users

Assisted living residences are designed for seniors who are no longer able to live on their own safely but do not require the high level of health care provided in a nursing home. Assistance with medications, activities of daily living, meals, and housekeeping are routinely provided. Three meals per day are often served waiter-style in a common dining room. Residents live in their own apartments, which frequently have a small pantry or "tea kitchen" with a sink, small refrigerator, and microwave. Staff is usually available 24 hours a day for additional safety. Some assisted living residences provide licensed nursing services, but hours vary from community to community. In fact, the extent to which residents require as-sistance with activities of daily living (dressing, bathing, etc.) can vary greatly. It is important to realize that over 40 percent of residents in assisted living have some form of cognitive impairment ranging from the mildly confused to the profoundly impaired.

Social activities and scheduled transportation are also available in most communities. In addition, a special unit for Alzheimer's residents is sometimes available, and many specialized assisted living residences have been developed. The assisted living industry has seen a period of phenomenal growth, which can be compared with the expansion of the nursing-home industry in the 1960s and 1970s. From the late 1980s to the late 1990s, the number of assisted living beds more than doubled. The National Investment Center for Seniors Housing and Care Industries (NIC) reports that assisted living facilities make up about 50 percent of the over 46,000 seniors' housing properties with supportive services in the United States today. The assisted living model has become a common alternative to nursing-home care for all but the most medically dependent or low-income residents.

(Also known as: Assisted-Care Community, Assistive Living, Adult Homes, Domiciliary Care, Personal-Care Homes, Sheltered Care, and Catered Living.)

Types of sponsors/owners

For-profit

For-profit developers have been the most aggressive sponsors of assisted living, having created the industry and defined its products. Sponsors like Sunrise, Manor Care, Atria, and Marriott have combined traditional real estate housing development with services, and at times a hospitality philosophy. These types of publicly traded companies have typically focused on upper-income residents in wealthy communities.

Not-for-profit

Not-for-profit sponsors have focused on providing housing and services to frail older adults in an assisted living setting. Like for-profit sponsors, they have typically focused on upper-income seniors who can afford to pay without public assistance. Not-for-profit sponsors have also developed a number of models that offer affordable housing and services through external and internal reimbursement, subsidies, and other programs.

Public

In a limited number of cases, public entities have sponsored assisted living—usually to offer an affordable alternative for their communities.

Types of settings

Freestanding

In the 1980s and 1990s most of the rapid development of new assisted living was done in freestanding new facilities physically separate from other senior housing and care options.

As part of a campus offering a continuum of services

In the growing effort to provide an environment that allows for "aging in place" with a spectrum of services that respond to the changing needs of aging residents, assisted living programs are now frequently being added to existing communities or being designed as a part of continuing care retirement communities (see CCRCs).

Major program elements and design considerations

Assisted living facilities have four major program components:

- Resident unit
- Common facilities serving each floor, wing, or cluster (often called a house or neighborhood) of residents
- Common facilities serving all residents
- Support spaces

Resident unit

Most of the growing number of sponsors, operators, and developers of assisted living bring their own interpretation to the specific program and project. As a result, there is a wide variety of unit types, unit mixes, and design features being incorporated in projects in North America. Some of the variety stems from differences in market expectations, cost, code, and program issues; but much of it is the result of each sponsor/developer's concepts.

Unit size and mix

The most apparent conceptual difference regards unit size. Some early for-profit developers of assisted living believed that a high proportion of their potential residents would find a small studio acceptable, so an emphasis on attractive communal spaces developed. Many early units were studios approximately 325–375 sq ft in size. Later sponsors, including the research group that developed the AAHSA (American Association of Homes and Services for the Aging) prototype and some for-profit sponsors, felt that the typical unit should be larger. The recommended basic AAHSA prototype unit, for example, was a 435–550 sq ft one-bedroom.

There have been many successful projects based on these program concepts, and it may be some time before there is definitive data related to user preferences and the success of facility operations over time to support any one approach. As more projects are completed and the field becomes more competitive, however, sponsor/developers are moving toward larger units. Even those that still build a high proportion of studio units are building larger studio units with more private sleeping areas.

Differences in program concept also appear in the unit mix. Today, most programs include various unit types and sizes. A typical resident mix might be 75–80 percent single women, 10–15 percent single men, and 5–10 percent couples. This accounts for some of the need for variety, but economics and market preferences are even stronger defining forces. Most sponsors prefer to offer a mix that appeals to as wide a variety of resident preferences and budgets as possible. Thus, it is not unusual for a project to contain both smaller and larger studios, minimum and larger one-bedrooms, and a few two-bedrooms or shared units. Most of the experienced sponsors also include a wing or "neighborhood" with special units for residents with dementia. Other sponsors, in particular many of the non-profits, use size differences to justify pricing. It is not uncommon to disguise an internal subsidy for lower-income residents by creating an artificially large spread between the larger and smaller units. The real debt-service and operating-cost difference between a small studio and a one-bedroom (where the size difference is often less than 100 sq ft) is less than $100 per month.

As the field has evolved, there are ten typical unit types. There are many differences within each unit type to be discussed later, but the following examples illustrate the most common program options.

Semiprivate

This option is likely to become less common for the reasons noted above, but it is still being included in some projects. It is an expanded nursing-home semiprivate, and it assumes that lower cost will make it acceptable as supportive housing for some residents. It is, however, an appropriate unit type for 10–20 percent of the units in a specialized facility or wing for residents with dementia. Often some residents with dementia bond with another resident, thereby requiring a shared living arrangement.

Small studio

This unit type—typically about 325 sq ft in size—is frequently used and has many of the features of a hotel room. It has the

▼ *The small studio. Perkins Eastman Architects PC.*

PROGRAM (PREDESIGN)

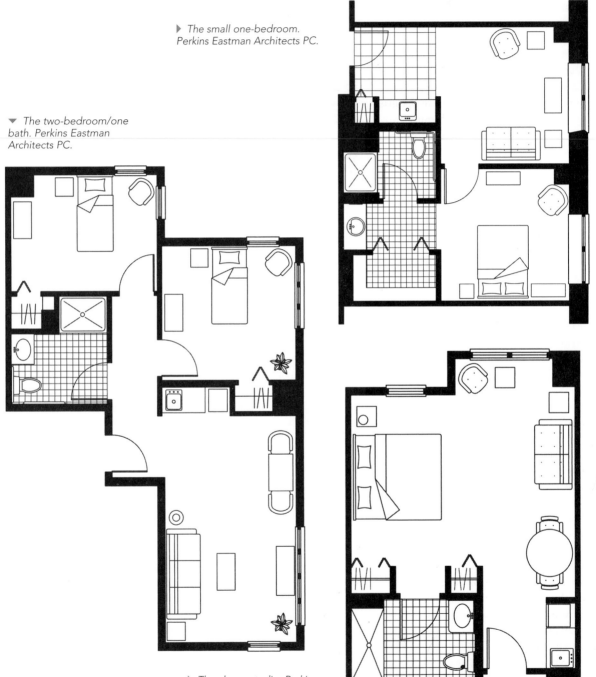

▶ The small one-bedroom.
Perkins Eastman Architects PC.

▼ The two-bedroom/one
bath. Perkins Eastman
Architects PC.

▶ The alcove studio. Perkins
Eastman Architects PC.

advantage of limited floor area and minimum building perimeter but lacks a private sleeping area.

Alcove studio

This unit type—typically about 350–375 sq ft in size—is a popular option because it provides a more separate sleeping area. It requires 16–18 feet of perimeter—often an issue in keeping the building size to a minimum.

Small one-bedroom

The smallest fully accessible one-bedroom is about 435 sq ft in size and requires 22–24 ft of perimeter. It has all the features of an apartment reduced to minimum dimensions.

Large one-bedroom

AAHSA (American Association of Homes and Services for the Aging) prototype research settled on a unit type with approximately 550 sq ft as its full one-bedroom. The living and sleeping rooms are each more generously sized, and typically there is more closet space.

Two-bedroom/one bath

Some sponsors build units with two bedrooms for single residents, couples, siblings, and even unrelated individuals. This unit is typically about 675–800 sq ft in size.

Double master

An increasingly popular option for the same market as the two-bedroom one-bath unit is one with two equal bedrooms and baths. Even some couples who no longer sleep together like this option; it also meets the needs of two siblings or friends sharing a unit. This unit typically is found in higher-income

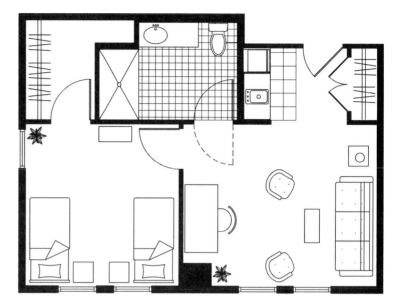

The large one-bedroom. Perkins Eastman Architects PC.

markets and in the assisted living wings of retirement communities.

Suite hotel unit

This unit is modeled after the suite hotel, with a two-room arrangement around a bathroom. Arranged like a dumbbell, it has one room that has no natural light and typically opens onto a corridor.

Shared suite style unit

Some sponsors have experimented with shared living arrangements where the assisted living unit is built similar to a three- or four-bedroom apartment: each person has a private room but shares a common living room, a tea kitchen (or full kitchen), and in some cases a bathroom.

Bedroom unit

This unit has historically been utilized in "room and board" type settings where residents share common areas and functions. Newer models have typically used

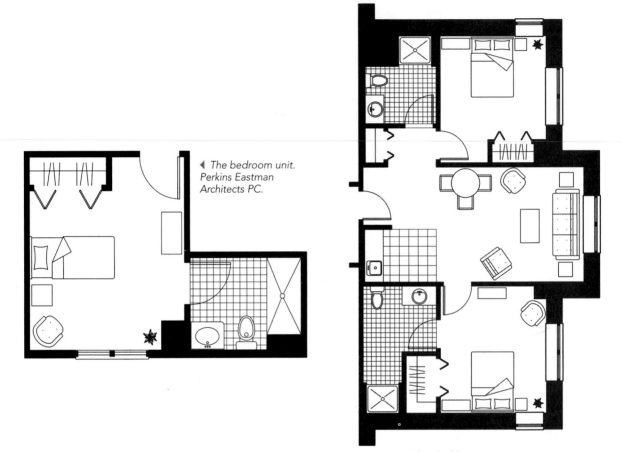

◀ *The bedroom unit.*
Perkins Eastman
Architects PC.

▲ *The double master.*
Perkins Eastman Architects PC.

▶ *The suite hotel unit.*
Berry Rio Architects,
Sunrise Assisted Living.

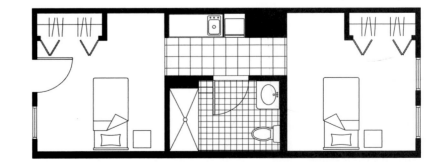

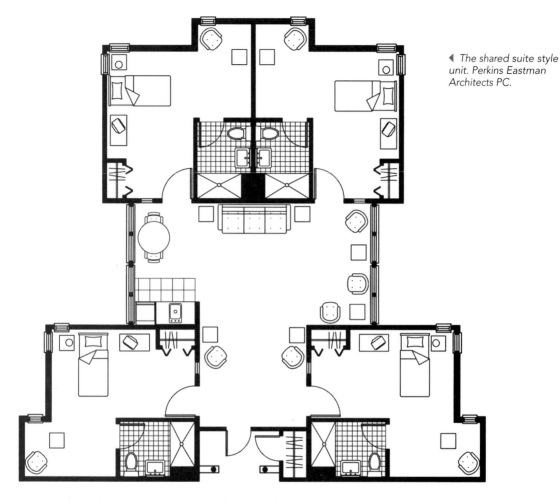

◀ *The shared suite style unit. Perkins Eastman Architects PC.*

this unit type in special programs for residents with dementia. These specially designed dementia programs generally have combined this unit type with a family-size house or cluster where the common areas of the house are shared by a group of 8–10 residents.

Unit features

Bedroom/sleeping area

The sleeping area must accommodate a bed and related dressing and clothes storage. It is important to remember that most residents furnish their own units,

with items of varying size and quantity. The transition from independent to assisted living can be difficult, particularly if related to a dramatic change in physical health and/or the loss of a spouse. Physical possessions take on enhanced meaning, and the full-size (or larger) bed may bring a significant sense of security to the individual. Also, as has been mentioned, couples may no longer be sharing a bed, and space for two twin beds may be essential.

In units without a separate bedroom, it is important to screen the view of the bed from the unit entrance, which maintains the appearance of apartment-style living and distinguishes it from other more institutional settings where the bed is (inappropriately) the focus of one's lifestyle. Creating a niche or alcove can be an important part of the unit design to distinguish the living and sleeping areas.

Bathroom

The bathroom requires significant planning to allow its intended users to remain functionally independent and to distinguish it from the traditional institutional product. It should be residential in appearance and detail. Based upon the aging-in-place and frailty issues of this population, it is important to design units that support functional independence. The bathroom design should acknowledge the fact that staff may provide assistance with various grooming and toileting functions. Accessibility standards provide a good beginning for planning adequate space, but many physical limitations are not covered by these standards. For example:

- Installing a shower big enough to use a portable shower chair (36" x 42" minimum; and 30" x 60" recommended)
- Installing shower controls as well as a shower wand that can be reached from a seated position
- Minimizing the height of the shower threshold to ease access or specifying a product such as Neoprene Threshold Adapter, whose flexible threshold depresses under weight yet provides a water dam
- Providing an additional heating source for increased comfort during bathing
- Installing an additional vertical grab bar at the entrance to the shower to steady the resident while entering and exiting

Most of the features noted in the skilled-nursing resident bathroom design are relevant here as well.

Living room

The unit living space should be familiar and relate to the resident's previous lifestyle. Whether that is watching television, doing puzzles or crafts, or using a computer, these are important factors in maintaining one's self-esteem and engagement with the world. Residents typically bring their furniture and attempt to crowd more objects and memories than

▼ *Most assisted living units have all of the components of an apartment but are very compact. Weinberg Terrace, Squirrel Hill, Pennsylvania. Perkins Eastman Architects PC. Photograph by Lockwood Hoehl.*

are practical into the room. Favorite furnishings include china cupboards, kitchen tables (or dining drop-leaf tables), lounge chairs/recliners, and large conversation seating groups with bulky sofas and several side chairs.

Unit kitchen/tea kitchen

In assisted living, the kitchen is commonly viewed as the element that defines the unit and distinguishes it from simply being a bedroom. While some sponsors may provide a full kitchen, it is more common to find a Pullman-style kitchen that provides a sink, small refrigerator, microwave, and cabinets in a 5–6 ft-long counter. This kitchen arrangement, frequently referred to as a "tea kitchen," originated in Europe. Assisted living sponsors typically provide three meals a day, so the tea kitchen is not seen as a food-preparation area; rather it is a snack kitchen that offers residents flexibility and choice. The kitchen also maintains continuity with past lifestyles, allowing residents to entertain in their units and retain important dishes and other objects. Tea kitchens are usually not provided in units specifically planned for people with dementia since the house or cluster kitchen meets the same need and decreases the risk of unsupervised injury.

The tea kitchen can be built of component parts but requires significant coordination of cabinetry, appliance venting, and dimensional concerns, and attention to the senior's special needs. Significant features that should be incorporated in the design include:

- A refrigerator with a separate freezer compartment that has the size and temperature controls to preserve ice cream, not just ice trays

- A refrigerator that is raised off of the floor 10–12 in. to reduce the amount of bending and stooping by the user

- A pantry cabinet with eye-level storage that is easy to reach

- An undercabinet shelf for the microwave, it to be used with convenient counter space below when removing hot items that must be set down

- An under-cabinet light for illumination of countertop tasks

- A removable base cabinet below the sink for accessibility

▼ The emergence of new housing options for the aging has encouraged manufacturers to work with architects and interior designers to create new specialized products such as this assisted living "tea kitchen." Perkins Eastman Architects PC. Photograph courtesy of Dwyer Kitchen.

Unit amenities

Emergency call systems

Emergency call systems have made great strides from the conventional hard-wired nurse call systems developed for nursing homes and hospitals. These systems can now be integrated with phone systems and wireless technologies. Systems integration consolidates most communication systems such as telephone, emergency call, fire alarm, passive notification systems, security, and staff paging/communication (see also Chapter 9).

Heating, ventilating, and air-conditioning

In assisted living units, sponsors and their design teams have generally employed relatively simple heating, ventilation, and cooling systems with individual controls in the units.

The typical assisted living resident is often more susceptible to chills than younger adults. As a result, assisted living units are often kept warmer than a normal apartment. Cooling, however, is also an issue, and virtually all new units are air-conditioned. (For a further discussion of this topic, refer to Chapter 8).

Unit personalization

A major issue for many residents is continuity with the past. As their new home, an assisted living unit must have features they associate with "home." The most common issues include:

- The ability to bring favorite pieces of furniture
- Wall space, shelves, or windowsills to accommodate photographs, memorabilia, and other personal items
- Flexibility to arrange the unit to fit the individual resident's lifestyle, including multiple telephone and cable TV outlets so that furniture can be arranged without extension cords that can become tripping hazards
- Window-treatment hardware that allows residents to install decorative drapes over building-supplied window blinds or shears for light and privacy control
- Neutral carpet and paint selections that work flexibly with various styles and color schemes

One of the most common efforts to individualize a unit has been at the hallway entry door. Sponsors who have provided "package" shelves at the unit entrance will find that it is also used for personal display of silk flowers, pictures, or other memorabilia. Providing ways for people to personalize their unit entry (much like their house) is important, whether it be a simple door hook for a wreath or a flexible signage system that identifies more than just unit number (name and sometimes photograph).

Storage

Storage is typically very limited and always an issue. Most storage within assisted living units is limited to one or two closets. Operating issues may also affect storage needs. For example, if sheets and towels are provided along with housekeeping, then there may be no need for significant storage of these items in the unit. If there is no central storage, then suitcases and other bulky items must be stored within the unit. Storage of medical supplies is a major issue if the occupants have equipment such as oxygen concentrators or other similarly large items. Power-operated vehicles are seeing increased use and affect the way senior housing is designed, because these vehicles take up lots of space when not in use and require electrical charging.

Common facilities

The center of the facility typically contains a number of common areas serving all of the residents. Typical common spaces include:

Connecting corridors. As a general guideline, the limit is 150 ft of corridor travel from the farthest resident unit to an elevator and to the main common spaces, such as the dining room. Most

◀ *Attractive common spaces are an essential element of a successful assisted living residence. Inn at Silver Lake, Kingston, Massachusetts. Perkins Eastman Architects PC. Photograph by Eric Cohen.*

▼ Dining is probably the most important common activity in senior housing. Private dining rooms for family dinners, birthday parties, and other special meals are a typical feature of newer facilities. Brookdale Living Community, Mt. Lebanon, Pennsylvania. Perkins Eastman Architects PC. Photograph by Jim Schafer.

corridors are designed to be six feet wide to permit two people with walkers to pass. A lean rail or handrail is needed on at least one side, but rails on both sides are recommended.

Dining. Dining is one of the most important daily resident activities, and its ambience is an important marketing tool aimed at prospective residents and families. Many facilities opt for one or two seatings per meal, depending on operations and facility size. It helps to break up the dining area into more intimate settings. This responds to

acoustic considerations by isolating small groups and thus minimizing background noise. Depending on the local codes 25–28 sq ft per resident is desirable.

Private dining. This is a residentially scaled and furnished space, which seats up to 15 people, accommodating family gatherings or smaller groups of residents. The private dining room is usually situated adjacent to the main area, and can be separated with French doors to allow this space to double as an extension of the main dining room.

Multipurpose/large group activity area. This space is meant to accommodate most of the building's population for movies, religious services, musical entertainment, exercise, or parties. These spaces can vary widely depending upon the culture and/or religious affiliation of the particular residence. As with any large space, special care should be given to acoustics and lighting and their impact on an aging population. (See Chapter 12 for acoustics, Chapter 13 for lighting, and Chapter 14 for design issues.)

Living room/library. Most facilities also have a smaller, more formal space that may double as a library. A library allows for small group activities as well as providing an information center. Access to Internet service provides an opportunity for socialization, and a reference source for medical information, the news, or genealogy.

Snack shop. The functions of a snack shop—depending on resident preference—could be a bistro, where alcoholic drinks are served, an ice-cream parlor, or even a small gift shop and convenience store. The goal of any of these variations is to provide a "street life" ambience and an informal opportunity for socializing.

*Specialized activity areas.*In addition to the above spaces, the traditional craft room can take on the character of activities particular to a region or community, including pottery, wood-working, and jewelry design. Once the messy activities are moved to a craft space, the pantries within resident clusters are available to be used for baking and other less messy small group activities. The aroma of baked goods enhances the residential quality of these neighborhoods.

Wellness center (health, nutrition and exercise). Most facilities have a nurse's office and an exam room. This may be combined with other wellness spaces. Like the general population, older adults have recently shown an increased interest in health main-tenance and wellness, rather than

simply seeking treatment for the diseases and challenges that plague them. Spaces for exercise and nutrition education are now supplementing or even replacing the traditional institu-tional models of occupational and physical therapies and clinic settings.

Spa/assisted bathing. While individual resident units generally provide full bathrooms with a shower fixture, some residents still prefer the occasional bath and may require some assistance with bathing. With the current accent on wellness, some have bathing areas that create a spalike atmosphere, offering massage, aroma therapy, beauty, and hairdressing assistance. Special tubs have been developed with doors or pull-up sides to permit easy access and exit, as well as staff assistance. The ability to control temperature and privacy are

◀ *Spalike common tub bathing areas are becoming a common feature. Harbour House, Greendale, Wisconsin. Architecture by KM Development Corporation. Interior Design by Mithun Inc. Photograph by Skot Weidemann.*

major issues associated with the design of these spaces (see Chapters 6 and 14).

Mail. Mail is an important feature that necessitates adequate space and a convenient location (often near or on the way to dining). Mail usually comes in two ways: U.S. Post Office mailboxes controlled by the local post office (local preferences will dictate front or rear loading) and a separate set of mail slots for facility-delivered notices, newspapers, and information. It is important that the two types of mailboxes/slots be no lower than 30" and no higher than 54" to minimize twisting, bending, and reaching. Shelves to set mail on, good lighting, waste containers, and comfortable seating nearby are important additional features.

Outdoor space (see Chapter 4). Easily accessible outdoor space is important for any assisted living program. An outdoor area adjacent to actively used program spaces will get more use and benefit from nearby staff. Attention to breezes, sunlight, glare, and insects may all be considerations, depending upon the region. It is important to provide a variety of types of outdoor spaces. These may include:

- Terraces/patios off of dining rooms for picnics and barbecues
- Screened porches
- Open porches and other shady/covered areas
- Gardening opportunities (raised planters)
- Formal gardens
- Walking paths

Parking. Parking will need to meet local zoning requirements. Typically, less than 10 percent of residents still retain a car, so parking needs are largely driven by visitor and staff requirements. (For more information on parking requirements, see Chapter 4.)

Neighborhood (or cluster) commons. A commons serving 12–20 resident units supports the idea of neighborhood and allows for informal gatherings. Among the spaces that may be included in this neighborhood commons are the following:

Sitting area. A small gathering space for informal activities is a common component of the neighborhood commons. It is sometimes associated with the elevator lobby. These areas may also be developed as libraries, living rooms, dens, or TV rooms. In addition, they may include a desk area for staff use.

Country kitchen/pantry. In some cases, the country kitchen is provided within a resident cluster. It is suitable for informal breakfast buffets, small group activities, and resident/family meetings.

Laundry. While many facilities contract with an outside service for general and even personal resident laundry, a laundry room on each floor gives residents or their families the option of doing their own laundry. Whether or not they take advantage of this opportunity is, of course, highly dependent on resident tastes and previous life patterns. It is desirable to associate the laundry room with pleasant views or adjacent activities, such as access to the Internet, cards, or snacks, any of which may be located in the dining area adjacent to the country kitchen.

Support spaces. All facilities offering meals and a variety of other staff support need a number of support

SAMPLE PROGRAM FOR A FREESTANDING 60–75 UNIT, 3-STORY FACILITY*

SPACE	AREA (sq ft)
Resident Common Areas	
(See optional spaces below)	
Vestibule	110
Lobby (Note: This may include an ornamental stair.)	900
Mail	150
Dining prefunction/carts	100
Dining (25–30 sq ft/resident)	1,600
Private dining	280
Library/living room	500
Large activity/multipurpose	500
Spa bathing	200
Toilets near dining (4 @ 50)	200
Special activity room	400
Beauty/barber shop	250
Resident common areas subtotal	5,190
Resident cluster common areas for 15–20 residents	
Sitting areas 4 @ 150–250	500
Country kitchen/pantry for 150–250	500
Resident laundry 4 @ 75	300
Guest toilet 3 @ 50	150
Cluster common areas subtotal	1,450
Resident cluster support linen 3 @ 15	45
Housekeeping closet 3 @ 50	150
Trash room 3 @ 25	75
Electrical closet 3 @ 25	75
Cluster support subtotal	395
Administration	
Administrator	180
Admissions/marketing parlor	200
Activities director	120
Business office (for 2)	150
Secretaries/waiting/receptionist	150
Workroom	120
Conference room	150
Administration subtotal	1,070

SPACE	AREA (sq ft)
General support	
(See optional spaces below)	
Staff lounge/lockers/toilet	500
Commercial kitchen	1,500
Housekeeping storage	300
Housekeeping supply	300
Central clean linen	250
Central soiled linen	300
Mechanical	800
Maintenance shop	300
Elevator machine room	50
Resident storage**	300
Cart wash	40
Loading/receiving	250
Trash***	150
Telephone closet	50
General support subtotal	5,090
Subtotal of all areas	13,195
× 1.4 Circulation	
Total	18,473
Optional Spaces	
Common spaces—resident	
Ice-cream parlor/cafe	500
Multipurpose/theater	400
Wellness Center	
Waiting/reception	120
Exam room	120
Office	120
Toilet	50
Exercise/meeting	400
Support—General	
Laundry****	500

*Resident units not included.
**Many facilities offer one storage space rather than individual lockers, as often found in independent living.
***If a compactor is used, equipment/size may vary.
****Many facilities contract with an outside laundry service.

areas. The most common are listed in the sample program on page 55.

Sample program

Square-footage amounts listed are general guidelines; licensed facilities may have varying code requirements. The total building area for typical facilities ranges from 600 to 1000 GSF per resident. Typically, anywhere from 45 to 50 percent of total space may be dedicated to circulation, support, and common areas, with the remaining 50–55 percent in the resident units. Unit sizes tend to be smaller than for independent living facilities because the common spaces replace or enhance what would otherwise be living space within the unit.

Payment/reimbursement and regulation

The residents—or their families—typically pay the full cost of rent and services at almost all newer assisted living facilities. Some states have limited programs to help Medicaid-eligible individuals pay their monthly charges (see Chapter 20).

Regulation

All states have some form of regulatory control for assisted living. Because it is licensed differently in each state, it is critical to verify how and by which agency it is regulated (department of health, social services/welfare agency, or department on aging). It is important to note that in some states like Massachusetts, the services are licensed and regulated, but the buildings/facilities follow state building codes for multifamily housing. Because of the physical and cognitive frailty of the residents, the local building officials may be concerned about their ability to evacuate the building without assistance.

Trends/opportunities for innovation

As a building type, assisted living has evolved from older models such as small board and care facilities for five to six people or the "old-folks home" into a residential alternative to nursing care. Assisted living in its present form is a set of services and an environment that reinforces the capabilities of the older resident while assuring safety and support in those areas of diminishing ability. Stretched to its limits, assisted living by definition is what allows people to age in place successfully. The building boom of the 1990s focused on a particular set of assisted living products, but there are many more opportunities to explore.

Assisted living services

Some retirement community sponsors are exploring a continuum of assisted living services that residents can receive in their independent living unit without having to physically move to a different unit type. Distance and cost are a major factor, which makes suburban communities on large pieces of land more challenging than a vertical/high-rise urban model. New models will need to think creatively to maximize the opportunity for residents to age in *one* place.

Urban models

Most of the products built over the past decade have focused on suburban models. Urban dwellers have typically found few options and have, with their own financial resources, networked supportive aging services through home health agencies and private duty aids and matched them with community resources such as the pharmacy, grocery store, and restaurants that deliver products to their door. In fact, a number of the sponsors of ur-

◀ Land and construcion costs, as well as other factors, have slowed the introduction of assisted living in many urban areas, but new models are now being developed. Carnegie East, New York City. Perkins Eastman Architects PC and Larsen Shein Ginsberg Snyder LLP. Photograph by Kyo-Young Jin.

> Memory loss alone is not a good enough reason to institutionalize an older person in a health care setting.
> (*Regnier 2002*)

ban models have found that "in-movers" to urban assisted living or residential communities are typically older and frailer than their suburban counterparts. It is believed that the network of available services coupled with personal financial resources often delay the need to move until a significant crisis has occurred. New urban models will need to be developed that address the cross-cultural issues of an increasingly diverse ethnic population. Affordable options in urban centers are typically missing because of the high costs of land and development. The housing options that exist for lower-income seniors are typically publicly subsidized and address only the need for shelter, not services. New models will undoubtedly find ways to utilize "generic" community-based services rather than developing a facility-based program.

Affordable models

The level of required services (and therefore staff) typically accounts for 60–70 percent of the daily fees in assisted living (the debt service on the physical building is typically 20–30 percent). Few affordable models have been built; those that exist are typically subsidized either internally by an organization or through public subsidy from a local or federal government source. Reimbursement and the need for more Medicaid waiver programs are central to the discussion. Assisted living has been proven to be an effective alternative to the nursing home for a large sector of the population, largely those with the resources to pay. Most of the people who could use this alternative cannot afford it.

Consumer expectations

In many markets there is increasing demand for larger units. Over the past decade the retirement living industry has seen a significant shift in product expectation as the generation of postwar homeowners has entered the marketplace. Assisted living is seeing, and will continue to see, a market sector with the personal resources to select a product that meets their expectations. The first assisted living products were largely studios with limited amenities, but new facilities are now opening with one-bedroom units exceeding 500 sq ft, and there is a demand for two-bedroom units. Because the units are typically the hardest things to change, it will be important to design models that have the flexibility to meet consumer expectations.

Niche products

Most assisted living products focus on the freestanding suburban model of 60–100 units, the "step" in a CCRC model, or specialized care programs for people with dementia (see next section). New models will emerge that need to meet specific demographics. Rural aging has been largely ignored and is not really covered by any of the existing models. Specialized programs for the younger physically disabled groups, persons who are blind or deaf, and even special groups such as gay and lesbian individuals, need to be created to address the variety of needs, expectations, and resources of the many people who would benefit from this housing option.

Residences for Persons With Alzheimer's and Dementia

Introduction/typical users

In recent years, one of the most important innovations in the field of design for the aging has been the development of successful models for special units serving persons with Alzheimer's and other forms of dementia.

There is perhaps no more diverse a population among the aging than those with Alzheimer's and dementia. Alzheimer's disease is one of the most common causes of the loss of mental function known broadly as dementia. As of 2002 there were at least four million persons in the United States suffering from this disease, and the number is expected to increase. This type of dementia proceeds in stages, gradually destroying memory, reason, judgment, language, and eventually the ability to carry out even the simplest of tasks. While the effects of the disease can vary greatly with the individual, even from day to day, the goal of specialized housing is to maximize what residents with Alzheimer's can do, so that they can live in a dignified residential (rather than institutional) environment.

The design of a residence for those with Alzheimer's moves away from conventional skilled-care models by avoiding traditional institutional symbols, objects, spaces and configurations, such as nursing stations and institutional finishes. Along with Woodside Place, one of the first national models of a specialized residence for those with Alzheimer's, nursing homes and other assisted living residences have begun to address the unique needs of those with the disease. First appearing in the 1980s, special care units (SCUs) have proliferated in a growing number of U.S. nursing homes with 30 or more beds.

SCUs can vary widely, depending on whether they are in skilled-care or assisted living settings and depending upon program. Some offer only one special feature, such as a sheltered area for wandering. Most have several special features, such as family counseling, support groups, and therapeutic activities for resi-

> We used to believe that mentally impaired people could not benefit from environmental design; now we have begun to recognize that they may be aided by design more than any other group and that our responsibilities to them do not end with "special" or secure units. We no longer focus on first impressions to the exclusion of other important issues like the significance of motion, socialization, and flow of activity.
>
> *(Hiatt 1991)*

dents. This section will focus primarily on assisted living licensed programs, but the program and design parameters will be similar to a long-term care model.

It is important to realize that seniors with cognitive impairment reside throughout the continuum and that many of the design issues discussed in this chapter are important considerations in a geriatric clinic or congregate living setting. In fact, retirement communities struggle to support couples where one has dementia and the other has become the caregiver without separating them. Assisted living facilities may have a special-care wing focused on those with profound confusion, but much of the rest of the population will also have cognitive difficulties that will vary in expression (benign confusion to aggressive elopement) and change over time. (*Also known as: Dementia Care Facilities, Special Care Units, Memory Support Units, and Residential Alzheimer's Facilities*)

Typical Sponsors
These facilities are being developed by many of the same not-for-profit and for-profit organizations responsible for other facilities for the aging. Most of the initial

innovative projects were accomplished by not-for-profits that saw a specific need and opportunity. For-profit sponsors have learned from these projects and have developed their own models, at times creating prototypes that can be built in almost any community.

Types of Settings

Freestanding

Most of the early examples and many of the new models are entirely freestanding. Because the residents are not typically involved in activities of a larger community, it is possible to create models that focus on their specific needs.

Special wing or neighborhood

Many programs are developed as a special section of a larger assisted living or nursing building to focus on those who need a special program to maximize their abilities and/or keep them safe. These programs usually have a full complement of program areas (such as dining, activities, bathing, etc.) that are separate from the larger population.

Integrated models

Some sponsors strongly believe in keeping people with dementia integrated in the larger community. These buildings may have special programs/activities for those residents who require a more structured day (or evening).

The following section primarily focuses on the first two models.

Major program elements and design considerations

Most assisted living facilities or special-care units designed for this group of residents are similar in services to basic assisted living facilities. There are, however, some significant differences in the way the following program elements are organized:

- The house
- The neighborhood
- The garden
- Service support

Major Program Elements

The house

Most models have focused on replicating the elements of a house, with an area of bedrooms, a kitchen and dining area, and a living room or activity space. While these elements may be organized differently, it is common to see "households" of between 8 and 12 residents with predominantly private rooms. Designs have created a zone of rooms off a private bedroom hallway or surrounding the dining/living areas. The major elements of the house are:

Resident room. The room is often sized to be more like a residential bedroom or small assisted living unit than an apartment. Most sponsors provide private room accommodations with a private bathroom but may reserve 10–15 percent of the rooms to be shared by couples or roommates. The room often has several significant features that have proven beneficial:

- *Dutch door.* A door that allows the bottom half to be closed to discourage entry and the top portion to be open for visual connection/orientation into the room.

- *Closet.* A two-door clothes closet that allows one side to be locked to secure seasonal and additional clothing while one door leaf is operable for residents to use with more restricted clothing choices. This concept has been utilized with an open wire dresser drawer unit so that socks, undergarments, and the like are visible.

- *Plate shelf.* A device to encourage personalization with artwork, objects, and hanging items (typically on pegs). It is typically mounted at 5–6 ft above the floor and is located on a wall visible from the hallway.

- *Window seat.* A built-in feature that provides additional storage (with a hinged and locked top), a place for family/visitors to sit, and an additional opportunity to personalize the room.

Resident bathroom. Models offer a full three-fixture bathroom with shower or a two-fixture bathroom with separate bathing facilities located elsewhere in the household. Sponsor experience indicates that the three-fixture arrangement provides the most familiar and comfortable bathing experience. The bathroom is typically designed to provide a direct visual connection from the bed to the toilet. Research has demonstrated that this visual reminder reduces incontinence and minimizes nighttime accidents. Other features include:

- Vanity countertop for toiletries

- Contrasting toilet-seat color to enhance visual contrast

- Mirrors, at times with shutters to cover from view for those who have fearful responses to mirrored images

- High shelf or storage cabinet for toiletries

- Low-threshold shower of at least 36" x 42" size for assistance by staff. A separate water shutoff valve may be provided to limit inappropriate resident use.

- Supplemental heat source, especially if a shower is provided

Kitchen/dining room. The typical model is a larger version of a residential country kitchen or great room. Planning of this space should encourage resident participation in this activity through visual connection to the food choices and stimulation of their olfactory senses. With the provision of an in-house kitchen, the staff are better able to meet the residents' needs whether they choose to eat during conventional meal hours (when food may come from a central source) or at times when it suits their personal rhythm. These residential-style kitchens can serve one or two houses, depending on the design, and are usually planned to provide a work space in the vicinity for direct-care staff. Other key features include:

- Residential appliances to support food service, snack/nourishment, and

▼ *This well-known early example of a specialized assisted living residence for residents with Alzheimer's incorporates many of the most widely used details: the Dutch door, the plate shelf for personalization of the room, and specialized signage. Woodside Place Alzheimer Residence, Oakmont, Pennsylvania. Perkins Eastman Architects PC. Photograph by Robert Ruschak.*

programs (baking, etc.). In many jurisdictions, licensure will require separate certified commercial refrigeration/freezers for the food-service program.

- Keyed switches for all major appliances and outlets so that staff can control safety
- Space for a large table for residents to use for cooking programs, informal activities or proximity to staff
- Separate hand-wash sinks for staff and food service personnel (typical code requirement)
- Dishwashing capabilities with an under-counter unit that meets temperature requirements (typically 180 degrees)
- Work space in the kitchen or vicinity for staff to maintain records, make calls, etc.

- Some type of connection to the outside with protected/shaded places to sit

Living/activity room. Depending on the size and design of the program, there may be a living room or informal activity space like a den or TV room associated with the house. Some designs incorporate it into a country kitchen as a dining/living room, whereas others plan it as a distinct space.

Spa/bathing. The quantity and location of spa/bathing spaces will depend largely on decisions made for the resident bathrooms. If showers are provided for all private rooms, then one central room will be sufficient to provide programs for hygiene, therapeutic whirlpools for skin care, and preferences for tub bathing over showering.

▶ A typical dining arrangement in an Alzheimer's residence is illustrated by this country kitchen serving the dining program for two 10-unit houses. Harbour House, Greendale, Wisconsin. Architecture by KM Development Corporation. Interior Design by Mithun Inc. Photograph by Skot Weidemann.

Programs without private showers will typically have some type of central spa/bathing room with a tub as well as a residential bathroom with shower in each house. Many of the planning criteria for the long-term bathing (see Chapter 10) are the same here, but more attention must be given to the selection of the mechanized bath tub so that it is not frightening in appearance or movement. Tubs that look more familiar have had success, and designing them within a niche, like a residential tub, adds some sense of security but forfeits flexibility in staff access.

The neighborhood

Most programs have 30–50 residents and have an area that programmatically joins all of the houses together. This common area usually contains a variety of program elements for both large and small group activities, such as:

Entry. The entry sequence for a specialized dementia program is different from that in other facility types. Because the residents do not come and go frequently (if at all), entrance identification is primarily a device for visitors, families, and staff. It should be welcoming, reassuring, and comfortable while providing direct access to administrative areas for staff and visitors. Entry, from the resident perspective, should not be featured and should be screened from the view from most active areas.

Great room. An assembly space that can be used for larger group activities (such as music/dancing, special dinners with

◀ *The common areas in this recent dementia-care facility reflect one design response that intends to evoke the local main street. Waveny Care Center, New Canaan, Connecticut. Reese, Lower, Patrick & Scott Ltd. Photograph by Larry Lefever Photography.*

families, exercise, etc.). This room is sometimes used for staff training and caregiver support group meetings.

Crafts room. Many programs like to have a room for messy or unstructured activities or projects that can be left out and completed over a long period of time.

Beauty shop. Due to issues of agitation, it is often difficult to incorporate an opportunity for hair care. This use can be incorporated into a spa/bathing area.

Private dining/activity. A place for families to be alone to share a meal, coffee or time together. This space is also useful for family conferences, staff meetings, and the like.

Living room/den. A place that contains comfortable seating and becomes the "heart" of the house or neighborhood.

Staff workroom. While direct-care activities occur in the houses and neighborhoods, there is still a need for a private workroom for care staff, health-care professionals, and supervisors for record keeping, medical supplies, resident medications (i.e., a locked cart), and private phone calls. It is often located strategically within the resident environment for easy access by staff but may also be located near administrative areas for backup services (i.e., copying) and access.

The garden (see Chapter 4)

A central feature in the planning of almost all special-care programs is easy access to a secure outside garden. Giving residents free access to the outside has proven to reduce agitation/frustration and improve overall physical fitness simply by providing walking space. It is im-portant that the area be safe and secure so that staff and families feel comfortable allowing residents unaccompanied access. Important design features are the following:

- A secure perimeter with fencing at least six feet high. Camouflage the fence so that it does not feel prisonlike or attract attention. Be careful that the fence design does not provide horizontal elements that can be used for climbing and that the site is planned to discourage residents from using site furniture to climb over the fence.

- Planting materials that are not toxic or thorny.

- Walking paths that are continuous and lead back to building entry points. Paths should be wide enough for two to walk side-by-side and built of a stable material so as not to create tripping hazards.

- Shaded areas with porches or trees for sunny days and protected areas for spring, fall, and pleasant winter days.

- Perimeter lighting for security at night in case someone does leave the facility.

- Good designs have all exit doors (except the front entry door) lead into this space for ongoing safety. If there are errant fire alarms, egress doors will open into a familiar area. (Note: An exit from the area will be required for evacuation in case of a true emergency.)

- Comfortable areas to sit.

- Passive and active recreation opportunities, from bird and squirrel feeders to patios for cookouts and places to putt golf or throw a basketball.

Services/support

As with other senior housing facilities, there are additional areas required to support the residential-care program. The key planning issues are the following:

- These facilities are usually small, so their infrastructure needs to be carefully planned to minimize cost.

- Staff retreat space is essential for relaxing and having some private time away from the demands and stresses of the job.

- Administrative areas may need to be separate from resident areas to minimize disruption from visitors, salespeople, mail deliveries, etc.

- Staff entries should be visually separate so that coats and bags at shift changes do not trigger reactions among residents.

- Staff training is an ongoing and important activity, so it will need to be accommodated in a separate space or thoughtfully planned to be shared with other program elements throughout the building.

Special design considerations

Research into designing for people with dementia has identified a number of important considerations. These concepts have been tested through several postoccupancy studies and informal observations published in *Aging Autonomy and Architecture*. Excerpts from this research are offered as an overview of special design considerations.

Acknowledging privacy and community

Postoccupancy studies at some of the early Alzheimer's facilities revealed a strong sense of community developed in those facilities where residents freely socialized

between houses. They were observed enjoying the common areas of the building as if they were a front porch or even a town square. It appears that the hierarchy of public to private spaces within a building is an important factor that helps individuals with cognitive impairment feel comfortable and gather more easily. Based on this research, several key points should be considered in the design of a facility:

- Provide a clearly defined hierarchy of public to private spaces. Avoid inappropriate adjacencies, such as bedrooms opening directly off living rooms, which may confuse residents, causing them to act inappropriately or to become frustrated.

- Provide private bedrooms with bathrooms that contain at least a toilet and a sink and access to a shower. (Note: Some accommodation for shared rooms should be made for couples or others who choose to share. One shared room for every ten private rooms should be sufficient.)

Research-based Planning Considerations in Designing for Residents with Dementia

- Acknowledging privacy and community
- Flexible rhythms and patterns
- Small group size
- Caregiver and family relationships
- Engaged wandering
- Alternative wayfinding systems
- Independence with security
- Focused and appropriate stimulation
- Residential qualities

(Hoglund 1985)

- Create a clear, private residential zone, preferably a private bedroom, where residents can choose to be alone and keep important personal items that help them feel secure.

- Maintain privacy and dignity by differentiating and locating public circulation away from private residential hallways and by locating and designing private rooms and bathrooms to reduce obtrusive visual observation. (Residents with Alzheimer's may behave immodestly. For example, residents may undress or use the toilet without closing the door.)

- Provide appropriate bathing facilities within the private zone of the house or room. Residents do not like to leave the privacy of a bedroom, go through common spaces and into a public zone to find a bathing room. Many facilities are now providing showers within the resident room toilet.

Flexible rhythms and patterns

Eliminating rigidly enforced schedules by substituting small group activities and allowing flexible eating patterns contributes to a noninstitutional environment. Because people with Alzheimer's and related dementias often have trouble adapting to changes and transitions, it is important to offer a setting that conforms to their needs and preferences rather than forcing conformity. These individuals cannot be expected to follow a rigid programming schedule; nor can they be expected to change their daily patterns drastically.

- Provide cooking facilities, such as a kitchen, that are available during off-hours or a warming cart that can be left in the country kitchen so that staff can meet residents eating requests or requests for alternative selections. In addition, a small residentially scaled refrigerator allows for the storage of snacks.

- Separate activity areas from resident rooms, so that residents can sleep or nap without interruption.

- Create a variety of settings, making a deliberate effort to include different room sizes, orientation, character, degree of stimulation, etc.

- Reinforce seasonal and daily rhythms by providing easy views to the outside, so it is clear whether it is day or night, summer or winter. Traditional institutions typically have few windows and depend on artificial light, often resulting in confusion.

Small group size

In a traditional nursing-care facility, people with dementia are sometimes overwhelmed or distracted by large groups of people or large spaces, especially at meal times. Staff report that people with dementia seem to be more successful in coping with smaller activity groups, generally not larger than 10–12 persons. Smaller groups at meals or in programmed activities can be accommodated in smaller spaces that are less noisy and less distracting. Other issues related to group size and space include:

- Arrange clusters or houses to accommodate no more than 10–14 persons.

- Provide small group spaces in each unit and visual separation from other spaces so that residents vulnerable to distraction can be comfortable.

- Create spaces for small groups that offer distinctive attractions, such as a large window, a fireplace, or special seating. Some spaces should be less enclosed than others, offering a place from which to watch other activity.

- Multipurpose spaces may be confusing to residents with dementia because they do not know how to alter their behavior to respond to changing uses. It is better to provide several different rooms that residents can associate with different experiences such as game activities, dining, cooking, sleeping, watching television, etc.

- On the other hand, a space should not be designed so specifically for one activity that it cannot be adapted to other uses, since the use of rooms will change over time in response to changing resident needs or as the management style of the facility evolves.

Caregiver and family relationships

The primary caregiver in a residential facility, a trained member of the staff, plays a key role in the quality of a resident's life. The quality of care is, of course, a function of the philosophy and management of the facility, but all of these are intertwined with the design and physical space. Both formal and informal research conducted at various residences for persons with Alzheimer's disease has led to the following recommendations:

- Integrate a staff workstation into each house as part of the residential furnishings (desk) or equipment (kitchen counter). Locate it near the main circulation path in the unit, where the residents and caregiver can enjoy casual meetings and participate in everyday activities. Provide a lockable file drawer at the workstation.

- Design the workstation as a social seating area in which residents can associate comfortably with the caregiver. A table or counter that the residents can share is desirable for common activities.

- Furnish suitable close-at-hand storage for supplies and services that caregivers need on a regular basis to minimize trips out of the unit: laundry machines, linens, and other supplies, and a well-equipped janitor's closet.

- Create a separate staff room that has a comfortable yet professional ambiance. Provide a conference/lunch table, shelves, and equipment for resource material, and a pleasant outdoor view. Lockers and toilet facilities should be nearby.

▼ *Staff stations should be integrated into the homelike furnishings of the residence's common areas. Copper Ridge, Sykesville, Maryland. Perkins Eastman Architects PC. Photograph by Curtis Martin.*

- Create an aesthetically pleasing environment in which residents can enjoy a variety of homelike settings with family members. Provide visitors with the option of an unobtrusive way out of the facility so that residents are not frustrated if they try to follow.

Engaged wandering

Wandering—that is, movement without apparent purpose—is a common behavior among people with Alzheimer's disease, though little is known about the physiological reasons for this. Rummaging, another common behavior, involves the apparent search for personal items.

Designers should view the wandering path as a major opportunity for innovation. Although some facilities strongly endorse loop-walking paths to eliminate dead ends (which can lead to frustration), such paths can also lead to an almost catatoniclike behavior or repetitive cycling without apparent purpose. One should not assume that wandering will be limited to corridors; creatively weaving rooms into the wandering path can help orient residents and provide activity spaces as destinations for socializing along the way. It is important that the path appear distinctive, with transitional changes in texture, lighting, and acoustics to help make physical segments memorable and the actual activity of walking more enjoyable. Issues to keep in mind when designing the wandering path include:

- Loops of circulation should be created to provide walking circuits. Multiple intersecting loops are preferable to a single one.
- Avoid dead ends that can lead residents to a destination without an obvious choice of what to do next. Specifically, avoid locked doors at the ends of corridors. Instead, a seating area at the end of a corridor, preferably with a good view, provides a destination, place to sit, and in effect helps to turn the resident around.

- Remember that people may shuffle and have gait difficulties, making them prone to falling. Minimize the number of flooring changes, particularly carpet to vinyl.

- Since residents can become easily disoriented, provide recognizable cues, such as artwork, furnishings, and changes in wall color or texture to lead residents back to an area that may seem more secure and familiar. Visible connection to destinations is important.

- Incorporate both interior and exterior wandering areas. Temperature, sunlight, and breezes can all reinforce daily rhythms and patterns, and assist in orienting people to place and time.

- Keep in mind that residents will tend to watch the floor as they walk and that sharp contrast in color or light value may cause them to perceive nonexistent steps or changes in depth. High-contrast spots in the flooring may appear to be items that need to be picked up.

- The scale of circulation paths should be kept small and residential, but there should be room for seating, especially near intersections and entrances to houses or other rooms.

- Minimize the choices a resident may need to make along the way or mark certain predetermined choices clearly with landmarks. Also, provide a hierarchy of walking places—some may be through public areas that offer one a range of experiences and others may be routed through more private areas that are only available for wandering at certain times. (See also Chapter 15.)

- Allow for unobtrusive staff observation of residents along the wandering path so that the staff will feel comfortable when residents are out of direct view. Consider using security systems to monitor/control door activity so residents cannot go into secure yards/gardens in bad weather without the staff being notified. Try not to use security systems to limit resident access, but rather use them to provide surveillance information so staff are aware of the locations of residents and can respond quickly should the necessity arise. Avoid devices with auditory signals, as this can lead to confusion or agitation.

- Make sure plants are nontoxic (see Chapter 4).

- Install open-wire baskets and similar storage systems that allow items to be directly visible. Provide appropriate places for rummaging where it is not destructive to personal belongings.

Alternative wayfinding systems
(see Chapter 15)

Cognitive impairment by its very nature reduces the value of common wayfinding, landmarks, and cueing techniques. The concept of wayfinding is based on the ability to connect objects and sensory stimulation with orientation to place. Research provides little evidence that residents are able to create a mental map of their surroundings. In fact, experience shows that some of the subtlest cues,

▲ Familiar residential furnishings, baskets of objects that allow for nondisruptive rummaging, and the smell of cookies baking or coffee brewing are program details common to Alzheimer's residences. Woodside Place Alzheimer Residence, Oakmont, Pennsylvania. Perkins Eastman Architects PC. Photograph by Robert Ruschak.

such as color changes, are lost even on staff and families. Environmental sociologist John Zeisel commented at a national conference on designing for people with dementia, "For people with dementia the concept of wayfinding needs to be thought of as 'place knowing.' People with dementia know where they are when they're there; they only know where they are going if they see the destination; and they realize where they were going when they arrive." The in-betweens—the connections between destinations—are lost on them.

For this reason, conventional signage, color-coding, and differentiation of finishes, flooring, hardware, and lighting will not provide perceptible cues for most people with dementia. The implications for design, while at this point still inconclusive, include the following:

- Reinforce visual connection between the path (or hallway or corridor) and important destinations. Residents may not be aware what they are searching for, but once they can see an activity or into a room, they may choose to join in.

- Provide flexibility so that visual connections can be controlled. Examples include dutch doors, which can be open, closed, or half open, and interior windows that can be curtained.

- Arrange public and shared spaces as a continuous progression. Clustered sitting arrangements, pets such as fish or birds, and the opportunity to view a programmed activity without actually engaging in it provide stimulation for residents as they move through the building. While still maintaining code standards for emergency exit, the traditional corridor design should be more residential in character. Low partitions and interior windows may help to increase visibility and enhance the feeling of openness.

- Use landmarks and objects that will attract a resident's attention.

- Create visual cueing for important activities. For example, design the bedroom so there is clear visual connection between the bed and bathroom (specifically the toilet). Be careful to arrange this view so that bathroom activities remain private and are not obvious from public spaces or hallways.

- Install objects that are important and memorable to each resident in "memory boxes" as a way of marking the entrance to their room. For some it may be photographs, for others it may be a familiar piece of clothing. Consider adding places that residents can personalize (plate shelf, deep windowsill, or window seat) in their unit or house entries.

Independence with security

For frail seniors, the aging process leads to a gradual decrease in independence and a constant adaptation to maintain those qualities of independence that are important to the individual. For those with Alzheimer's disease, independence becomes increasingly elusive. Physical measures to make the environment accessible answer only a small part of the issue—especially since those in the first stages of Alzheimer's disease are generally ambulatory and physically healthy. Offering choice is important, in maintaining independence, but for those with dementia, choices must be restricted to limit confusion, distress, and emotional disturbance. Maintaining continuity of lifestyle is clearly important, because it reinforces positive behaviors and patterns. Also, the environment can support an individual's abilities and enhance remaining skills.

▼ The ability to personalize room décor is an important cueing aid for residents with Alzheimer's. Woodside Place Alzheimer Residence, Oakmont, Pennsylvania. Perkins Eastman Architects PC. Photograph by Robert Ruschak.

Complicated procedures or directions, or the necessity to choose from among an abundance of options, can cause confusion and lessen a person's feelings of independence and self-esteem. At the same time the facility must build in safety and security as follows:

- Organize the building so that high-risk areas (such as kitchens, outdoor areas, etc.) are visible or accessible from areas where staff are commonly present.

- Secure only doors that lead to high-risk places, such as mechanical rooms, commercial kitchens, rooms storing cleaning chemicals, or exterior doors that open on to unsecured areas. Design these doors to be unobtrusive. Similarly, provide locks on cabinet drawers and doors that contain potentially harmful products, but allow access to other cabinets.

- Restrict access to areas or equipment (storage, bathtubs) that may be hazardous. Provide staff-controlled power switches for equipment and keyed electric outlets for kitchen equipment.

- Provide a secure outdoor area with appropriately designed six-foot-tall fences and allow free access from the interior into the safe yard. Select garden plants to be nontoxic, with leaves that are not abrasive or sharp-edged.

- Use carpet rather than hardwood floors wherever possible to limit slipping and cushion falls (see Chapter 13).

- Provide good lighting levels and supply night lighting at resident bathrooms (see Chapter 13).

- Use windows that open, but restrict opening to 8" or less.

- Install handrails on at least one side of major indoor walking paths.

Focused and appropriate stimulation

The degree to which sensory stimulation is therapeutic for persons with Alzheimer's has been an ongoing source of debate among mental health professionals. For example, a current trend is the use of light stimulation. In the field of designing for people with dementia, the goal is a constant and careful balance that attempts to offer interest and raise curiosity without becoming distracting or stressful. There is no easy formula to find this balance.

There does appear to be some consistency in that many persons with Alzheimer's experience an increased level of physical activity in the late afternoon, often referred to as "sundowning."

The design implications of adjusting stimulation to meet the needs of people with Alzheimer's are numerous, ranging from the size and locations of rooms to the color of the walls, the lighting sources, and the print on the wallpaper (see Chapter 14). The following points are offered as a range of design issues to address:

- As noted earlier, provide rooms that will comfortably accommodate small groups of 6–14.

- Provide rooms with auditory privacy so that noise from one activity is not distracting to participants in another. Use carpet where possible because it reduces unwanted noise, reverberation, and glare from floor surfaces.

- Be aware of the confusion that can occur for residents that use rooms for a variety of activities. A resident who knows a particular room to be a dining room may find it difficult to understand that it is now acceptable to exercise or dance.

- Provide a staff exit/entrance away from the public front door so that leaving will not cause feelings of despair and abandonment. Channel late-afternoon activities into dinner preparation, freshening up, or other appropriate late-day events. Orient some rooms to the west to gain from sunsets. Provide TV rooms for watching the news and kitchens for preparing dinner.

- Screen the public entrance from resident view. Provide a vestibule or lobby between the building entrance and residential entry door—this will allow deliveries, visitors, and others to come and go without intruding into the resident's domain.

Residential qualities

Although there is almost universal support today for a "residential" environment, there is very little agreement as to what the term means. Rural, suburban, and urban locations all affect the way we perceive housing, and many dementia facilities are much larger than a single-family home. The inclusion of homelike qualities in the design of the building touches on many issues, ranging from the overall size and appearance to the use of interior and exterior materials and the purpose, scale, and detailing of interior rooms. Lighting, finishes, and furniture are also important in evoking feelings of home for the resident. Some common suggestions are as follows:

- Break up the building volume into smaller elements so that the exterior does not appear monolithic or institutional.

- Organize spaces from public to private as in other residential prototypes such as houses, inns, and hotels.

- View rooms and spaces as they are in a house. Living rooms (not day rooms), bedrooms (not private or semiprivate rooms), family rooms or dens (not lounges), and bathrooms (not toilets) all add to the ambiance.

- Avoid using hard finishes, which are typically found only in institutional settings, such as vinyl tile, ceramic tile, sheet vinyl, plastic laminate, and stainless steel and metal doors. If these materials are used, apply them in limited quantities in appropriate locations.

- Locate spaces so that necessary operational equipment (carts, fire-alarm panels, nurse call stations, etc.) is hidden from view.

- Select furniture that appears familiar and comfortable. Some of the specially designed geriatric furniture lines, while meeting hygienic and physical comfort requirements, are the least attractive options. Fortunately, there are better choices. In addition to other ergonomic criteria, check furniture for stability (especially tables and chairs), as residents will use them for physical support.

- Treat surfaces the way they would be in a home setting. For example, windows often have fabric curtains or valances to soften their appearance.

- Install light sources that are residential; 2 x 4 fluorescent lights with acrylic lenses do not look residential and are not good sources of lighting because of their glare.

Payment/reimbursement and regulation

Payment and reimbursement models are the same as those described in the assisted living and long-term care sections. Regulatory control will also be the same, except that some states and local building officials have begun to require higher construction standards based on this population's inherent inability to reliably evacuate the building in an emergency situation without assistance.

SAMPLE PROGRAM FOR AN ASSISTED LIVING RESIDENCE FOR 40 PERSONS WITH DEMENTIA

SPACE	AREA (sq ft)	SPACE	AREA (sq ft)
Residential areas, 4 Houses of 10		Staff workroom/medication	235
Residential cluster (10)		Beauty/barber	150
8 Single rooms with bathrooms @ 220	1,760	Subtotal	2,075
Shared room with bathrooms (2 residents)	400	**Administration/public–residential**	
Shower with toilet*	80	Vestibule	60
Linen closet	15	Lobby/reception/waiting/secretary	350
Cluster sitting area & private alcove	250	Public toilet	50
Dining room for 10	250	Staff toilet	50
Subtotal	2,755 NSF	Director's office	140
x 4 wings	11,020 NSF	SW/admissions office	140
		Recreation/activity director office	120
Shared areas for each cluster		Conference room	200
Country kitchen/staff work area	350	Workroom/copy/supply/file/ storage	200
Bathing room with toilet/grooming	150	Subtotal	1,310 NSF
TV/Den	250	**Service support**	
Laundry room	50	Kitchen	1,200
Soiled holding room, janitor's closet		Storage	400
& housekeeping	100	Soiled holding (assumes bulk laundry	
Storage room	15	elsewhere)	150
Toilet	45	Clean holding	150
Subtotal	960 NSF	Housekeeping storage	150
x 2 Clusters	1,920 NSF	Mechanical/electric	1,020
		Staff lounge/retreat	280
Residential areas total	12,940	Staff lockers	40
Activity/program areas		Subtotal	3,390
Great room	700	**TOTAL (subtotal x grossing factor*)**	30,735 GSF
Fireplace room	400		
Arts & crafts	250		
Private dining/activity	250	*Grossing factor at 1.4, required only if resident rooms do not have individual showers.*	
Toilets 2 @ 45	90		

▶ *Adjacent to the country kitchens, this living room is often kept at a relatively low light level, which in combination with the fireplace has been found to be calming to the residents. Marjorie Doyle Rockwell Center, Cohoes, New York. Perkins Eastman Architects PC. Photograph by Randall Perry.*

Trends/opportunities for innovation

Research is focusing on identifying the causes and medical interventions to manage/control dementia. Because of the many forms and sources, it is unlikely that this unfortunate deterioration will be eradicated from the aging process. New models will need to focus on supporting the individual's remaining capabilities and provide a supportive setting throughout the continuum. These models will explore:

Integration throughout the continuum. Retirement-living sponsors must confront the reality that dementia occurs throughout the continuum and not only as part of end-of-life issues in long-term care. Over the past decade, specially designed assisted living settings have offered new opportunities in less restrictive settings. Adult day care provides services for those who wish to remain at home and outside traditional residential-care options. Senior living services will need to provide support for cognitive deficits, and environments will need to be carefully planned to enhance capabilities. Spouses/family caregivers will need programs and training to assist them in their own caregiving abilities along with complementary respite services to meet their own needs.

Affordable options. Dementia care is intrinsically expensive because of high ongoing staff labor cost. Cost-effective buildings are only a small portion of the solution. New models have focused on a variety of ways to support spouses and family caregivers to continue to provide those services without jeopardizing their own health status. Unfortunately, some home settings are not appropriate, safe, or easily altered to meet the needs of the individual or their caregiver. A few experimental models have been developed with "caregiver cottages," where the spouse/family member can continue to be the primary caregiver while physically networked to on-site staff and respite resources in an appropriately planned setting.

Cottages. Some sponsors are developing "group home" type models where 6–10 residents share a large house in a conventional residential neighborhood or apartment building. These models can be dispersed easily in a neigh-borhood, provide options for rural and smaller communities, and meet smaller-scale expectations.

Independent/Residential/ Congregate Living

Introduction/types of users

Several residential-living options are available for people who are able to live independently but have made a lifestyle choice to address individual needs and concerns. These options assume the residents can live without significant health-care support but want to begin to direct and control their quality of life in their later years. Average age at entry is late seventies to early eighties where specific needs have arisen through change in health status, lifestyle expectations, or future planning. They are also designed for those who want to begin downsizing their homes and in turn their upkeep and maintenance responsibilities. Among the living options available, congregate living, which combines traditional residential-

living options (typically an apartment) with availability of services, is often the preferred choice.

Similar to pure independent living, congregate care was the first model to offer an alternative to the extremes of custodial care and complete self-sufficiency. Congregate care provides supportive services to accommodate the changing needs and varied populations in residential surroundings. There can be broad differences between facilities with regard to size, services, staffing, and social programs. The several forms of residential-living facilities provide units in which services such as one meal per day (versus three in assisted living and skilled nursing), housekeeping, transportation, and social activities may be included as part of the rent or cost of the unit. Additional services may be available on-site and purchased by residents for an additional fee. Independent-living sponsors do not usually provide health care, as it generally triggers a measure of regulation. To avoid regulation, health-care services are sometimes offered as an á la carte option provided by a separate licensed health-care provider (such as a home health service).

Congregate housing offers independent living in self-contained apartments, duplex units, or cottages and provides opportunities to share activities of daily living with other residents, as one chooses. These facilities encompass a broad array of facility types, ranging from developments that are similar to assisted living facilities to developments that mimic the independent-living components of continuing care retirement communities. *(Also known as: Catered Living, Adult Congregate Living Facility (ACLF), Senior Service Apartments.)*

Typical sponsors/owners

An independent-living/congregate-care developer may be a not-for-profit entity, a for-profit, a propriety corporation, a partnership, an individual, a syndicate, or an association of residents. Many not-for-profit sponsors have historically been faith-based, fraternal, or community organizations. The type of organization that sponsors a facility often has a significant impact on the design itself. In addition to providing funding, the sponsoring organization may be dedicated to creating a certain sense of community. It may provide a common link among residents, be it by shared interests or shared beliefs, which can be utilized in the design process to maximize the effectiveness of the facility. For example, a community organized under the aegis of a religious organization would certainly differ from a community brought together by a love of golf.

Types of settings

Independent/congregate living is found in three major models.

- *Freestanding.* A conventional apartment building with services that may be any size.

- *Blended service/living options.* Apartment and/or cottage-style living that may be physically associated with another level of care such as assisted living.

- *Retirement community.* A multiple-level-of-care continuum that includes independent/congregate apartment/cottage living with assisted living and long-term care.

This section will focus primarily on the first two models.

Major program elements and design considerations

Congregate living typically resembles an apartment building with enhanced public areas that include dining, activities, and social spaces. The most significant program elements are the residential-living units and the public spaces, as well as the services that support them.

Residential-living units

Independent/congregate living apartments continue to get larger to match the expectations of postwar retirees whose housing expectations and standards are higher than the previous generation's. Few new projects, including those with government subsidies, are being developed with studio apartments. In fact, in many markets there is a limited ability to market standard-size one-bedroom apartments. Most consumers are looking for larger accommodations that offer guest space or office space and find a one-bedroom with den to be the minimally acceptable unit configuration. The typical unit configurations and their design criteria include the following:

One-bedroom. The conventionally arranged apartment of 600–700 sq ft with a full kitchen, living room, bedroom, and bathroom. New models are typically arranged with the bathroom directly off the bedroom.

One-bedroom with den. An apartment unit that adds a den of 90–120 sq ft to a one-bedroom apartment. Some models will include an extra half-bath (powder room).

Two-bedroom. A two-bedroom unit of 750–950 sq ft with all the features of a one-bedroom and the added amenity of a second bedroom that can be used as a sleeping room (for couples that sleep in separate bedrooms) or as an office, music studio, or art studio. Most models include a full bathroom and a powder room or two full bathrooms.

Two-bedroom/double master. A two-bedroom unit that provides two bedroom suites (bedroom with full bathroom), usually located on either side of the living room.

Two-bedroom with den. A unit with the features of a two-bedroom unit as well as a 90–100 sq ft den.

Deluxe units. Variations of the previously defined models that may include a special spatial feature such as a dining alcove/area, eat-in kitchen, dining room, or larger living room.

Cottages. See section on continuing-care retirement communities.

Unit features

Bedroom/ sleeping area
In addition to conventional bedroom planning features, senior residents may expect amenities such as:

- Additional space and clearances around/between furniture for easy maneuvering (especially if a mobility device is required)

- Space for two twin beds, for couples who sleep separately

- Ample storage space with walk-in closets in the master bedroom of larger units

- Either hardwired or flexibly installed wireless emergency-response systems

- Sufficient power, telephone, and computer outlets for TV's, computers, and fax machines that may or may not be located in the bedroom

Bathrooms
All of the features identified in an assisted living apartment bathroom should be included. Units with multiple bathrooms may include a tub/shower in the second bathroom or a smaller shower (36" x 36") unit.

Living room
The standard features of a residential living room with the added flexibility to create a small office or dining area and a wide variety of furniture pieces.

Kitchen
In general, residential kitchen designs have become more sophisticated, with

▲ *Independent living units resemble a typical apartment but have built-in features: wider doorways, accessible hardware, emergency call systems, towel bars that double as grab bars, and many other details that facilitate aging in place. Classic Residence by Hyatt, Yonkers, New York. Perkins Eastman Architects PC. Interior Design by Bonnie Manson. Photograph by Hyatt.*

more features and appliances. There are few senior markets where the following amenities would be questioned:

- Full-size refrigerator with self-defrosting features
- Four stovetop burners, and a self-cleaning oven with front-end controls for safety (usually electric to avoid open flame)
- An undercounter microwave with convenient counter space below
- Dishwasher
- Single-or double-bowl sink with garbage disposable (subject to local jurisdiction)

Designers of senior living units should also consider incorporating special features, such as:

- Pantry cabinet to provide eye-level, easily reachable storage
- Space for a small table for dining as well as seated food preparation
- Cabinet accessories that glide out and turn, to maximize easily reachable storage space that doesn't require excessive bending, twisting, or extension
- Side-by-side refrigerators so that both freezer and refrigeration compartments have shelves that are easily reachable and at eye level

Washer/dryer

Most developments are meeting growing consumer expectation for laundry facilities within the unit. Stacked washer-dryer units are a minimum expectation in the unit, with growing demand for conventional side-by-side units.

▶ *Activity spaces for both men's and women's varied interests are a common program element in many retirement communities. Brookdale Living Community, Mt. Lebanon, Pennsylvania. Perkins Eastman Architects PC. Photograph by Jim Schafer.*

Common areas

Public areas vary greatly, making it difficult to generalize about projects and markets. The basic common areas—dining, a living room, library, etc.—will generally be similar to those found in assisted living. Because of the generally larger size of the communities, there may be more variety in spaces, as well as more activity options, to respond to the varied interests of the residents. Game rooms (with billiards), card rooms, gardening rooms, and similar spaces are not unusual. Another area of significant difference is in the education and fitness programs offered.

Education

There has been an increased interest among seniors in lifelong learning opportunities and an active engagement in the world around them. New independent/congregate-living sponsors are expanding their library resources, Internet connectivity, and classroom spaces for lectures and academic-style classes.

Fitness

Exercise equipment rooms and swimming pools were not formerly part of the image for retirement living. They are now a large and significant part of the common area programs of many buildings. Swimming pools are being developed that have level (or slightly sloped) bottoms three to four feet deep that accommodate 10–20 participants for aquatic-based aerobic exercise. Land-based fitness programs have also expanded in popularity, with space needs for

◀ Fitness facilties such as swimming pools and exercise equipment are increasingly popular program elements in retirement communities. Glenmeadow Retirement Community, Longmeadow, Massachusetts. Perkins Eastman Architects PC. Photograph by Jeffery Yardis.

exercise and weight training equipment separate from aerobic exercise rooms.

Support areas

Service and support areas vary with the size of the community, the range of programs offered, and the integration of other services and settings (such as assisted living). Typical areas are identified in the sample program on the next page.

Key planning issues

The key planning issue in this building type is to plan for aging in place. Over time the residents will become older and frailer, needing more services and mobility aids. The facility should be fully accessible and allow for the addition of programs and services so that most residents can remain safely in their apartments.

Payment/reimbursement and regulation

Independent/congregate-living facilities may be rental or ownership units or may include an up-front entry fee in addition to a monthly rent or maintenance fee. Rents charged vary widely and may either be market-rate or include some type of rent subsidy. Persons with limited income and assets may qualify for government-subsidized housing or services.

There are several major types of federally funded housing, and some of these are mimicked or supplemented by similar state and local programs:

- Public and assisted housing—rental units that are available to low-income families under programs run by HUD (the U.S. Department of Housing and Urban Development) or the

Rural Housing Service. Families usually pay no more than 30 percent of their income for rent.

- Section 8-a program that covers the difference in rent above 30 percent of family income through rent vouchers to low-income families living in approved housing

- Section 202-a housing program for low-income seniors that sometimes includes other supportive services, such as activities and transportation. (This program is currently being modified to permit assisted living services due to the aging in place of many 202 residents.)

- Section 221(d)(3) and 211(d)(4) provide mortgage insurance for new and substantially rehabilitated multifamily housing.

- Section 811 provides funding for rental housing with support services for very-low-income adults with disabilities.

In addition to rent, some developments charge an entry fee coupled with a monthly fee. The entry fee may be fully or partially refundable, or refundable on a declining basis, when a resident dies or leaves the facility. Whether the development is based on entry fee or rental, the impact on the space program is usually related to unit size, and the range and quality of the common spaces.

Independent/congregate living is not typically licensed but may need to meet consumer protection laws through state controls imposed by an office on aging. Building standards in most states follow traditional multifamily building codes.

SAMPLE PROGRAM FOR A CONGREGATE LIVING APARTMENT

Program Category	Program Space	No.	Unit Size (NSF)	Total Area (sq ft)
A. Summary	Independent living (IL)	226		186,235
	IL Common areas			640
	IL Support areas			1,040
	Subtotal IL NSF			187,915
	Assistive living (AL)	34		14,100
	AL common areas			1,935
	AL support areas			400
	Subtotal AL NSF			16,435
	IL Subtotal GSF (net x 1.3)			244,290
	AL Subtotal GSF (net x 1.3)		21,366	
	Total RU GSF (net/gross factor 1.3)			265,655
	Non-RU GSF			315,879
	Garage			71,380
B. Independent living:	IL - Studio s	15	450	6,750
resident units	IL - 1 BR, 1 bath	80	650	52,000
	IL - 1 BR, 1.5 bath, den	56	900	50,400
	IL - 2 BR, 2 bath	69	1,015	70,035
	IL - 2 BR, 2 bath, den	6	1,175	7,050
	Subtotal	226		186,235
C. Independent living:	Resident laundry	8	80	640
common areas	Subtotal			640
D. Independent living:	Housekeeping/storage	8	60	480
support areas	Trash room	8	30	240
	Telephone/CATV closet	8	20	160
	Electrical closet	8	20	160
	Subtotal			1,040
E. Assistive living:	AL-studio	30	400	12,000
resident units	AL-1 BR	4	525	2,100
	Subtotal	34		14,100
F. Assistive living:	AL dining 34 @ 20 sq ft	1	680	680
common areas	AL servery	1	150	150
	Living room	1	775	775
	Activity room w/ toilet	1	250	250
	Resident laundry	1	80	80
	Subtotal			1,935

continues

PROGRAM (PREDESIGN)

SAMPLE PROGRAM FOR A CONGREGATE LIVING APARTMENT (continued)				
Program Category	**Program Space**	**No.**	**Unit Size (NSF)**	**Total Area (sq ft)**
G. Assistive living:	Staff work areas	1	100	100
support areas	Staff toilet	1	50	50
	Clean linen	1	20	20
	Soiled linen	1	70	70
	Housekeeping/storage	1	60	60
	Trash room	1	30	30
	Telephone/CATV closet	1	20	20
	Electrical closet	1	20	20
	Janitors' closet	1	30	30
	Subtotal			400
H. Common	Porte-cochere	1	500	N/A
public areas	Vestibule	1	150	150
	Entry lobby	1	700	700
	Reception	1	100	100
	Mail/package room	1	375	375
	Coffee shop/convenience store	1	600	600
	Public toilet	2	180	360
	Subtotal			2,285
I. Common	Reception/waiting	1	150	150
administration	Office	1	200	200
	Office	2	150	300
	Office	2	150	260
	Marketing open office	1	300	300
	Administrative assistant	1	80	80
	Conference room	1	300	300
	Copy/workroom	1	80	80
	File storage	1	54	54
	Coat closet	1	10	10
	Staff toilet (M/F)	1	50	50
	Subtotal			1,834
J. Common	IL Dining 113 @ 20 sq ft (2 seatings)	1	2,260	2,260
resident areas	IL servery	1	150	150
	Private dining for 16 @ 20 sq ft	1	320	320
	PD servery	1	75	75
	Billiards/game room	1	850	850
	Library/media room	1	600	600
	Gathering lounge w/ fireplace	1	1,000	1,000

Program Category	Program Space	No.	Unit Size (NSF)	Total Area (sq ft)
	Community room w/ stage	1	1,200	1,200
	CR storage	1	100	100
	Card/club room	1	700	700
	Activity/crafts room	1	650	650
	Supply storage	1	75	75
	Computer room	1	300	300
	Wood shop	1	400	400
	Resident association office	1	100	100
	Barber/beauty shop w/ toilet	1	450	450
	Branch bank/personal finance	1	200	200
	Decentralized toilets	2	120	240
	Guest rooms	2	350	700
	Subtotal			10,370
K. Common resident care	Reception/nurse/files	1	200	200
	Exam room	2	100	200
	Physician office	1	120	120
	Office	1	120	120
	Toilet (unisex)	1	50	50
	Lab/supply room	1	65	65
	Wellness coordinator	1	80	80
	Exercise/lap pool/spa	1	1,825	1,825
	Pool equipment & storage	1	80	80
	Pool mechanical room	1	240	240
	Fitness room	1	600	600
	Changing/ showers/ lockers/toilets	2	375	750
	Subtotal			4,330
L. Service/support: Food service	Kitchen	1	3,200	3,200
	Dry storage	1	300	300
	Storage	1	300	300
	Janitor closet	1	45	45
	Director of food service office	1	120	120
	Dietician office	1	90	90
	Director of human resource office	1	100	100
	Staff lounge/vending	1	275	275
	Staff lockers	2	200	400
	Staff toilets (M & F)	2	175	350
	Subtotal			5,180

continues

Program Category	Program Space	No.	Unit Size (NSF)	Total Area (sq ft)
SAMPLE PROGRAM FOR A CONGREGATE LIVING APARTMENT (continued)				
M. Service/support: housekeeping	Director of housekeeping office	1	65	65
	Central housekeeping supply	1	325	325
	Central laundry	1	650	650
	Central clean linen holding	1	200	200
	Central soiled linen holding	1	65	65
	Subtotal			1,305
N. Service/support: maintenance	Maintenance shop	1	450	450
	Maintenance storage	1	250	250
	Office	1	100	100
	Subtotal			800
O. Service/support: maintenance	Mechanical rooms/AHUs	1	1,000	1,000
	Boiler room	1	1,200	1,200
	Chiller room	1	1,200	1,200
	Domestic/fire pump	1	300	300
	Electrical equipment room	1	500	500
	Emergency generator	1	250	250
	Telephone/CATV equipment room	1	150	150
	Elevator equipment room (roof)	1	450	450
	Subtotal			5,050
P. Service/support: miscellaneous	Central building storage	1	800	800
	Resident storage (IL)	226	12+6=18	4,068
	Resident storage (AL)	34	12+6=18	612
	Receiving/loading dock/trash/compact	1	2,000	2,000
	Subtotal			7,480
Q. Totals	Public areas, H			2,285
	Administration, I			1,834
	Resident areas, J			10,370
	Resident care, K			4,330
	Subtotal common NSF			18,819
	Food service, L			5,180
	Housekeeping, M			1,305
	Maintenance, N			800
	Mechanical, O			5,050
	Miscellaneous, P			7,480

Program Category	Program Space	No.	Unit Size NSF	Total Area (sq ft)
	Subtotal service/support NSF			19,815
	Total nonresidential unit NSF			38,634
	Common subtotal GSF (Net x 1.3)			24,465
	Service/support subtotal GSF (Net x 1.3)		25,760	
	Total non-RU GSF (Net/Gross Factor 1.3)		50,224	
R. Parking	Garage			
	Resident (0.5/Unit)	130	415	53,950
	Staff	18	415	7,470
	Visitor	24	415	9,960
	Total garage area	172		71,380
	Site			
	Staff	22		
	Visitor	16		
	Total site parking	38		
	Total parking spaces	210		

Trends/opportunities for innovation

Housing and service integration
Significant new options are emerging in independent/congregate-living products as sponsors look to combine apartment-style living with a wide range of services and programs to allow people to age in place. Industry-wide aversion to developing new long-term care beds due to cost, lack of reimbursement, regulation, and low market acceptability are creating CCRC look-alikes that provide a wide continuum of services without licensed nursing care.

Naturally occurring retirement communities (NORCs)
In many communities, older apartment buildings have evolved into senior housing due to the average age of the residents. The residents of these buildings have chosen a community-based housing option (rental or condominium/cooperative) but may be in need of more services and programs. Sponsors, particularly not-for-profit organizations, are examining ways to add an array of services (meals, home health care, housekeeping, senior centers for socialization, scheduled transportation, etc.) to maintain older seniors in their apartments.

Service house model
Several European countries have experimented with the service house model, where an independent/congregate-living facility is developed with supportive program areas that provide meals, activities, and health services to age-qualified seniors in the neighborhood. This model meets several needs:

- Provides neighborhood-based services to maintain seniors in their own homes
- Increases the use of services and spaces provided by the independent/congregate-living program
- Develops additional revenue sources (membership fee or fee-for-services) to support staff and operating costs
- Integrates the building and residents into the larger community
- Generates a natural marketing base before seniors may need to move to the housing portion

Ownership/payment

Preference for payment structures varies by income, geographic region, and cultural background. In areas where the tradition of home ownership has been strong, it can be expected that there will be an increasing interest in ownership options (condominiums, cooperatives, or fee simple) and a declining interest in entry-fee models. Financial structures that increase financial control, retain value (investment), and build equity may be of increasing interest to future generations of seniors.

Continuing Care Retirement Communities (CCRCs)

Introduction/types of users

Continuing care retirement communities (CCRCs) are residential communities that offer housing and health-related services that permit residents to remain in the community for the rest of their lives.

They are designed to offer older adults an independent lifestyle through the provision of varying levels of supportive services, while allowing individuals to maintain the privacy of their own home within the facility and obtain the care they need as they age without hav-

ing to relocate to a different facility. In addition to the residential unit, CCRCs typically offer:

- Access to coordinated social activities
- Dining services
- Housekeeping
- Scheduled transportation
- Emergency call monitoring
- Health care when and if the course of aging raises the need
- A fully accessible or adaptable environment

CCRCs are sometimes referred to as life-care communities or lifecare retirement communities because they provide a continuum of care including independent living, assisted living, and long-term care facilities all within one community. While the average age of residents in each of these settings varies, it is not unusual to find average age at entry into independent living to be mid-seventies to early eighties, and slightly younger into cottage/villa products.

Typical sponsors/owners

Historically, sponsors of most CCRCs have been faith-based organizations that desire to provide supportive settings for their constituents during their declining years. Such organizations continue to play a major role in developing and operating CCRCs as not-for-profit organizations, though most also serve people who are not affiliated with the organization. During recent decades, a number of for-profit or proprietary organizations have entered this field. Many of these organizations have emphasized the social and hospitality aspects of CCRCs and often focus on independent living environments for residents with limited health-care needs.

Types of settings

Typically, CCRCs have been set in suburban or rural locations on sites that provide campuslike environments with low-rise buildings in parklike settings. These communities usually offer a mix of independent living apartments and cottages, with a complement of assisted living units and long-term care beds, together with common facilities. As land has become more costly and development approvals more difficult to secure, CCRCs, especially those near large cities, have been built on smaller properties with mid- to high-rise structures offering independent living apartments exclusive of cottages and often with assisted living units and long-term care nursing units stacked in a single building.

Recently, as both urban and nonurban dwellers recognize the convenience and benefits of residing in urban areas to be close to family and friends and to take advantage of the varied lifestyle and range of facilities cities offer, urban CCRCs have begun to develop.

Many older CCRCs were small, with fewer than 100 independent living units, as they were community based and often supported by volunteers through their religious affiliations. As residents have come to demand a greater number and variety of common facilities, a range of dining options, convenient medical support, and more staff, communities have had to grow to remain financially viable. As a result, few CCRCs under development in the early 2000s had fewer than 100 independent living units; most had 200–300 independent living units, and some CCRCs—usually developed in phases—had more than 1,000 independent living units.

Major program elements and design considerations

The major program components of CCRCs include independent living, assisted living, and long-term care. Each of these components of the continuum has a residential living environment and shared common areas similar to those described in the previous sections of this chapter. CCRCs, however, develop a layer of community programs that are used by all residents of the community. This distinctive characteristic, depending on the overall size and configuration of the community, redistributes the common areas in varying fashions.

Large CCRCs

Large communities of over 400 residents may have multiple dining options dispersed throughout the building/site to

▼ This representative CCRC has skilled nursing, assisted living, and independent living along with common activity, dining, and support areas in a main building that is centrally located and surrounded by 130 independent living units in cottages. Buckingham's Choice, Adamstown, Maryland. Perkins Eastman Architects PC. Photograph by Tom Lesser.

minimize walking distances, foster smaller-feeling neighborhoods, and meet expectations for choice and variety. Large communities may also duplicate living rooms, activity areas, and staff support spaces to meet these same goals. The various care components of the continuum (assisted living and long-term care) typically have their own dining and living-room spaces, but as the overall community gets larger they may also have their own activity, larger gathering/multipurpose, wellness, and staff service/support areas. Even large communities may have only one fitness center/swimming pool area, auditorium, or religious/chapel space, so it is important to plan the community to assure easy and proximate access to these areas for the assisted living and long-term care residents.

Medium-size CCRCs

Communities with 200–400 residents typically have a wide array of program and activity areas but will work off of one service support chassis for services such as the kitchen, laundry, loading, and administrative staff. These areas become critical to the efficient planning and design of CCRCs to minimize staff resources, maximize product/service quality (especially food), and eliminate cross-traffic between residents and service/delivery functions. While assisted living and long-term care programs usually have their own dining and living spaces, they share some activity, gathering, and wellness spaces with independent living residents. Major program areas such as fitness/swimming pools, auditoriums, and religious/chapel spaces cannot be duplicated and need to be proximate to assisted living and long-term care residents.

Small CCRCs

CCRCs with less than 200 residents may find it difficult to afford the type and variety of spaces expected by the marketplace. Small communities find that the core components of the continuum are quite small and that there is a need to have more shared spaces, staff, and resources. Smaller CCRCs may find that they need to affiliate with other organizations and facilities to provide the full range of fitness, activity, and social opportunities desired by residents.

A number of market considerations impact the design of a CCRC. These include:

- The unit size, level of service, and common/support facilities that can be afforded by a facility are directly dependent upon how much the target residents are able to pay in entry fees, rents, and monthly fees. A facility that seeks to cater to a clientele with a higher disposable income and greater real estate equity will be able to provide more space, better services, and more common/support facilities.

- The interests of potential residents will help determine the nature of common facilities, such as provision of a spa/wellness center, swimming pool, music and lecture rooms, art studio, a theater and the like.

- If a high percentage of couples is anticipated, more common space for male-directed activity space is desirable, such as a woodworking shop, billiards, a room for Monday-night football, card/poker room, barber shop, and golf. Otherwise, it can be assumed that the majority of single residents will be female, as women have a significantly longer life expectancy.

- Destination-type CCRCs that attract residents based on a special attraction often develop common spaces or other facilities related to the focus of the community. These may be a college or university affiliation, a historic location like Williamsburg, an area rich with cultural institutions or music, or a recreation/outdoor-directed location.
- Some CCRCs market themselves to a select population, such as a branch of the military or a religious or fraternal organization affiliation.

Major program components

Distinctive program elements of CCRCs include more variety in independent living and common areas. The following items identify those elements that are either different or in addition to those discussed previously in this chapter under independent/congregate living, assisted living, Alzheimer's and dementia residences, and long-term care.

Residential living apartments/ congregate living

The unit types, design features, and amenities are similar to those previously discussed, but CCRCs can offer more variety in their housing products. CCRCs, particularly rural and suburban models, are typically developed with cottage-style housing units. These units can come in a variety of styles:

- Detached single-story single-family-style units with garages
- Duplex single-story units with garages
- Attached single-story units with 3–6 units arranged to appear like a larger house
- Attached single-story units with 6–15 units arranged in a cluster with carports or detached garages nearby

Cottages are usually larger than their independent living apartment counterparts. In CCRC communities it is not unusual to find units with three bedrooms, two-car garages, and eat-in kitchens, which are over 2,000 sq ft. These units are occupied by a majority of couples who have made a lifestyle choice and do not desire apartment-style living, or require the added safety and proximity to common areas. Many CCRCs with cottage units develop pedestrian circulation paths that are sometimes covered or partially enclosed for weather-protected access to common areas. Communities on large sites will find resident use of motorized carts and need additional parking spaces near common areas for those who drive from the farthest units.

Common areas

Resident common areas will vary in size and variety with the size of the community. Some distinctive characteristics of CCRCs include the following:

Dining programs in new CCRCs usually provide more variety to respond to the different expectations of the consumers. In addition to the formal dining room with waiter/waitress service, informal dining options are provided in a more casual bistro, grill room, or café setting. Snack/coffee shops with coffee, beverages, and a limited sandwich and snack option are also gaining in popularity and sophistication. Dining options respond not only to casual setting and dress expectations but menu preferences (smaller portions and à la carte options) and flexibility in dining times. Other dining options are expanding with interest in popular options like buffets, display cooking, and take-out.

▲ More sophisticated spaces for movies, lectures and other presentations are now becoming a popular element in some retirement communities. The Osborn, Rye, New York. Perkins Eastman Architects PC. Photograph by David Lamb.

libraries, multipurpose/auditoriums, and fitness programs are being expanded and reinvented to meet new expectations.

Libraries are no longer just locations for donated books, but are becoming active resource centers with a wide variety of publications, work/study spaces, Internet connectivity, resource volumes, travel guides, and comfortable reading areas. Interest in lifelong learning is expanding opportunities with classrooms and meeting rooms for lectures, discussion groups, and book clubs.

Multipurpose rooms/auditoriums are evolving from simple large gathering spaces to more sophisticated rooms for performance arts, lectures, and music. Attention to acoustics, theater lighting, and sound systems is becoming more important, along with "back-of-house" spaces for staging shows that may have sets, props, costumes, and musical instruments.

Fitness programs have evolved with increased awareness of healthy aging and the benefits of exercise for remaining independent with better endurance and a wider range of motion and mobility. A wide range of fitness programs may be offered with classes ranging from Tai Chi, to aerobics offered in chairs or on floor mats, to aquatic aerobics. Strength training on specially designed equipment, stationary bicycles, and rowing machines is also gaining popularity. The most sophisticated and expensive space to build and operate is the swimming pool, and it has very specific requirements:

In addition to the living rooms and informal meeting places found in most senior living settings, there is a growing expectation for spaces that allow residents to continue lifelong interests and hobbies. Craft rooms are evolving into art studios with space for painting, drawing, ceramics, and weaving. Art/craft studios are also places to offer classes and training opportunities, since many individuals may continue their activities within their unit if space permits. Specialized interests are being recognized with working greenhouses, woodworking shops, music/recital rooms, and photography labs. Traditional CCRC spaces like

- Adequate size to permit lap swimming and/or aquatic aerobics. (Pool sizes should be a minimum of 18' × 42' with a level or slightly sloping bottom and water depth of three to four feet.)

- Variety of access points and means, including ladders, gradual steps, ramps, and chair lifts

- Pool water temperature of 88–95 degrees with air temperatures a few degrees higher

- Environmental controls to keep higher-than-average air temperatures, minimize humidity, and prevent drafts/breezes

- Aprons around the pool large enough for safe walking areas, with places to sit while waiting and for instructors to conduct classes

- Space for storage of kickboards, floats, and other equipment

- Space for instructors and lifeguards, with visual control of the pool area and entrance

- Locker rooms sized with multiple showers and changing areas, since residents may take a bit longer getting changed and are generally coming in groups for classes

- A showerhead on the pool apron to provide the rinse option for those going into the pool without tying up the locker room showers

- Family locker room for one-person use with an assistant (spouses may need to assist with showering or dressing)

- Privacy in pool areas, since residents may prefer not to be seen in swimming attire

- Bathrooms immediately adjacent to the pool if locker rooms are more remote

Outdoor space

In addition to passive activity areas such as porches, terraces, patios, and covered outdoor areas, it is important to include active recreational opportunities for walking, gardening and other resident interests. Some communities have included fishing, tennis, and putting greens.

Assisted living residences

Assisted living is provided in the CCRC for those who need a more supportive environment due to frailty or cognitive impairment. These services are usually provided in a wing or floor of the CCRC dedicated to the care needs of those residents. In addition to residential units tailored to their needs, residents have use of common and support facilities designed specifically for their use. Some residents or spouses with Alzheimer's or dementia may live in this area as well. If the CCRC is large enough it may have a separate cluster of units dedicated to residents with Alzheimer's disease and related dementia. In general, the design guidelines for assisted living and Alzheimer's facilities defined earlier in this chapter apply here as well. Typically, the number of assisted living units in a CCRC ranges from 10 to 20 percent of the number of independent living units.

Health center (long-term care)

CCRCs also offer residents short-term care, such as rehabilitation after a hospital stay or for short-term illness requiring 24-hour care. These beds are often combined in a health center with beds reserved for long-term care residents. Both are provided with round-the-clock nursing services similar to those in a nursing home. Residents who require short-term or long-term care may also require assistance in most activities of daily living including help in eating and walking. (See section on skilled-nursing facilities on pages 27–41. However, note that CCRCs

PROGRAM (PREDESIGN)

REPRESENTATIVE CCRC PROGRAM

RESIDENTIAL LIVING UNITS

Apartments	Area (sq ft)
1 BR; 1 bath 40 @ 750 sq ft	30,000
1 BR/Den; 1.5 baths 50 @ 950 sq ft	47,500
2 BR; 2 baths 45 @ 1,200 sq ft	54,000
2 BR/den; 2 baths 15 @ 1,400 sq ft	21,000
Subtotal: 150 apartments @	152,500
Total (Grossing @ 1.3):	198,250

Cottages	
1 BR; 1 bath 10 @ 875 sq ft	8,750
1 BR/den; 1.5 baths 20 @ 1,050 sq ft	21,000
2 BR; 2 baths 20 @ 1,250 sq ft	25,000
2 BR/den; 2 baths 10 @ 1,550 sq ft	15,500
Subtotal: 60 units	70,250

Garages & Covered Parking for Cottages	
Covered parking 40 spaces @ 190	7,600
Detached garages 20 spaces @ 440	8,800
Subtotal	16,400

Assisted Living Units	
45 Units @ 550 sq ft	24,750
Dining room for 45 @ 20 sq ft	900
Living room 2 @ 200 sq ft	400
Assisted bathing 2 @ 200 sq ft	400
Resident laundry 2 @ 75 sq ft	150
Resident kitchen	110
Activity room	250
Offices 2 @ 100 sq ft	200
Wellness/nurse office	120
Soiled utility 2 @ 80 sq ft	160
Clean utility 2 @ 50 sq ft	80
Resident toilets 2 @ 50 sq ft	100
Staff toilet @ 50 SF	50
Janitor/housekeeping 2 @ 50 sq ft	100
Lobby/waiting	250
Subtotal	28,020
Total (Grossing @ 1.4)	39,200

HEALTH-CARE CENTER

Pvt. long-term care rooms 42 @ 240 sq ft	10,080
Dining for 42 @ 30 sq ft	1,260
Pantry	150
Activity	400
Cluster living rooms 2 @ 225 sq ft	450
Shower rooms 2 @ 150 sq ft	300
Bathing/grooming 2 @ 200 sq ft	400
Nurse station	150

	Area (sq ft)
Medication	100
Charting	100
Nurse alcoves 2 @ 75 sq ft	150
Nurse office	100
Conference room	175
Staff toilet	50
Resident toilet 2 @ 50 sq ft	100
Medical records/unit clerk	100
Social worker	100
Activities office	150
Staff lounge/lockers	200
Clean utility 2 @ 50 sq ft	100
Soiled utility 2 @ 80 sq ft	160
Janitor/housekeeping @ 50 sq ft	100
Wheelchair storage	50
Medical supplies	75
Subtotal	15,000
Total (Grossing @ 1.6)	24,000

COMMONS

Public Areas	
Lobby	800
Vestibule	150
Reception	100
Public toilets	450
Mailboxes/package room	200
Subtotal	1,700

Resident Areas	
Dining for 175 @ 16 sq ft	2,800
Private dining for 20	400
Multipurpose room	1,200
Gathering lounge	1,200
Coatroom	75
Gift shop	400
Store	200
Snack bar/grill	800
Meeting rooms 1 @ 600 sq ft	600
Library	600
Barber/beauty salon w/ toilet	500
Billiards/game room	350
Activity/art room	350
Health spa/exercise	600
Pool/changing	2,800
Greenhouse	150
Workshop	400
Resident council room	600

	Area (sq ft)
Volunteers	0
Resident bank	600
Guest suite	550
Misc. toilets	300
Subtotal	15,475

Ambulatory Clinic

Reception/nurse office	250
Exam room 2 @ 100 sq ft	200
Specialty exam/treatment	150
Medical director	150
OT/PT suite	750
Toilets 4 @ 50 sq ft	200
Lab/workroom	100
Records/workroom	150
Subtotal	1,950

Central Administration

Executive director	250
Assistant director/nursing home administrator	150
Dir. of social work/admissions	125
Dir. of finance	125
Dir. of development	125
Dir. of housing	125
Chaplain	150
Waiting	0
Business office	200
Secretaries	225
Marketing office	150
Marketing reception/waiting	150
Human resources office	100
Human resources waiting	150
Workroom/copy/supplies	150
Conference	200
Staff toilet 2 @ 50 sq ft	100
Subtotal	2,475

Service/Support

Kitchen	3,200
Dir. of food service & asst. food service	175
Dir. of housekeeping	125
Training	300
Plant manager/asst. plant manager/plans	200
Maintenance shops	600
Central storage	800
Resident storage	1,500
Staff locker rooms 2 @ 300	600
Staff lounge/cafeteria	500
Housekeeping	600

Body holding	100
Cart wash	100
Trash holding	150
Central laundry	800
Mechanical	3,000
Subtotal	12,750
Total Net Area	34,300
TOTAL (Grossing @ 1.4)	48,000
Maintenance Building	1,500

SUMMARY OF BUILT AREAS

Independent Living Units

Apartments	198,250
Cottages	70,250
Garages and covered parking	16,400
Assisted living units	39,200
Health-care center	24,000
Commons	48,000
Maintenance Building	1,500
Grand Total	407,100

Total Development

Use	Total
Independent living apartments	150 units
Independent living cottages	60 units
Assisted living units	45 units
Health care	42 beds

PARKING	TYPICAL NEED	TYPICAL ZONING REG.
Apartments		
90 1BR	@ 1.0 = 90	@ 1.5= 90
60 2 BR	@ 1.25 = 75	@ 2.0 = 120
Subtotal	165	255
Cottages		
30 1 BR	@ 1.0 = 30	@ 2.0 = 60
30 2 BR	@ 1.25 = 38	@ 2.0 = 60
Subtotal	68	120
Assisted Living		
45 units	@ 0.33 = 15	@ 0.33 = 15
Health Care		
42 units	@ 0.33 = 14	@ 0.33 = 14
Central Building		
Staff	75	0
Visitor	45	0
Subtotal	120	0
Total	382 Spaces	404 Spaces

typically include a higher proportion of single rooms than a traditional nursing home.) The table on pages 92–93 tabulates a typical program for a CCRC with 210 independent living units (150 apartments and 60 cottages), 45 assisted living units, and 42 long-term care beds.

Regulations and payment/ reimbursement

CCRCs are regulated in many states, though these regulations vary greatly. The specific regulatory requirements should be verified with the responsible agency for the state in which the facility is located. Typical regulations protect future residents through review of proposed resident contracts and agreements, the financial feasibility of the proposed community and its long-term viability, and other financial matters. States also have varying provisions to allow for long-term care beds within CCRCs. Some states have no restrictions, whereas others permit a fixed ratio, such as one bed per five independent living units. Finally, physical and environmental standards and requirements for long-term care and assisted living facilities within CCRCs are controlled by state regulations for these uses.

Types of contracts

CCRCs usually offer residents one or more of four types of agreements or contracts:

- Extensive, or life-care, contracts provide independent living and health-related services for a fee, usually consisting of both an entrance and a monthly fee. Entry fees may be fully refundable, partially refundable, or refundable on a declining scale at the death or withdrawal of the resident.

- Modified contracts provide independent living and a specified amount of health-related services for an entrance and monthly fees. Some health services, such as a stay in the health center, are covered, but the cost, number of days covered, and other terms vary. In some cases, the sponsor may require residents to purchase long-term care insurance to cover this cost.

- Equity contracts involve an actual real estate purchase, with a transfer of ownership of the unit. Health-related service arrangements vary but usually require an additional monthly fee.

- Monthly rental contracts that cover the cost of the housing accommodation, utilities and a specified service package, such as the provision of 20 meals per month.

Trends/opportunities for innovation

When current communities were built, most responded to the needs and desires of potential residents born before or during World War I who lived through the Depression. Communities are now starting to serve the needs of the next generation, who raised families after World War II and benefited as the first generation of largely college-educated homeowners. Looking ahead, communities will need to address the desires of the baby boomers and their influence on the choices their parents are making. These are groups that came of age during a period in which the ideal of individual expression flourished. They believe that things not to their liking can be changed and that quality, value, and service are researched and measured. As senior living facilities look to appeal to these generations, they will have to keep the following trends in mind:

- Residents' lifestyle preferences will reflect a heightened health consciousness with ongoing provisions for better health and more active interests in exercise and wellness.

- Residents' attitudes, personalities, and expectations will demand greater self-determination. This will be manifested in demands for resident participation in management decisions and resident councils setting their own agendas, using staff for support rather than for organizing and directing.

- Residents will be more impatient and demanding, more analytical about value (i.e., what they get for their money), more culturally and ethnically diverse, more high-tech, more casual in dress, more geographically mobile, and better educated than prior generations.

New models, opportunities, and ideas are emerging as new retirement communities are built and existing ones reposition themselves to meet marketplace expectations. New concepts and ideas include the following:

Common areas that borrow from retail concepts

- Copy/mail center: With interest in life-long learning, second careers, and continued involvement in organizations on the rise, there is increased need for sophisticated copying, color printing, express mail delivery, and computer capabilities. Kinko's-style business centers that may be adjacent to or affiliated with the administration area are becoming more popular.

- Theaters: With the availability of videos, DVDs, and other electronic media, some communities provide small home theaters with fixed theater-style seating. These rooms can also be used for lectures and distance-learning opportunities with colleges and universities.

- Display cooking: Dining options are increasingly following restaurant trends, with themes and customer participation. Display cooking can provide residents with "visual theater" and the opportunity to customize food orders to meet specific dietary needs or preferences.

- Take-out/fast food: Expectations for flexible eating opportunities extend to speed and choice. Facilities have turned to offering take-out menus and pre-packaged chilled or frozen meals that may be sold in the CCRC's store or café.

Unit size, amenities, and features

Retirement living unit design continues to mimic the features found in the private homes from which residents relocate. Watching residential design trends will help inform retirement living unit design. Current concepts include:

- Great-room living style that combines the den, kitchen, and dining room into one large informal area

- Bathrooms that feature multiple sink and counter areas (his/hers), more storage, more space, and accessories

- Technology with remote-controlled lights, temperature, and security systems.

- Multiple telephone lines for separate voice, fax, and data as well as prewired units for community-wide computer networks

Community integration

Intergenerational responses provide opportunities for older adults to make housing choices that meet their specific retirement needs but do not remove them from the larger fabric of the community. European "new towns" have planned senior living options to be integrated into the community, often at its center, with direct connections to the town library, retail core, or civic center. Current U.S.-based interest in traditional neighborhood design and New Urbanism should yield unique products that reinforce access to community-based services such as schools, libraries and recreational centers.

Urban models

Shifting demographics and aging populations in the cities are giving rise to new CCRC models in urban centers. The opportunity to stay connected to cultural institutions and meet diverse ethnic needs are dictating models that are inherently more flexible and built upon existing urban resources. Restaurants, groceries, pharmacies, and laundries/dry cleaners all offer delivery services that can minimize the costs and infrastructure for CCRCs that need to be more cost-effective.

Active Adult Communities (AACs)

Introduction/types of users

Active adult communities, also known as empty nester developments, provide residents with a distinct, adult-oriented lifestyle choice rather than simply with a place to live. The market for these communities differs in many ways from the market for primary family homes, especially with respect to buyers' motivation, the needs and preferences of residents, and housing product design. As a rule, the lifestyle choice is more important to the consumer who may want to shed both the space and maintenance responsibilities of the large family home. *(Also known as: Empty Nester Developments)*

Typical sponsors

Sponsors for active adult communities have typically been for-profit, proprietary developers. In recent years, not-for-profit sponsors of CCRCs have looked to entering this market niche to provide a feeder source for their CCRCs as well as to expand the potential customer pool for selected CCRCs services such as housekeeping, yard maintenance, and health care within the private home setting.

The active adult community market typically attracts people 55–74 years of age. The potential market for active adult communities is diverse and controls substantial wealth. In addition, baby boomers will swell this market pool considerably over the next few decades. Individual households within the target group vary considerably—they may or may not have children at home, though most do not; they may or may not be retired; and they have various income levels.

Types of settings

Most active adult communities are large, but they vary considerably in size. Active adult communities, all of which compete for the older home buyer, encompass various types of communities that can generally be differentiated on the basis of size, target market, and location.

Active adult communities with more than 1,500 units are categorized as large, 300–1,500 units as moderately sized, and fewer than 300 units as small. Large communities feature diverse offerings in their site plans, amenity packages, and choice of housing types. They also attract buyers from a large market area. These communities can be broken down further into age-restricted and not-age-restricted developments. Both types are typically amenity-rich and are often centered on golf or other recreational amenities.

Moderate-size communities may be age-restricted or not, and typically offer a clubhouse but may or may not have a golf course within the development. Some moderate-size communities may offer linkages to golf courses or a country club. Small age-restricted and age-targeted communities generally offer fewer home choices and fewer amenities within the development.

Based on data in the *National Directory of Lifestyle Communities*, in 1999 over 60 percent of existing communities were located in the Sunbelt—in Florida, Arizona, California, South Carolina, and North Carolina—but this project type was growing in popularity in other regions in the early 2000s.

Major program elements and design considerations

These communities appeal to empty nesters and retirees who want to leave homes that are too large, too difficult to maintain, and too lonely as their neighbors and friends leave and are replaced by younger and less compatible neighbors.

Developers of active adult communities must decide whether to develop an *age-restricted* or an *age-targeted* community. From a market standpoint, there are advantages and disadvantages to either choice. Some older people prefer age-restricted communities because they want to be among people like themselves who have similar time availability and interests. They also want to live in a commu-

◀ *Many active adult communities incorporate golf courses in their amenities packages.*

nity in which all facilities and programs will be directed toward their interests.

Conversely, a large group of prospective buyers may balk at the idea of age restrictions, either because they prefer to live among a more diverse group of residents or because they, or their younger spouse, think of retirement communities as places for old people. If a community is not age-restricted, the developer can market and sell to a larger pool of buyers; however, it cannot then prohibit children and teenagers.

Other types of products that compete for the 55–74-year-old market include age-targeted country club communities, second home and preretirement communities, and resort/empty-nester communities. Often such communities evolve over time into age-targeted active adult communities.

Lifestyle is determined to a great extent by the design of the community and its components. Nature is a key amenity for active adults and contributes significantly

▲ In some communities, the existing natural environment becomes the central focus. In developments with uninteresting land, a natural environment is created.

• A hierarchy of vehicular and pedestrian circulation

Because socialization is important, the overall plan should encourage contact among residents. To achieve this, homes can be clustered in neighborhoods, and places should be created where people will naturally gather, such as miniparks, mail/postal centers, shopping areas, and a clubhouse.

Residents generally want the architectural style of their homes and common facilities to be strongly associated with the area in which they choose to live. Therefore, the community design normally reflects the architectural style and materials of the region.

For larger communities with over 300 units, creating smaller neighborhoods within the community helps residents find their way and identify with their neighbors. The best neighborhoods contain a balanced mix of units of different types and costs, with the goal of accommodating people of various socioeconomic levels. The lot configuration and design should be efficient and promote privacy. Efficient planning entails providing a lot that is proportional to the size of the house. Promoting privacy means limiting visibility into a house or private yard from neighboring houses and yards.

The primary program components of active adult communities consist of lowrise, usually single-story, residential units with supporting amenities. Unit sizes vary widely, depending primarily on the financial means of the target market of a particular development. Most residential units are single-story or feature all main living spaces and the master bedroom on the ground floor, reflecting market preferences of a population that is starting to

to a feeling of relaxation. Natural features such as open space, landscaping, and water, and the way in which they are incorporated into the project design, create the resort or country club atmosphere that characterizes active adult communities. The outdoor environment is not only important for aesthetic reasons but because it provides a pleasant setting for activities like golf, fishing, boating, walking, and hiking.

Many buyers are drawn to active adult communities because they are controlled environments. To promote a sense of order, communities should be designed with the following:

• Readily identifiable entrances that often include signage, a guard booth, and gates

• A sense of arrival

• Well-defined boundaries (many are gated communities)

• A hierarchy of spaces from public to private

consider the realities of aging. Unfinished attics or basements offer the flexibility for larger living spaces to meet individual expectations and lifestyle needs. Median sizes of residential units, excluding the garage, are:

Detached home	1,900 sq ft
Attached home	1,690
Manufactured home	1,500
Condominium	1,410

Based on a profile of 353 communities (from the *National Directory of Lifestyle Communities*), the provision of amenities in communities is as follows:

• Clubhouse	88.7%
• Outdoor swimming pool	87.0
• Fitness center	69.8
• Arts and crafts room	62.6
• Walking trails	62.6
• Tennis courts	55.3
• Recreational vehicle storage areas	50.0
• Shuffleboard	48.8
• Ballroom with stage	45.3
• Computer center	40.9
• Golf course	39.7
• Bocce court	38.2
• Restaurant	34.6
• Community gardens	29.8
• Indoor swimming pool	22.7

Regulation and payment/reimbursement

Generally, active adult communities must conform to local zoning regulations, which impact allowable land uses, building density, setbacks, roadway standards, open-space requirements, building height, parking requirements, and the

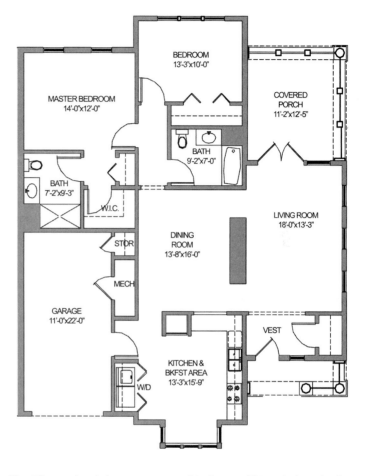

▲ *This typical two-bedroom single-story cottage offers such amenities as a garage, fireplace, and covered porch. Hunterbrook Ridge, Yorktown Heights, New York. Perkins Eastman Architects PC.*

like. If a condominium-type ownership is proposed, the development may be subject to certain disclosures and approvals from a state agency as part of the development's offering plan.

All communities are subject to the terms of the Civil Rights Act that prohibit discrimination in the provision of housing on the basis of race, color, religion, sex, or national origin. Communities are also subject to the Fair Housing Act, which among other things prohibits discrimination against persons based on familial status. However, the act recognizes the need for housing that excludes

▲ *An increased emphasis on exercise and health characterizes the activities available at many of these communities.*

children and for communities created solely for persons above a minimum age threshold and provides for three types of communities designed for older persons based on specific criteria.

- Criterion 1: At least 80 percent of the occupied units in the "housing facility or community" must be occupied by at least one person 55 years of age or older.
- Criterion 2: The facility or community must publish and adhere to policies and procedures that demonstrate intent to comply with the requirements of the Fair Housing Act.
- Criterion 3: The community or facility must meet the rules for verification of occupancy through surveys and other means of data collection to determine occupants' ages and update other information.

Ownership

Active adult communities may be developed either as rental or ownership models. Rents charged are usually market rate. Ownership models include fee-simple or condominium-type of ownership. In addition, a monthly fee is usually charged for the use of the development's amenities and other services such as yard care and housekeeping.

Program standards

Common facilities for large communities are derived from the list above. Programs usually fall within the following ranges (from the *National Directory of Lifestyle Communities*).

100-unit or less community

1,200–1,500 sq ft meeting/social building with a meeting room, efficiency kitchen, and restrooms

250–300-unit community

5,000–7,000 sq ft recreational building with social activity spaces, small library, exercise room, meeting area, small kitchen, and restrooms

300–1,500 unit community

16–18 sq ft per residential unit

1,500-unit or more community

13–15 sq ft per residential unit

Trends/opportunities for innovation

Empty-nester housing products that are not necessarily recreation-oriented are gaining in popularity in many regions of the country. Modern housing conveniences, single-story living, and lack of maintenance make this product an attractive lifestyle option that will gain in popularity. The following significant trends impact active adult communities:

- Need to recognize the realities of aging in place (Units should build in accessibility or adaptability.)
- Desire for larger, more open-feeling residential units
- Increasing emphasis on health and exercise
- Ongoing interest in continuing education
- Desire to be near family and friends and familiarity of hometown
- Interest in resort-type escape destinations that offer a special environment such as water or mountains or form of recreation such as golf.

Summary

The eight building types defined above are only a snapshot of the most common facilities for the aging in 2003. The rapidly growing population of older people in North America, and around the world, is an increasingly sophisticated and demanding part of the overall population. As a result, we should expect that new building types, services, and programs will emerge to respond to their needs.

We need bold thinking that questions the status quo and calls for more humane environments. Between now and the end of this century's first decade, millions of people will enter environments for the frail. Let us hope that these places will be more like the homes they left and less like the institutional environments they fear.
(*Regnier 2002*)

CHAPTER 2

PROJECT PROCESS AND MANAGEMENT

This chapter focuses on two major issues in planning, design, and construction:

- The major steps and tasks involved in planning, designing, and implementing a building program

- The most common management problems that occur in senior housing and care building programs

PLANNING, DESIGN, AND IMPLEMENTATION PROCESS

Design of facilities for the aging typically involves many client representatives, outside agency and public reviews, complex functional issues, rapidly changing technology, restrictive codes, and other significant design influences. Even relatively small projects can take two to three years, and larger projects take from four to seven or more years from initial conception to completion. The design professionals who are successful in dealing with this combination of issues are those who understand not only the issues but also the implementation process during which these issues are resolved.

The implementation process for most facilities for the aging involves 11 steps:

1. Strategic planning

2. Feasibility analysis and scoping of market need

3. Selection and organization of the project team

4. Programming and predesign work—defining scope of the proposed facility

5. Schematic design

6. Obtaining public approval and/or financing/premarketing and sales

7. Design development

8. Construction documentation

9. Selection of the construction and FFE installation teams and purchasing

10. Construction and FFE installation

11. Occupancy

The first part of this section discusses the design team's tasks for each of these steps. Understanding all the steps—as well as the design team's potential role in each—is an essential responsibility of any design professional. On page 104 is a typical schedule for these eleven steps in a new CCRC building project.

Strategic Planning and Preliminary Definition of Need

Many projects are done within existing facilities or on existing campuses. Therefore, any project needs to be planned within the framework of a long-range plan. Even in new facilities, the initial design has to assume growth and change in the future.

An effective strategic plan will respond to more than site and facility issues; it has to take into account the potential impact of changing approaches in technology, demography, funding, and other factors that will determine the future need for and use of the facility. For example, experienced owners and architects recognize that many of the initial occupants of a facility will age in place, and the facility must be designed to accommodate increased frailty over time. The role of the

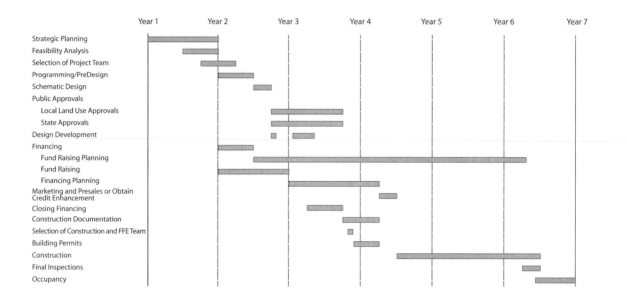

	Year 1	Year 2	Year 3	Year 4	Year 5	Year 6	Year 7
Strategic Planning							
Feasibility Analysis							
Selection of Project Team							
Programming/PreDesign							
Schematic Design							
Public Approvals							
Local Land Use Approvals							
State Approvals							
Design Development							
Financing							
Fund Raising Planning							
Fund Raising							
Financing Planning							
Marketing and Presales or Obtain Credit Enhancement							
Closing Financing							
Construction Documentation							
Selection of Construction and FFE Team							
Building Permits							
Construction							
Final Inspections							
Occupancy							

▲ *Typical minimum time frame, major tasks for a CCRC or large senior housing project. Source: Perkins Eastman Architects PC.*

> We were once content to focus on improving the appearance of nursing homes, but now we realize that design for older people must transcend appearances and curbside appeal. It must work.
> (Hiatt 1992)

design professional in this initial phase can be very important.

Typically, design professionals evaluate existing conditions—from mechanical systems to interior finishes, operational issues, code compliance, site conditions and constraints, and the ability of facilities to support their mission. Once these issues or problems are defined, the design team can develop possible solutions as well as the cost and schedule of each major facility action implied by a potential development strategy. In most strategic plans, the facility's addition/expansion/modernization options are then evaluated according to how well they help achieve the institution's key goals. Then the options can be reduced to a preferred strategic direction.

Feasibility Analysis

Once the strategic-planning framework is set, the next step is to define the scope of the specific project. The sponsor may choose to do this, but it is often more ef-

ficient and productive to include specialists in market or need analysis, as well as design professionals, in this process.

The primary tasks of this step include establishing an outline program and statement of project objectives, setting a realistic schedule, outlining a preliminary project budget, and defining the professional services that need to be retained. In certain cases, this step also includes some preliminary test of feasibility. Because projects must be planned within significant market and financial constraints, clients need to have early confirmation that the project is financially viable. As discussed in Chapter 20, the owner may retain a market and/or financial consultant at this point to provide an independent professional opinion of the market and financial feasibility—a basic requirement for the financing of most projects. All the project parameters—program, budget, schedule, and feasibility—need to be

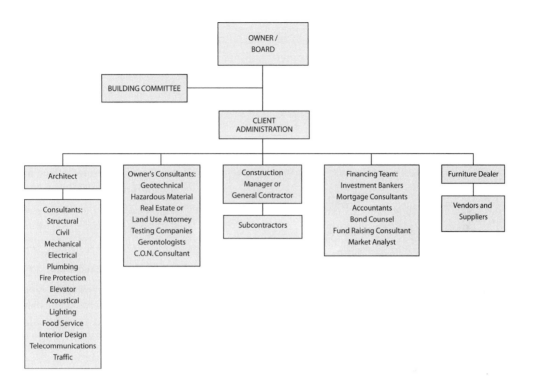

```
                        ┌─────────────┐
                        │   OWNER /   │
                        │    BOARD    │
                        └─────────────┘
                               │
┌────────────────────┐         │
│ BUILDING COMMITTEE │─────────┤
└────────────────────┘         │
                        ┌─────────────┐
                        │   CLIENT    │
                        │ADMINISTRATION│
                        └─────────────┘
```

| Architect | Owner's Consultants: Geotechnical Hazardous Material Real Estate or Land Use Attorney Testing Companies Gerontologists C.O.N. Consultant | Construction Manager or General Contractor | Financing Team: Investment Bankers Mortgage Consultants Accountants Bond Counsel Fund Raising Consultant Market Analyst | Furniture Dealer |

Consultants:
Structural
Civil
Mechanical
Electrical
Plumbing
Fire Protection
Elevator
Acoustical
Lighting
Food Service
Interior Design
Telecommunications
Traffic

Subcontractors

Vendors and Suppliers

reconfirmed and refined after the full team is selected, but it is important to have a realistic outline of the project before selecting the full team.

SELECTION AND ORGANIZATION OF THE PROJECT TEAM

The design of any facility is a team sport. It is not uncommon for ten or more professional disciplines to be involved. Typically, the architect retains most of these different disciplines to form a single cohesive team, thereby providing the owner with a single source of responsibility. The team may include:

- Architects
- Gerontologists
- Food-service consultants
- Equipment specialists
- Interior designers
- Civil engineers
- Mechanical engineers
- Structural engineers
- Electrical engineers
- Plumbing and fire-protection engineers
- Cost consultants and/or construction managers
- Telecommunications and technology consultants
- Lighting designers
- Landscape architects
- Acoustical consultants

▲ *Typical project organization, large nursing home or senior housing project. Source: Perkins Eastman Architects PC.*

There is, in addition, a second group of consultants that often includes:

- Accountants
- Financial consultants
- Market analysts
- Certificate-of-need or other public-approval specialists
- Development-management consultants
- Investment bankers
- Attorneys
- Bond counsel
- Fund-raising consultants
- Environmental and hazardous materials consultants
- Traffic analysts
- Parking consultants
- Zoning consultant

The client typically focuses on the lead professionals (usually the architect), who, in turn, often select the remainder of the design team. The key issue is to have a team that incorporates all the critical professional skills. The complexity of many projects demands that the team find a way to cover most of the specialist disciplines listed above, even if financial limits curtail the scope of their involvement.

The selection process for the lead professionals varies considerably, but a thorough process would include the following:

1. Research is done into firms with relevant experience.

2. A written request is sent to a "long list" of firms asking them to submit letters of interest, lists of references, and information on relevant projects. This request, sometimes known as a request for qualifications (RFQ),

would include a statement of the project objectives, an outline of the program, a schedule, and an assumed budget.

3. After a review of the submittals, four to six firms are selected for a shortlist and asked to make a formal presentation.

4. In some cases the short-listed firms are sent a request for a written proposal, sometimes known as a request for proposal (RFP), summarizing:

   - The firm's understanding of the project
   - Proposed work program
   - Proposed schedule
   - Key personnel and subconsultant firms involved, and their relevant experience
   - Proposed fees and expenses

Following the formal presentation and interviews, a contract is negotiated with the selected firm. In some cases, the fee is discussed only after the team is retained based on qualifications and there is a comprehensive discussion of scope, schedule, proposed specialist consultants, and other variables. No two projects are the same, so the appropriate fees should be carefully calculated on a case-by-case basis to reflect the full scope and cost of the services provided. The form of contract is typically based upon one of the standard AIA contract forms, but the client may edit these. Once the lead firm is selected, the entire team must be organized.

This organization must begin with the client, because only the client can:

- Select the team or the lead professionals who will assemble the full team

- Set the overall project goals and monitor whether they are being met
- Select the program and design solutions that best meet the objectives from among the options prepared by the design team
- Resolve differences and problems between team members (i.e., design team and builder)
- Administer the contracts with the team members
- Lead the relationship between the project team and the public

Most successful projects have clients who create a clear decision-making structure and a strong team relationship with all the firms involved in the process. Some clients have even used one- to

three-day "partnering sessions" at the beginning of a project to build the team relationships. Recognizing the importance of the client's role in this relationship, the renowned Finnish-born architect Eero Saarinen liked to start a project by saying to the design team, "Let's see if we can make this guy into a great client."

Programming and Predesign

For the design team, one of the most challenging steps is to translate market data, owner objectives, state codes, and other input into an architectural program and initial concept. In the past, the client would often prepare a detailed statement of the requirements or program for a project during the scoping phase. Today the increased complexity of the average project has meant that the full detailed

▼ Conceptual diagram for the first floor of a typical suburban assisted living residence. Perkins Eastman Architects PC.

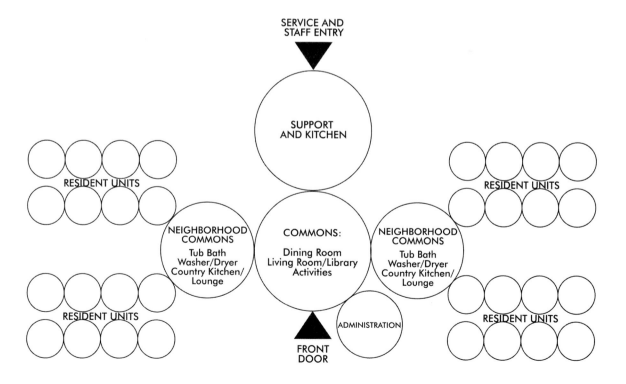

AIA B141 Definition of Schematic Design: Schematic design documents shall establish the conceptual design of the project, illustrating the scale and relationship of the Project components. The Schematic Design Documents shall include a conceptual site plan, if appropriate, and preliminary building plans, sections, and elevations.

scope must be analyzed and defined with the assistance of the design team.

Program analysis has become a basic service provided by the architects, planners, and interior designers on most projects. Among the additional issues the design team and specialists must define are the number of each type of space, the detailed functional and equipment requirements (type of food service to be provided, number and type of physical and occupational therapy equipment to be accommodated, etc.), mechanical/electrical/plumbing and other service needs, dimensions of each space, and the relationships between spaces. This important initial step is discussed in more detail in Chapter 1. The project team also has several other tasks before design can begin, including:

- Detailed assessment of existing conditions in the project area
- Preparation of base plans showing the conditions of the existing structures, a site survey, utility analyses, and subsoil analyses (if new construction is involved)
- Analysis of the zoning, building code, and public-approval issues that will influence the design
- Special analyses of any other issues (asbestos, structural capacity, and so on) that could affect the design, cost, schedule, or feasibility of the project

The results of the programming and related analyses are then combined into one or more preliminary concepts, an expanded statement of project goals, and an updated project schedule and budget.

Once the material is available, many projects will start two important parallel series of tasks: land-use approvals (zoning, site plan approvals, wetland permits, etc.) and financing.

When required, the local land-use approvals typically start with informal meetings with the municipal officials or planning department staff. They help outline the steps in the process, identify whether any special approvals (such as zoning variances) are necessary, and define the information required at each step in the process. Most local approval processes for projects that involve more than interior renovation require detailed site design and schematic building design for land-use approval. On larger projects, the process may also require detailed analyses of the environmental impact of increased traffic, noise, storm drainage, and other issues before local officials give their approval. It is not unusual for the land-use approval process to take one year or more to complete. In many cases, the design team must take the lead in this effort.

The second task that typically begins during predesign is securing financing for the project. Few major projects are paid for from the sponsor's current income, cash reserves, or endowment. Most involve borrowing and/or fund-raising. The financing process can take more than a year to complete. During this process, the design team is often asked to assist in the required documentation, public presentations, and other steps. This is covered further in Chapter 20.

Once these predesign tasks near completion, it is time to start the traditional design process.

Schematic Design

Schematic design is the first phase of the traditional design process. On most senior housing and care projects, this phase may not begin until preliminary

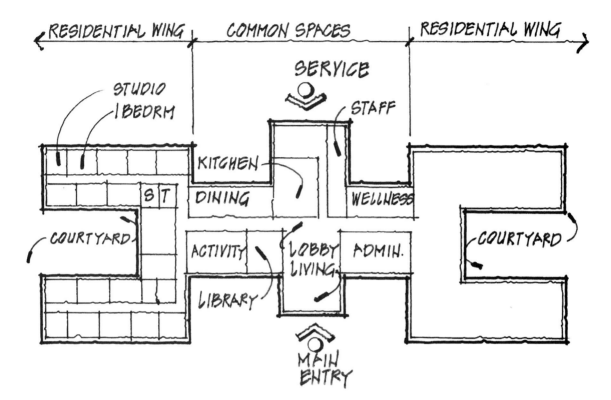

RESIDENTIAL WING | COMMON SPACES | RESIDENTIAL WING

SERVICE

STUDIO
1 BEDRM

STAFF

KITCHEN

S | T

DINING

WELLNESS

COURTYARD

ACTIVITY

LOBBY
LIVING

ADMIN.

COURTYARD

LIBRARY

MAIN
ENTRY

▲ *A schematic plan.
Perkins Eastman Architects
PC. Drawing by Ty Kaul.*

fund-raising or additional feasibility studies confirm the project's viability. During this first design phase, the basic design concept is developed for all the major components of the project. The standard forms of agreement for design services provide brief definitions of schematic design as well as the subsequent phases.

The standard contractual definitions of design services are based on a process that would theoretically permit the design team to move in an orderly way through the most common steps in the design, documentation, and construction of a building. This theoretical process assumes that a clear definition of the client's program exists and that the design process can progress in a linear fashion from that definition through a series

of steps—each of which results in a more complete definition of the design—until the project is sufficiently detailed to go into documentation for bidding (or negotiation) and construction.

The reality is not so orderly. Evolving program requirements, budget realities, increased knowledge of site considerations (such as subsoil problems), and many other factors make it necessary to go back and modify previous steps. Design moves forward, but rarely in the clear linear fashion implied by the standard two-phase description of design. In fact, most design professionals agree that design choices occur at every step of the process. In other words, building design neither starts with schematic design nor ends with the completion of the second phase, design development.

The process by which a design team and its consultants convert all of the design influences into a specific design solution varies from firm to firm. In schematic design, however, most firms begin with a period of analysis of the key issues (function, cost, codes, aesthetics, etc.) followed by a period of synthesis into a single concept.

It is common for the design team to consider several conceptual solutions to a design problem. For this reason, most have developed a process for narrowing down to a single concept. Selection may be based on a formal grading of a concept against the original project objectives, on an intuitive judgment based on experience, or, as is often the case, on a combination of both.

Underlying this diversity of approaches are some common themes and design tasks. The first is an expansion of the

original client's goals statement to include clear design goals. These will help in making the inevitable decisions on trade-offs of budget and quality, appearance and energy efficiency, as well as the thousands of other major decisions where competing priorities must be reconciled.

The next basic task is the development of a "parti" or basic conceptual diagram for the project concept. Sometimes this concept evolves from the site and program, other times it starts with a strong formal concept. As architect Edward Larrabee Barnes, FAIA, put it, "It is not just a case of form following function. Sometimes function follows form."

Designers also choose a design vocabulary. The vocabulary includes the formal or asthetic ideas that will govern the development of the design concept. Some designers develop a personal vocabulary of ideas, details, preferred materials, and

DESIGN OPTIONS					
	1	2	3	4	5
Program Fit	●	●	⊖	●	●
Appropriate Adjacencies	●	⊖	⊖	⊖	●
Clear Circulation	⊖	⊖	⊖	○	●
Code Compliant	●	●	○	●	●
Impact on Staffing	⊖	⊖	●	⊖	⊖
Potential Disruption	⊖	⊖	⊗	⊖	⊖
First Cost	⊖	⊖	⊖	⊖	○
Life Cycle Cost	○	○	○	○	⊖
Site Utilization	⊖	⊖	⊖	○	⊖
Conformance with Zoning	●	○	●	○	●

●   Good

⊖   Acceptable

○   Poor

⊗   Prohibitive

Source: Perkins Eastman Architects PC.

so on, and refine it on each project. Others approach each project as a unique problem, and select a vocabulary appropriate to that problem. In senior housing projects, there has been a debate for years on this subject. Most specialists in the field try to incorporate residential scale, materials, and detailing appropriate to the region. Others, however, argue for a break from what they see as overly traditional design vocabularies.

Beyond the first conceptual steps, the process becomes more complex. In all but the smallest and simplest projects, the steps that follow the original planning concepts involve a team of people. While it is true that significant projects are usually developed under the guidance of a single strong design leader, it is important to realize that for most projects more than ten people are involved in the decision-making process. Thus, design excellence is dependent upon the effective management of a complex team, all of whose members contribute to the quality of the final result.

The result of all these steps is a completed schematic design. While different projects, clients, and design teams have different definitions of the completion of this phase, there are certain commonly agreed upon objectives and delivered documents.

Objectives

The primary objective is to arrive at a clearly designed, feasible concept and to present it in a form that achieves client understanding and acceptance. The secondary objectives are to clarify the project program, explore the most promising alternative design solutions, and provide a reliable basis for analyzing the cost of the project.

Products

Communicating design ideas and decisions usually involves a variety of media. Typical documentation at the end of this phase can include:

- A site plan
- Plans for each level, including conceptual reflected ceiling plans
- All elevations — exterior and conceptual interior elevations
- Two or more cross-sections
- An outline specification: a general description of the work indicating major systems and materials choices for the project
- A statistical summary of the design area and other characteristics in comparison to the program
- A preliminary construction cost estimate (See Chapter 19 for a more detailed discussion.)
- Other illustrative materials— renderings, models, or drawings— needed to adequately present the concept

Other services

As part of the schematic design work, the design team may agree to provide energy studies, life-cycle cost analyses or other economic studies, special renderings, models, brochures, or promotional materials for the client.

Approvals

The final step in schematic design is to obtain formal client approval. It is important that the schematic design presentation is clear enough to gain both the understanding and the approval of the client. As a sign of this approval, each item in the presentation should be signed and dated by the client so that the design-development phase may begin.

Obtaining Public Approval and/or Financing

At this stage, the design may also be subject to review by state, local, and sometimes federal agencies. A certificate of need (CON) may be required for nursing homes, medical-model adult day care, some assisted living facilities, and most other projects where the care will be reimbursed by Medicaid, Medicare, or other public programs. Some clients will apply for a CON during conceptual design, but most approvals require plans and reliable cost estimates.

Most CON applications also require comprehensive demographic analyses, analyses of staffing, care plans, protection plans for existing residents during construction, and many other studies. Other specialist consultants prepare most of these, but some require input from the design team.

Continuing care retirement communities and some active adult retirement communities also require state approval in most states. State approval usually requires a detailed offering plan for potential residents describing facilities, services, and costs that cannot be defined without at least schematic-level design information.

Though less common, many nursing homes and assisted living projects use federal mortgage guarantee programs as part of their financing plan (see Chapter 20). These typically require review and approval of both the schematic drawings and cost, and later the contract documents and final pricing.

At the same time they are undergoing state and/or federal review, most projects also proceed with local land-use approvals. For reasons that are hard to understand, there has been widespread resistance to the development of senior care and housing options in many regions. As a result, the most complex task in many projects has become obtaining local land-use approvals and permits (site plan approval, wetlands permits, approval for curb cuts, etc.).

Local land-use approvals also typically require detailed site engineering (public utility demand, sanitary waste disposal, etc.) and special impact studies (traffic, visual, etc.) that are far more detailed than the architectural design at this stage. The local land-use process must be carefully planned and executed. Failure to manage any of the public approvals is one of the most common reasons for projects not to proceed.

Design Development

The primary purpose of the design-development phase is to define and describe important aspects of the project so that all that remains is the formal step of producing construction contract documents.

As schedule pressures and the amount of fast-track construction have increased,

---

In recent years, the local public-approval process has become one of the hardest tasks to complete. Indicative of the increasing opposition is a comment made during a public hearing for site plan approval of a nursing home in a small upper-income community: A local resident: "How many people die in your facility each year?" Answer from the proposed facility's executive director: "The average age is 88, and about one-third pass on each year." Now irate local resident: "Do you realize that you will raise our village's death rate from 2 to over 60, an increase of 3000 percent ? Do you realize that you will make us the death capital of New Jersey?"

some clients and design firms have attempted to cut down or even eliminate this phase. However, there are strong arguments against doing this. Design development is the period in which all the issues left unresolved at the end of schematic design can be worked out. If this phase is eliminated, there is an increased possibility of major modifications during the construction contract documents phase. These changes are costly and more likely to lead to coordination problems during construction.

For continuing care retirement communities requiring formal state approval of their marketing materials and offering plans to prospective residents, most experienced clients ask for design-development documentation. This minimizes the need for amendments after the marketing has begun.

Effective design development results in a clear, coordinated description of all aspects of the design. This typically includes fully developed floor plans, interior and exterior elevations, reflected ceiling plans, wall and building sections, and key details. This also includes the evaluation of alternative interior finishes and furnishings. In addition, the basic mechanical, electrical, plumbing, and fire-protection systems are accurately sized and defined, if not fully drawn. No major issues should be left unresolved that could cause significant restudy during the construction contract documents phase.

The products of the design-development phase are similar to those of schematic design drawings and specifications that fix and describe the size and character of the project, as well as any recommended adjustments to the preliminary estimate of construction cost. It is important to bring the design-development phase to a close with formal presentation to, and approval by, the client.

Construction Documentation

The design process does not really end with the completion of the design-development phase, but the emphasis shifts to producing a complete coordinated set of documents to guide the purchasing, construction, installation, and initial operations steps that follow.

The construction documents typically include drawings, specifications, contract forms, and if the project is being bid, bidding requirements. Each of these documents plays an important role:

1. Drawings provide the graphic description of the work that is to be done.

2. Specifications outline the levels of quality and standards to be met.

3. Contract forms include the actual contract, bond and insurance requirements, and general conditions outlining the roles, rights, and responsibilities of all parties.

4. Bidding requirements set the procedures for this process.

The professional design organizations (such as the AIA and others) have model documents for the specifications, contract forms, and bidding requirements that can be adapted to incorporate each project's unique requirements.

The largest part of this step in the process, however, is the production of a comprehensive set of drawings and technical specifications. This often takes four to six months. A new building or a large renovation of a nursing home or retirement community can involve over 100 sheets of architectural drawings and

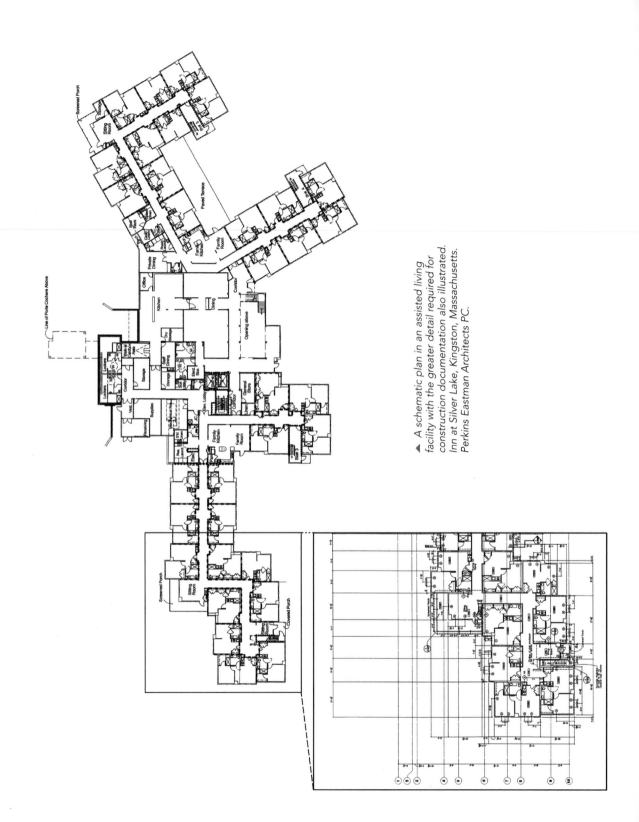

▲ A schematic plan in an assisted living facility with the greater detail required for construction documentation also illustrated. Inn at Silver Lake, Kingston, Massachusetts. Perkins Eastman Architects PC.

several hundred pages of technical specifications. Each sheet of the drawings may involve 100–200 hours of work to complete, because the drawings must provide a clear, accurately dimensioned graphic description of the work to be done. Moreover, each drawing must be coordinated with the many drawings of the other design professionals working on the same project.

Selection of the Construction and FFE Installation Teams and Purchasing

Once part or all of the construction documents are available, the next critical step is the selection of the builders, furniture, finish, and equipment (FFE) manufacturers, and others who will provide the construction and other installed elements of the facility. Typically, the design team either manages the selection process or is an active participant with the client, as any experienced architect or owner will attest.

A number of selection strategies are available. For selection of the builder, there are five major alternatives:

1. The most common is for the construction documents to be completed and put out for a bid to companies attracted by public advertisement, solicited by the owner and design team, or selected from a list of prequalified general contractors.

2. For many projects, it is a good idea to hire a construction manager (CM) to work side-by-side with the design team. During design, the CM provides advice on cost, schedule, and constructability issues. When the construction documentation nears completion, there are two ways in which the CM may continue to be involved in the project. In the first scheme, the CM bids all of the various subtrades and then provides a guaranteed maximum price (GMP) and becomes the general contractor. In the second scheme, the CM is a consultant to the client during construction as well. The CM may replace the general contractor on a fee basis. The construction subcontracts may be bid, but the CM—in its professional service form—does not guarantee the price. If the price is guaranteed, too much power is placed in the hands of the CM, and he or she can no longer be expected to work solely in the client's interest— the risks are too great.

3. For projects where the scope is unclear or where construction must start long before the completion of design, some clients will retain a builder to work on a cost-plus basis. Most clients do not like the open-ended nature of this method, but there are times when it is necessary.

4. A variation sometimes occurs on projects where common components such as sheetrock walls, electrical outlets, light fixtures, and doors can be identified. The client may negotiate unit prices for each component and can then choose to buy as many units as it needs or can afford. This works for projects such as window replacement programs, repaving of parking lots, replacement of light fixtures, and repetitive interior renovations.

5. An increasingly common option is design-build. In this alternative, the client typically retains a team that includes both a builder and a design

team, or a design team that includes a "builder" component. Some clients like the simplicity and the assumed higher degree of cost control. The success of the design-build approach, however, depends upon the selection of a design-build team committed to the client's interests, since the normal quality-control check provided by an independent design team is compromised. Because the design team works for or with the builder, it often cannot communicate quality and value concerns directly to the client. For furnishings, the equivalent is the furniture procurement specialist, who bids furniture packages within the framework of a performance specification.

The selection of an approach, as well as the selection of appropriate companies, is important and should be carried out in a systematic fashion. Advertising for bidders and hoping the right people show up to bid is rarely enough. Most experienced design teams will research the options, identify the most qualified firms, solicit their interest, confirm their qualifications, and then limit the final proposals to the four to six best candidate firms. As is the case for many of the other steps in the process, the AIA and other professional organizations have standard forms to facilitate this.

The purchasing of interior finishes, furnishings, and equipment involves some of the same options. Dealers, who may represent one or several manufacturers, will provide fixed-price bids for furniture and/or finishes. There are also many firms prepared to provide cost-plus services with or without a guaranteed maximum price, and there are a growing number of services offering the equiva-

lent of a design-build approach. Finishes and furnishings are not typically purchased by the same team. Finishes are typically handled by the GC or CM; furniture is usually not included in their scope of work.

Construction and Installation

With the start of construction and the production and delivery of furnishings and equipment, many additional companies and individuals take on major roles. In most senior housing and care projects, the design team is expected to provide both quality control and management throughout this process. The management role typically includes administration of the various construction and supplier contracts; review of payment requests, change orders, claims, and related contract issues, and assistance in resolving problems in the field. It is not uncommon for 20–25 percent of the design team's total project effort to be spent during this phase.

Occupancy

Most clients need their buildings to be effectively complete one to two months prior to occupancy. This time is necessary for staff to learn to operate the new facility and prepare for resident occupancy. There are also several final inspections required for licensed facilities such as nursing homes.

The design team's work is not complete when the facility is ready for occupancy. Virtually all clients moving into new facilities require assistance during the first few months. The design team's task during the occupancy or "commissioning" phase often falls into two categories: following up on incomplete or malfunctioning construction, furnishing, and equipment issues; and organizing and transferring the information necessary to occupy and maintain the facility.

Occupancy frequently reveals construction, furnishing, and/or equipment that do not perform as intended. It is helpful for design teams to prepare their clients for the probability of some lingering issues and assure the clients that they will be there to help resolve them.

It is important, however, for clients to be weaned from dependence on the design team for routine operation and maintenance. This begins with the collection and transfer of operation and maintenance manuals, training information, and related materials to the client. This information should include a set of record drawings (in both electronic and hard-copy forms) describing what was actually built based on the contractors' marked-up working drawings. In addition, some design teams prepare a reference manual containing samples, supplier data, and other information on all furnishings and finishes.

COMMON PROBLEMS AND CAUTIONS

The design team (in conjunction with the facility's owner/sponsor) is the thread that ties all of the 11 above steps into a unified planning, design, and construction process. Experienced design professionals know how this process should proceed and understand how it can go wrong. Twelve of the most common and serious problems are outlined in the following section.

Failure to Plan

A building program begins with a clear definition of why this type of building or facility is needed, its feasibility, and the potential alternatives to meet the need. Too many clients start projects without real feasibility or market studies. Others fail to translate the finding of these initial studies into a clearly defined program/list of spaces for the proposed project.

In some cases, careful planning can even reduce or eliminate the need for large new construction. For example, the need to build new structures or enlarge existing ones may be avoided by more limited planned-renovation programs. In other situations, mergers with or acquisition of another existing facility might accomplish the same objectives at lesser cost.

Unclear and/or Unrealistic Goals

An unrealistic initial budget can haunt an entire building program. No team should ever publicly announce a budget target that is not based upon a clear outline of all goals to be accomplished with-

---

Common Problems

- Failure to plan
- Unclear and/or unrealistic goals
- Inadequate client leadership
- Selecting the wrong professional team for the wrong reasons
- Ineffective management
- Poor planning and execution of the public approval process
- Placing too low a priority on quality
- Failure to plan a facility to maximize staffing efficiency
- Poor cost management
- Failure to plan for maintenance
- A drawn out or interrupted schedule
- Failure to match the project with the best available construction resources

in the building program, because the first publicly discussed budget estimate often takes on a life of its own. Meticulous planning precedes reliable budgets.

Do not expect too much from a renovation program. "Parity" between older and newer facilities is often virtually impossible. In some instances older facilities cannot be renovated to support resident expectations, a more efficient operation, or even current life-safety requirements. Replacement may end up being the better course of action.

Inadequate Client Leadership

Selection of a strong professional team does not relieve the sponsor from the role of team leader. You cannot create a good building without a good client.

Selecting the Wrong Professional Team for the Wrong Reasons

Few clients can analyze their needs and present a realistic plan without help. Clients and professionals should be wary of basing decisions on proposed fees and cost estimates or free or inexpensive up-front work. Fees are usually negotiable, and free up-front work is rarely of any real value. A successful design comes from a careful process carried out by a design team that can bring design and management skills to bear over the several years that it takes to carry out a building program.

Ineffective Management

Poor management by the client often compounds problems with construction programs. In some cases the client fails to establish and organize clear decision-making procedures. In others, micromanagement or poor relationships among the client and team members interfere with the team effort necessary for a successful building program.

There are several ways to organize management responsibilities for a building program.

- The client's executive or administrative staff provides the day-to-day leadership while the board reviews and approves the major policy issues (budget, team selection, major design choices, etc.).

- The administration and board assume joint leadership and are supplemented by a building committee and/or additional staff with the skills to help manage the program. This building committee typically includes a design professional, an attorney with construction experience, and a builder among its members.

- Clients may retain a professional project representative to act as a day-to-day liaison with the design team and builder. For this "clerk of the works" to be effective, he or she must have experience and be vested with sufficient authority.

Regardless of which approach is used, one individual should have the authority to make day-to-day decisions. This individual should build a consensus among the committee and, when necessary, make the decisions needed to advance the project even if a consensus does not exist. Clear allocation of responsibilities is crucial.

Poor Planning and Execution of the Public Approval Process

Failure to effectively plan and manage the public-approval process can be fatal even to worthwhile projects that fill a real need. A rejection at the state or local level can be difficult and costly to reverse. Therefore, it is essential that the project team:

- Clearly define the issues that will come up in the process (traffic, environmental impacts, utility impacts, etc.) and prepare appropriate analyses, recommended mitigation measures, and other responses

- Carefully prepare any CON application or other public-approval submittals so that there are no major gaps, errors, or inconsistencies that lead to criticism, attack, or rejection

- Seek out and meet with those who may have an interest (positive or negative) in the project to solicit support and mute opposition based on ignorance

- Use only experienced and knowledgeable personnel when presenting the project in a public meeting

Placing Too Low a Priority on Quality

No client wants to build a low-quality building, but nevertheless poor quality may result. The most common reasons include an overemphasis on cost, an initial budget that is too low, planning only for the short term, failure to build in the capacity to grow or change in the future, and overreliance on outdated and unimaginative models. For example, too many nursing home operators continue to build traditional hospitallike semiprivate rooms (supposedly to save first cost) even though this is a proven problem for future market acceptance.

The client must understand the trade-off between cost and quality. The team must ensure that all participants in the planning process understand the con-

cepts of first vs. life-cycle costs and short- vs. long-term needs. In addition, the design team should challenge traditional senior housing and care models and present the client with alternatives that reflect their current and future needs.

Failure to Plan a Facility for Staffing Efficiency

Too few sponsors look at the staffing implications of their proposed plans. The salary of one registered nurse is often equal to the debt service on over $500,000 of construction.

Therefore, such key building blocks as the nursing unit must not only maximize care for the residents but also be structured to minimize overstaffing. One common approach is to design nursing units so that they can be operated as smaller subunits during the staff-intensive morning and afternoon shifts but combined under the supervision of just one nursing station during the night shift.

The same planning approach should be applied to every aspect of the operation. Keep in mind that:

- Different approaches to food service, preparation, and delivery have different staffing requirements.

- The selection of mechanical, electrical, and other systems needs to consider the skills and number of maintenance and engineering staff.

- The use of durable finishes, long-life light fixtures, and other selections can be a significant factor in the number of maintenance staff required in the future.

Poor Cost Management

Most building programs are dominated by a focus on first cost. This stems from a fear of cost overruns. Construction costs—and even life-cycle costs—can be managed. There is no reason why a building program should not finish within budget, but this can be accomplished only with the help of an effective cost-management process. (See also Chapter 19).

One of the single most common sources of serious budget overruns in any building program is a team that changes decisions and adds scope during construction.

Failure to Plan for Maintenance

No matter how well built the facilities, they will not last unless they are maintained. An overemphasis on low initial construction cost (vs. life-cycle cost) or poor choices in the initial planning can accelerate the need for a maintenance program. When owners fail to plan for maintenance or balance their budget by deferring essential repairs and preventive measures, they are increasing long-term liability and cost. Clients across the country continue to pay a high price for this short-term thinking.

A Drawn-out or Interrupted Schedule

The project's leadership should not ignore the importance of momentum and continuity. A project that does not proceed in a steady, orderly fashion is often more expensive and can lead to a lack of continuity in decision-making as key leadership or design team members change. In addition, key team members can simply become exhausted by a drawn-out process. Once a building program is initiated, it should be completed as quickly as possible, while the understanding of the need is clear and the team is fresh.

Failure to Match the Project with the Best Available Construction Resources

It is essential that the project team seek out the best construction resources available—both at the management level and at the subcontractor level.

Conclusion

All building programs—even the most successful—face some problems, but a well-run program will surmount these challenges. The difference between a successful program and one with problems does not depend on the wealth of the sponsor but on sound planning and effective management.

CHAPTER 3

UNIQUE DESIGN CONCERNS

The first part of this chapter takes the program and planning guidelines defined in the first chapter and illustrates how they are typically organized into the conceptual plans created at the beginning of the process described in Chapter 2. The second section includes a discussion of some of the major issues, trends, and concepts that are shaping the planning, design, construction, and operation of senior living and care facilities.

TYPICAL CONCEPTUAL DIAGRAMS

The most common organizational diagrams or parties for the major building types are based on the logic described in the program descriptions outlined in Chapter 1. Most plans are organized around the grouping of resident units into nursing units, neighborhoods of assisted living units, or the "houses" of Alzheimer's residents.

Geriatric Clinics and Adult Day Care

These facilities are not typically located in new freestanding facilities. The required spaces usually must be fit into existing buildings. Therefore, no single plan diagram governs their design.

Skilled-Nursing Facilities

As noted in Chapter 1, the floor plans of most skilled-nursing facilities are based on a building block that resembles one of several letters of the alphabet. These building blocks, which account for the majority of the program area, are then joined to the central common spaces in the middle of the plan. Some of the most common alphabet building blocks are illustrated in the diagrams on pages 122 and 123.

Assisted Living

There are a wide variety of assisted living plans, but the conceptual plan of most such residences is probably best illustrated by the diagram on page 125.

Alzheimer's/Dementia Residences

This is an evolving building type, but the most frequently referred to models are illustrated in the diagram on page 124.

Independent/Congregate Living

These buildings use the full range of forms used for other multifamily apartment projects, but in most regions the simpler forms are the most common.

Continuing Care Retirement Communities

CCRCs in suburban and rural locations are typically low-rise and heavily influenced by their sites. There is usually a common building that provides the centerpiece, surrounded by the independent units. Projects on tight sites must bring these units into one or more large buildings containing all kinds of care. For the typically more site-restrictive urban models the vertical organization of the different programs, types of units, and levels of care becomes even more complex.

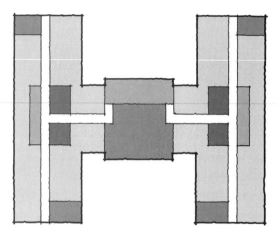

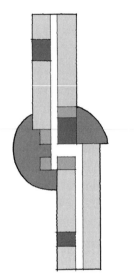

▶ These eight floor plans are drawn from existing skilled-nursing facilities. They illustrate the alphabet of common nursing unit planning diagrams. Perkins Eastman Architects PC. Drawing by Ty Kaul.

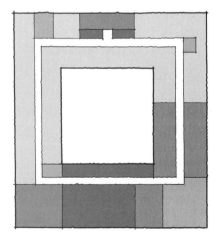

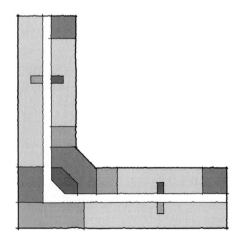

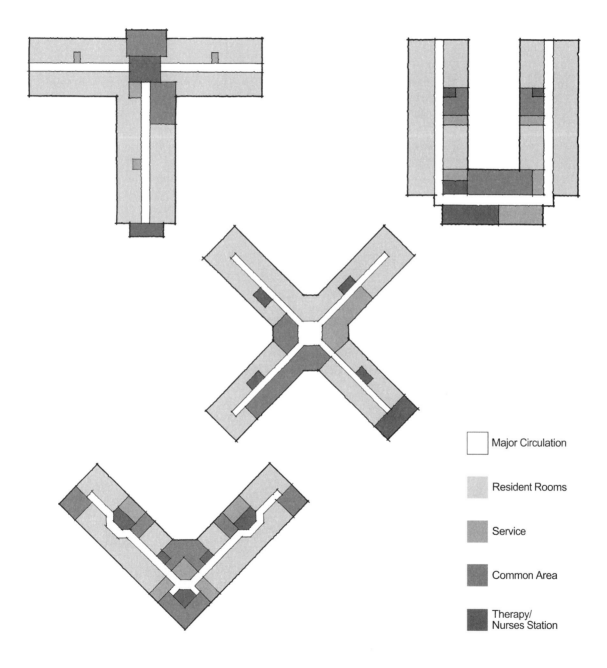

Major Circulation

Resident Rooms

Service

Common Area

Therapy/
Nurses Station

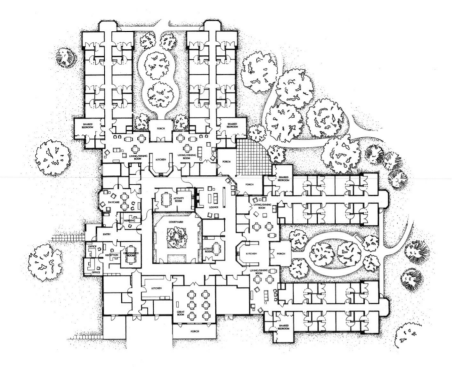

▲ These two plans illustrate
typical planning based on the
house concept for
Alzheimer's residences.
Asbury Place, Mt. Lebanon,
Pennsylvania. Perkins
Eastman Architects PC.

▶ Woodside Place Alzheimer
Residence, Oakmont,
Pennsylvania. Perkins
Eastman Architects PC.

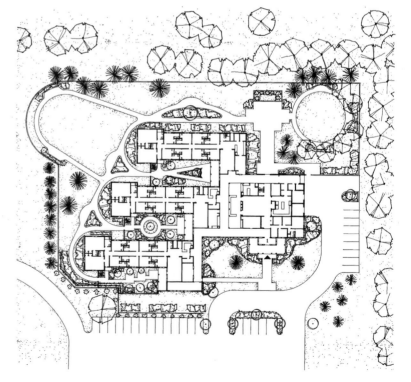

▶ Urban CCRCs are typically larger towers on small plots of land. Sun City Ginza East, Tokyo, Japan. Perkins Eastman Architects PC.

▼ This diagram was created for the American Association of Homes and Services for the Aging. It represents to its members the typical planning diagram for an assisted living residence. Perkins Eastman Architects PC.

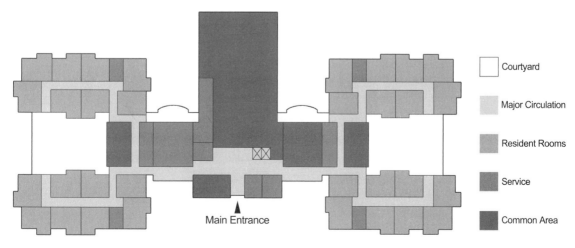

Main Entrance

Courtyard

Major Circulation

Resident Rooms

Service

Common Area

UNIQUE DESIGN CONCERNS

▶ In suburban locations, the typical CCRC has a larger centrally located building with the major services and amenities as well as housing for the frailest members of the community. These two typical CCRC site plans illustrate a central building surrounded by independent living cottages. Cloverwood Retirement Community, Pittsford, New York. Perkins Eastman Architects PC.

▼ Harbor Ridge, Port Washington, New York. Perkins Eastman Architects PC.

ISSUES, TRENDS, AND EVOLVING CONCEPTS

Senior living and care facilities are influenced by many of the same general changes and trends that influence all building types, such as the general economy, construction costs, and the development of new systems and materials. Issues that are specific to this segment of the population, however, also affect the facilities that must meet their unique needs. Among the most important issues, trends, and evolving concepts are the following.

Demographic Trends

All demographic projections point to a rapid growth in the number of elderly in the United States and most other developed countries. Particularly striking are the projections for the number of "old-old" (those over 85) for whom supportive housing and care options are particularly important. As was noted earlier, in the introduction to Chapter 1, the need for a growing inventory of such options will expand.

Mortality Curves

Balancing some of the growing long-term demand is the fact that people are living healthy longer and moving to senior housing and care options later—often after they are very old and frail. This trend has surprised some sponsors of assisted living and other senior housing and care projects, because the average length of stay is far shorter than their past experience, largely due to the fact that residents are entering at an older age and dying sooner than expected. This has reduced the effective demand for assisted living and other forms of senior housing in some markets.

Privacy

As noted in Chapter 1, this issue is changing the design of senior living and care facilities. A recent study of assisted living commissioned by the American Association of Retired Persons found that only four percent of respondents over 50 years old preferred a shared room. Low-income households had the same preference as the national sample. In fact, the study found that an overwhelming majority preferred a smaller private room to a larger double room. While quality of care ranked as the top concern, sharing a bedroom with a stranger was the next greatest concern for women and third highest among men.

Lifelong Learning

Accompanying the trend toward healthier lifestyles is a growing interest in lifelong learning. Many older persons continue to seek intellectual stimulation, and perhaps even new or different vocational opportunities that were unattainable during earlier years. This interest has changed the ac-

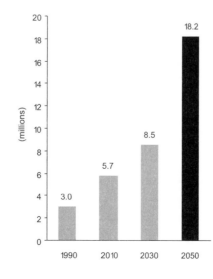

◀ Americans age eighty-five and older; historically and projected. The aged are the fastest-growing segment of the U.S. population.

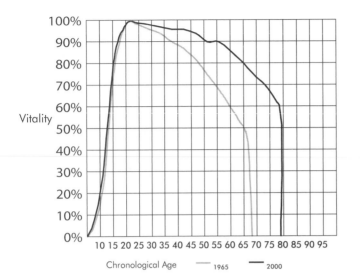

Vitality

Chronological Age — 1965 — 2000

▲ The aged are staying healthy longer, but once physical decline begins it is steeper. (Fries 1980; Rowe and Kahn 1998.)

▼ Lifelong learning is a higher priority for many retirees.

tivities and programming, and provided a market for a growing number of retirement communities adjacent to colleges and universities. These communities, which now number in the hundreds across the country, are able to provide cultural and intellectual stimulation along with the availability of medical care if needed, often in an area with a relatively low cost of living. The Kendal Corporation has pioneered this concept with five continuing care retirement communities adjacent to college campuses, including Dartmouth College, Cornell University, and Oberlin College. Another way in which lifelong learning has impacted design has been through the inclusion of libraries and public and resident-unit computer terminals (see Chapter 9).

Ethnic and Cultural Diversity

Traditionally, many sponsors have been faith-based organizations that have built and operated for their own religious or ethnic groups. The population of the United States and Canada, however, is changing rapidly; Americans are becoming ethnically and culturally more diverse and more accepting. Moreover, they are increasingly basing senior housing choices on shared interests, quality, location, and factors other than religious and ethnic background. In the future there will probably still be a strong demand for facilities focused on one faith or segment of the population, but more facilities will have to reach out to the broader population to maintain sufficient occupancy levels.

Integration into Existing Communities vs. Isolation of the Aging

One of the myths about the aging is that older adults want to be off in a compound of people their age looking at the countryside. In fact, most would prefer to stay in their communities and remain near their children, grandchildren, and friends. The primary market area for a new assisted living facility is usually defined as being within a five-mile radius of the site. In other words, the majority of potential residents live, or have children who live, within five miles of the facility.

Creating a Range of Housing and Care

The vast majority of senior housing and care options are freestanding facilities providing just one service—skilled nursing, assisted living, etc. Most leading sponsors, however, recognize that a significant percentage of their future residents want to make only one move. They do not want to move to congregate or assisted living and then have to relocate if they need skilled nursing. Therefore, where economically feasible, existing campuses are offering a range (i.e., a continuum) of care and services on one campus. CCRCs already offer this range of care and service, but more and more of the other leading sponsors are trying to create virtual CCRCs by adding the missing parts. Moreover, some multiproject sponsors such as Hyatt and Brookdale, who entered the field to provide independent living, are now offering a broader range of housing and services in their newer communities.

Aging in Place

One of the issues driving the interest in a full care continuum is the fact that the residents in senior housing continue to age within a particular facility and therefore often require increasing levels of care. "Aging in place" is happening in all facilities, and the average age (and needs) of the residents is growing over time. Hyatt, for example, saw the average age of one of its early "classic residences" grow from 80 at move-in to over 87 ten years later.

NORCs

The same trends exist in many apartment buildings and neighborhoods. As residents age, they often choose not to move, and "naturally occurring retirement communities" (NORCs) develop. Support services (home health care, delivered meals, social-service support organizations, etc.) make it possible for a significant percentage of seniors to live in these NORCs.

The Challenge of Urban Models

Some of the senior housing markets with the fewest new options are in the major cities. Various factors including higher cost, security, and land-use controls, as well as the natural development of NORCs, which serve the same role as planned senior communities, account for the limited number of urban models. The need is there, however, and a growing number of urban models are being developed.

Obsolescence

Many of the existing facilities serving the aged are obsolete. In some cases, superior service helps mask the deficiencies of the facilities, but as the market becomes

◀ *These three women illustrate the growing diversity of America's aged.*

▶ *The aged do not want to be segregated from the rest of the community. Integration into the community and intergenerational programming are now common goals for both new and existing communities.*

▼ *Building retirement communities adjacent to colleges and universities has been a successful strategy. Kendal on Hudson, Sleepy Hollow, New York. Perkins Eastman Architects PC.*

steadily more demanding and sophisticated, obsolete facilities will suffer. Therefore, one of the most common assignments for architects and interior designers is to overcome the physical factors creating obsolescence (see also Chapter 16). In some cases, it may be as simple as an interior face-lift to make the facility more homelike and attractive. In others, it may mean reconfiguring existing units to offer larger apartments or building additions to increase the proportion of private rooms in a skilled nursing facility.

No amount of renovation or interior design can revive some existing facilities in North America. Too many were poorly planned, designed, built, and/or maintained. As newer, more appropriately designed facilities are built in the same market, some facilities will have to be replaced in order to stay competitive on any basis other than price. In a growing number of cases renovation is not a viable option. (For a more detailed discussion of this issue, see Chapter 16.)

Regional Influences
There are no universally appropriate design guidelines. Climate, regional tastes, building traditions, market expectations, and other factors create a framework that should influence program, design, and operations. Most of the better facilities built in recent years try to reference the better housing and hospitality design traditions in the market area. Companies that use prototype designs have usually found that they need to adapt these prototypes when they move into new markets or regions.

Security
Security is a growing issue in facilities for the aging, just as it is in most other aspects of life today. The aged, and through them their families, feel increasingly vulnerable. Therefore, an environment for seniors must not only be safe and secure but also create the feeling of safety and security.

Noninstitutional Environments
One of the major arguments made against large facilities is that they seem institutional. The market has made it clear to most sponsors that residents and their families prefer a homelike (or at

▲ Experienced operations such as Classic Residence by Hyatt found that "aging in place" required them to add services. In their first New York–area project, they only designed for independent living. Ten years later, their second project in the area included assisted living and dementia care. Classic Residence by Hyatt, Yonkers, New York. Perkins Eastman Architects PC. Photograph by Chuck Choi.

◀ Classic Residence by Hyatt in Teaneck, New Jersey. Courtesy of Classic Residence by Hyatt.

▶ Some national
developers tried to
use a standard
design in all regions
but found that
adaptation to
reflect the region
was more
successful. Sunrise
of Bellevue,
Bellevue,
Washington.
Mithun Inc.
Photograph by
Robert Pisano.

▶ Sunrise of
Norwood,
Norwood,
Massachusetts.
DiMella Shaffer
Associates.
Photograph by
Mike Powell.

least a hotellike) environment. Many of the major design assignments in the last two decades have been commissioned to achieve this change in existing facilities, and virtually all new environments are designed with this idea in mind. (See also Chapters 14 and 16.)

Cluster Concept

As described in Chapter 1, there has been a movement to decentralize staff—in particular the nurses and aides in skilled-nursing facilities. In many facilities this means locating staff stations closer to smaller resident room clusters.

Affordability

In the senior housing building boom of the 1990s, a large part of the demand was for luxury options. Medicaid, various federal and state housing programs, and some of the mission-driven nonprofits care for lower-income individuals. The group that has been largely left out are those who cannot afford the luxury options and yet do not qualify for one of the subsidized options. Thus, one of the most important current and future challenges for sponsors and their design teams is affordability. Building design is only one part of the answer. Financing, creative reuse of existing land and facility resources, containment of operating costs, technology, and other factors must also contribute.

Operating Cost Containment

As with most institutions, the cost of the facility (debt service and depreciation) is far outweighed by the cost of staff, supplies, and energy, and other ongoing expenses. There is a growing interest in designs that can help contain operating costs through reduction of staffing

needs, use of longer-life products needing less maintenance, energy conservation, and other measures.

Sustainability

As discussed further in Chapter 6, a growing number of sponsors are interested in "green" or "sustainable" design. For some the issue is life-cycle cost reduction, but for others it reflects the growing interest in environmentally sensitive design (see Chapter 6).

Technology

As discussed in Chapters 9 and 10, information and other technologies are beginning to show promise for improving the quality and reducing the cost of care. For example, changes in emergency call, the monitoring of care delivery, the delivery of supplies and medications, and management tools are increasingly serious design considerations.

▼ *This CCRC recycled an existing building and used low-cost land and an inexpensive design to create a financially viable CCRC with entry fees and monthly charges far below those of other communities in the region. Redstone Highlands, Greensburg, Pennsylvania. Perkins Eastman Architects PC. Photograph by Lockwood Hoehl.*

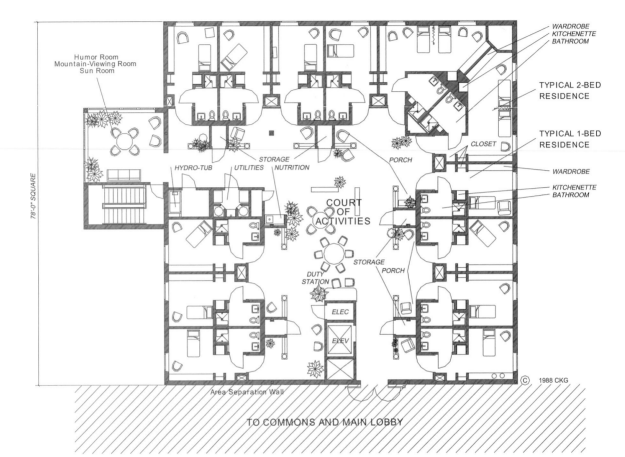

WARDROBE
KITCHENETTE
BATHROOM

TYPICAL 2-BED
RESIDENCE

TYPICAL 1-BED
RESIDENCE

WARDROBE

KITCHENETTE
BATHROOM

CLOSET

PORCH

Humor Room
Mountain-Viewing Room
Sun Room

78'-0" SQUARE

HYDRO-TUB   UTILITIES   NUTRITION

STORAGE

COURT
OF
ACTIVITIES

STORAGE   PORCH

DUTY
STATION

ELEC

ELEV

© 1988 CKG

Area Separation Wall

TO COMMONS AND MAIN LOBBY

TYPICAL RESIDENTIAL POD

0   10'   20'   30'

▲ In larger residences, the cluster concept
may be implemented by organizing the plan
into smaller pods, each with dedicated staff.
Mary Conrad Center, Anchorage, Arkansas.
Christopher K. Graeff Architect.

◀ Mary Conrad Center, Anchorage, Arkansas.
Christopher K. Graeff Architect. Photograph
by Chris Arend.

The Ideal Size

There are sponsors who seek to size facilities for economic efficiency. There is no consensus, however, on what the right size is. There are major variations in labor costs, building costs, and other variables. Some clients have created profitable CCRCs of 150 units, while equally experienced sponsors in adjacent communities insist 300 or more units is the minimum.

In assisted living, the AAHSA research concluded that 64 units could be economically viable in most suburban locations and less than 40 in more rural communities. Others in the field think 90–100 units are needed for feasibility. (Most agree that more than 120–150 assisted living units in one facility is too big for most markets.) In nursing homes, there is a debate between the advocates of small (120–160 beds) and those who feel 300 or more beds are needed to support the cost of the services for quality care.

The Greenhouse Project

The Greenhouse Project argues for a different approach to facilities. In this concept, the buildings themselves are proposed to be small 6–8 person community homes, linked with a sophisticated management and an Internet-connected health-care delivery network that can ensure quality, provide expertise, organize back-up staffing, and deliver accounting/billing support.

Pioneer Movement

The Pioneer movement represents a philosophy of care that advocates a change in the culture of nursing homes by one of four approaches, each of which has its own leaders and advocates. All of these have the potential to change the design and operations of a facility. These approaches are summarized by their advocates as follows:

1. *The Eden Alternative.* Developed by Judy and Bill Thomas of Sherburne, New York

   - It creates a "human habitat," with plants, pets, and young children.
   - It combats residents' loneliness, boredom, and sense of helplessness.
   - Residents and staff have continuing contact characterized by variety and spontaneity.
   - Residents can give care as well as receive it (involvement in daily activities).
   - Direct caregivers and residents are decision-makers.

2. *The regenerative community.* Developed by Debora and Barry Barkan of El Sobrante, California

   - Staff members act as community developers, augmenting conventional work responsibilities.
   - Regular community meetings are opportunities for residents and staff to socialize and discuss problems with the aim of building a life of shared experience and concerns.
   - Residents are regarded as esteemed elders, regardless of physical or mental disability.

3. *Resident-free/individualized care.* Developed by Joanne Rader of Mt. Angel, Oregon

   - It is used particularly with residents who have dementia; these persons still have the right to direct their own care.
   - Staff must be creative and compassionate when addressing behavior; and make decisions through the eyes of the resident.

- There are no physical constraints or psychosocial medications; bathing is personalized, based on residents' preferences and comfort levels.
- Staff learns to "speak the language of dementia."

4. *Resident-directed care.* Developed by Charlene Boyd and Robert Ogden of Seattle, Washington

- Nursing homes should be made up of small "neighborhoods" instead of large units. Each community has its own budget for social work, activities, housekeeping, nursing, personal assistance, and management. Each also has its own laundry and family-style kitchens.
- Residents choose their own daily routine; for example, when to get up, when to go to bed.

- There are fewer managers and more front-line staff.
- There is extensive cross-training of workers; everyone can make a sandwich or answer a phone call.
- Nurse aides, called residents' assistants, are well paid and highly respected.

New Products

Generally, new senior housing products will continue to reflect an increasingly sophisticated market demand, based upon the rapidly growing population. Smaller-scale decentralized settings that are more a part of traditional neighborhoods are reflecting a national planning interest in New Urbanism. With this mind-set, senior housing is less insular and relies on the services, support, and socialization of multiple generations from multiple sources, within a familiar neighborhood.

CHAPTER 4
SITE PLANNING/PARKING/ACCESS

Most buildings for the aging have important site-planning issues, but they are not particularly complex. Most of the site issues revolve around the following: the amount of land required; relationship to adjacent land uses; resident, staff, and service circulation; appropriate parking ratios; and recognition of the need for features that protect the residents from environmental hazards. This chapter discusses and illustrates each of these issues.

SITE SIZE

The size of a site for a senior housing or care facility can vary significantly due to differing zoning requirements for buffers or setbacks, height limits, parking, and other land-use restrictions. The building design, resident unit mix and density, outdoor program areas, use of structured parking, and other variables can also have a major impact. See the table on page 138.

▼ *This 70-unit Sunrise assisted living residence was designed to fit on a very compact half-acre site. Sunrise of Bellevue, Bellevue, Washington. Mithun Inc.*

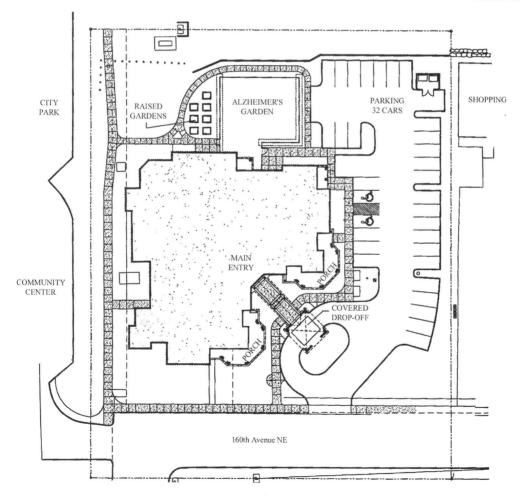

CITY PARK

RAISED GARDENS

ALZHEIMER'S GARDEN

PARKING 32 CARS

SHOPPING

COMMUNITY CENTER

MAIN ENTRY

PORCH

PORCH

COVERED DROP-OFF

PORCH

160th Avenue NE

TYPICAL SITE SIZES BY FACILITY TYPE			
	Small	Medium	Large
Long-Term Care	120–60 beds	161–250 beds	251–400 beds
	4–10 acres	6–12 acres	10–20 acres
Assisted Living	Under 60 units	61–100 units	101–200 units
	3–5 acres	4–8 acres	6–20 acres
Active Adult Communities	Under 300 units	301–1500 units	1501+ units
	Median size: 181 units	Median size: 566 units	Median size: 2,999 units
	Median land: 43 acres	Median land: 282 acres	Median land: 1,600 acres
CCRCs	100–200 units	201–400 units	401+ units
	15–20 acres	20–50 acres	50+ acres

*These estimates are for suburban and rural locations. Many suburban, town center, or urban sites are one acre or less, even for large facilities

▲ *This 297-unit CCRC, Buckingham's Choice in Frederick, Maryland, covers almost all of its 40-acre site. Buckingham's Choice, Adamstown, Maryland. Perkins Eastman Architects PC.*

RELATIONSHIP TO ADJACENT LAND USES

As discussed in Chapter 3, it is a myth that all seniors want to live in their own isolated campus or building. This may be true for some, but it is completely untrue for the majority. Most experts in the field argue that the best place for many of these facilities is in the center of the community convenient to public transit, shopping, services, health-care providers, and family.

In spite of the logic of central locations, various historical factors including site availability, zoning, development re-sistance, and other issues have forced many developments from the center of their communities. This is hard to explain, since hundreds of studies of existing facilities consistently demonstrate that these building types usually have minimal traffic impact, generate positive tax revenues (if tax-exempt, facilities usually contribute to community revenues through a PILOT—payment in lieu of taxes), and are quiet neighbors. Moreover, they meet a growing need in virtually every community: appropriate, supportive housing for the growing number of the aging.

▲ The buildings and parking of Kendal-on-Hudson's 288-unit CCRC in Sleepy Hollow, New York, cover only 9 acres of the 20-acre site. Kendal on Hudson, Sleepy Hollow, New York. Perkins Eastman Architects PC.

▲ A covered drop-off, such as this one at Copper Ridge, in Sykesville, Maryland, is an important feature. Copper Ridge, Sykesville, Maryland. Perkins Eastman Architects PC. Photograph by Curtis Martin.

VEHICULAR CIRCULATION

Because the staff is not typically large (20–30 on the morning shift in a typical assisted living facility and approximately twice that for a skilled-nursing facility), shift changes do not coincide with rush-hour traffic, and staff often utilize public transit if available, it is rare for the traffic impact to be significant.

The majority of senior housing facilities have 24-hour staffing. CCRC and assisted living facility shift times vary and overlap, with a day, evening, and night shift. In long-term care the shifts are typically 7 A.M.–3 P.M., 3 P.M.–11 P.M., and 11 P.M.–7 A.M. The first (morning shift) is the largest, since this staff has the most tasks (helping residents get up and dressed, preparing and serv-

ing lunch and breakfast, assisting with bathing, leading activities, etc.). Thus, most traffic studies focus on the two shift changes at each end of the morning shift.

During the morning, the facility's peak hour usually precedes the street peak hour, whereas in the afternoon the peaks do not overlap. The table on page 141 details the traffic generated by each facility based on surveys conducted by the American Association of Housing and Services for the Aging (AAHSA) and the Institute of Transportation Engineers (ITE).

This table shows that in general trip-generation rates for the facility peak are higher than the street peak (commuter peak). It should be noted that peak-hour trip-generation rates for the assisted care facility are based on a survey of more

WEEKDAY PEAK-HOUR TRAFFIC GENERATION*								
	AM PEAK HOUR				**PM PEAK HOUR**			
Type of Facility	**Street Peak**		**Facility Peak**		**Street Peak**		**Facility Peak**	
	in	out	in	out	in	out	in	out
Senior Housing/ Independent Living Units	0.08	0.09	0.15	0.14	0.15	0.12	0.19	0.15
Congregate Care	0.04	0.02	0.08	0.08	0.10	0.07	0.13	0.08
Assisted Care	0.12	0.08			0.11	0.10		

*Expressed in vehicle trips per bed.
Sources: Institute of Transportation Engineers, Trip Generation Manual 6th Edition; American Association of Housing and Services for the Aging, A Study of Traffic & Parking Implications.

than 100 facilities, whereas trip-generation data for senior housing and congregate care facilities are based on samples of less than 10 facilities.

Service vehicles are also not typically a major issue. There are a few truck visits (primarily food deliveries and garbage pick-up) each day. Most facilities can schedule deliveries so that they do not aggravate rush-hour traffic or annoy neighbors.

Most facilities are planned with a service entrance and/or loading dock. This is typically also the location of the employee entrance, because it is operationally desirable to concentrate staff access and egress from the building at a single location for control, security, and monitoring purposes. This is not an attractive area and should be hidden or screened.

Residents and visitors usually enter through the facility's front door; in CCRCs and independent living communities, they come in from an open or covered parking space convenient to their unit. Almost none of the residents in assisted living or skilled nursing drive. All facilities for the aging should provide a covered drop-off area at the main entry to protect residents from the weather, ice, and other hazards.

PARKING

Parking demand varies by building type, as well as with the location of the facility (i.e., whether it is in an urban area in proximity to services and public transportation or in an area with limited services). For the purpose of assessing parking demand, the distinction is made between (1) senior housing and independent living facilities that offer very few if any services, (2) assisted living facilities (i.e., a housing facility that includes additional staff to help with daily activities), and (3) continuing care facilities that contain a full spectrum of housing types, from independent living to nursing care. The following summarizes the results of parking surveys undertaken at the three types of facilities.

Based on a research paper prepared for the Institute of Transportation Engineers, a survey using assisted living, CCRC, and independent living found actual parking need of 0.3 – 0.5 cars per unit. Most zoning codes, however, mandate at least 0.3 spaces per bed for nursing homes, 0.5 spaces per unit for assisted living, and one or more spaces per unit for market-rate independent living. Active adult communities typically must comply with normal residential zoning. Since the parking required by zoning is often excessive, some local planning boards permit a lesser amount with a portion of the site land banked for additional parking should it be required.

The above parking ratios include residents, employees, and visitors, and they represent the peak parking ratio on a typical weekday. Do not segregate visitor parking demand from employee and resident parking; because the individual demands do not peak at the same times, they can share the same spaces. Peak parking demand on weekdays generally occurs during the early afternoon, when the number of visitors is relatively high and staff shifts overlap. The impact of the shift overlap can be minimized if a

portion of the day shift leaves before the bulk of the evening shift arrives. The peak day of the year is generally Mother's Day. Temporary parking overflow possibilities should be provided for this once-a-year event as well as other major holidays.

For all of the above facility types, the proximity to public transportation and the provision of shuttle services affects parking demand. These services are important for the employees working at the facility as well as for the residents. Access to public transportation or a shuttle service allows staff to get to work without driving, thereby decreasing the need for parking spaces, and allows residents to travel to nearby shopping areas and visit friends and relatives in the area.

▶ ▶▶ *Multiple environments were created from one site, providing interest and variety. Hebrew Home of Greater Washington, Rockville, Maryland. Perkins Eastman Architects PC. Photographs by Eric Cohen.*

▲ BEFORE

▲ ▶▶ AFTER

LANDSCAPE DESIGN

In every community, to add interest and support memory, it is desirable to provide settings that stimulate the senses, both inside and outside a building. In CCRCs and active adult communities, landscaped and natural areas should be developed for walking, contemplation, golf, lawn sports, shuffleboard, gardening activities, fishing, and other recreational activities.

Outdoor spaces should resemble their interior counterparts, responding to the site and to the cultural and activity needs of the specific residential setting. A hierarchy of spaces, as one makes the transition from indoors to outdoors, might include the following:

- Indoor-outdoor blend: spaces within the building that have an indoor-outdoor character or porches that extend from the building to provide shelter, shade, security, vistas, and an experience for residents who do not want or are unable to venture from the building. For those with dementia, spaces that feel like rooms are more easily understood.

- Paved program area: areas large enough to accommodate community activities, such as a concert, barbecue, etc.

- Meaningful walk: pathways with things of interest, including an area for butterflies, bird feeder, benches for resting, water fountain, etc.

▲ An accessible outdoor patio for ambulatory Alzheimer's residents at Copper Ridge. Copper Ridge, Sykesville, Maryland. Perkins Eastman Architects PC. Photograph by Curtis Martin.

- Landmark/destination: an outdoor structure, such as a gazebo, that can serve as a small-group activity spot, an enticement to venture further outdoors, or as a landmark for those returning to the building from a walk.

- A nature walk: if site space permits, a natural walking path that allows for greater exercise and a more natural experience.

- Children's play areas: attractive places for grandchildren to play while their parents are visiting.

- Outdoor exercise/therapy: areas, site details, and equipment to support appropriate exercise, stretching, and physical therapy.

If the residents are frail, cognitively impaired, or vulnerable, these outdoor areas must be carefully planned and landscaped. Among the issues to consider when designing these spaces are the following (note that these apply equally to the general population):

- Use of flowering trees, shrubs, and perennials that provide seasonal change to reinforce awareness of life's rhythms and cycles, as well as features such as bird feeders to attract wildlife, such as birds and butterflies, and to stimulate the senses and provide a focus of interest.

Appropriate Plant Material

- Select plants for fragrance, color, tactile qualities, movement, and color change of foliage and flowers and seasonal interest.
- Research which species might have special cultural or sacred meanings for the residents.
- Avoid poisonous vegetation or vegetation that is irritating to the touch, as well as plants that tend to attract an inordinate amount of stinging insects. Plants vary in level of toxicity, as well as which parts are toxic; for example, the flowers may be toxic and the leaves not, and vice versa. A good source in researching plant qualities is *Plants for Play* by R.C. Moore (1993). The local horticultural society is another good source.

- Accessible outdoor areas for ambulatory residents with Alzheimer's or other forms of dementia. The ability to walk freely has been found to slow the physical deterioration that often comes with the disease, and it also reduces agitation.
- Incorporating outdoor areas into an activity program can be important. Gardening can be a popular activity, reinforcing memories. Gardens can also be designed to provide an outdoor physical therapy area.
- Shade, since an older person is more vulnerable to the skin damage and vision problems caused by too much direct sunlight. A mix of umbrellas, vegetation, and building elements, such as porches and trellises, provides effective means of introducing shade.
- Seating with backs/arms near entrances encourages socialization (see Chapter 14 for furnishing guidelines).
- Tables and chairs are good for picnics or snacks, or just for resting.
- Entrances to gardens and the width of pathways should accommodate walking side-by-side.

CHAPTER 5
CODES

Because of the importance of the health and safety of the aging, senior housing care facilities are among the most carefully regulated. Many states, for example, have at least eight to ten codes that govern program areas and the construction of all of the major building systems.

The National Conference of States on Building Codes and Standards Inc. (NCSBCS) publishes an annual guide, the *Directory of Building Codes & Regulations.* Volume 1 is for states, and Volume 2 is for cities and for other jurisdictions that have codes. They address general building compliance and indicate the referenced standards including building codes, mechanical, plumbing, electrical, energy, gas, fire prevention, life safety, accessibility, and elevators. In addition, the NCSBCS addresses where one can get copies of these codes, the responsible parties, and a general idea of how often they are updated. Their website is www.ncsbcs.com.

In addition, most states have detailed regulations written specifically to govern certain senior housing and care building types, including nursing homes, adult day care, outpatient diagnostic and treatment facilities, some forms of assisted living, and others. These regulations cover everything from space and environmental standards (also discussed in Chapter 1) to resident rights and staffing requirements. A table of contents from one of the typical state regulations for long-term care is included on the next page. Many of these regulations are also available on the Internet.

Regulations promulgated by state licensing agencies go hand in hand with building code requirements and are often more rigid and even less susceptible to revision. Because building codes specify the conditions for a broad range of building types, they are constantly being questioned, tested, and revised. Licensing standards, on the other hand, are less likely to be scrutinized on a regular basis.

To illustrate the links between codes and regulations that affect building design, note the collection of requirements that must be satisfied when designing a "typical" nursing home. A nursing home can be required to comply with the basic mandates of all six of the following regulatory standards:

1. *Legislative acts, such as the 1987 Federal Omnibus Budget Reconciliation Act (OBRA 87) and the Americans with Disabilities Act (ADA):* These are intended to control quality of life and are enforceable as civil rights issues.

2. *Certificates of need (CON):* These are processes intended to contain costs borne by the public through entitlement programs. They vary by state (some have none) and typically control:

   • How many beds can be constructed

   • Project size and programming requirements (total gross-square-foot building area per bed)

   • Project cost

   • Scope of new construction/renovation

TABLE OF CONTENTS
TYPICAL LONG-TERM CARE STATE REGULATIONS

1. Definitions
2. License Required
3. Licensing Procedure
4. Licensed Bed Capacity
5. Rights of Applicant If License Denied or Revoked
6. New Construction, Conversion, Alteration, or Addition
7. Administration and Resident Care
8. Admission and Discharge
9. Resident-Care Policies
10. Physician Services in Long-Term Care Facilities
11. Nursing Services
12. Dietetic Services
13. Specialized Rehabilitative Services—Occupational Therapy Services, Physical Therapy Services, Speech Pathology, and Audiology Services
14. Special Care Units—General and Respiratory Care Unit
15. Pharmaceutical Services
16. Laboratory and Radiologic Services
17. Dental Services
18. Social Work Services
19. Clinical Records
20. Infection Control
21. Reports and Action Required in Unusual Circumstances
22. Transfer Agreement
23. Disaster Plan and Communication
24. Physical Plant Requirements
25. Patient-Care Unit
26. Resident Bedroom and Toilet Facilities
27. Equipment and Supplies for Bedside Care
28. Rehabilitation Facilities—Space and Equipment
29. Dayroom and Dining Area
30. Dietetic Service Area
31. Administrative Areas
32. Housekeeping Services, Pest Control, and Laundry
33. Resident-Care Management System
34. Resident Status Assessment
35. Care Planning
36. Special Skin Record
37. Geriatric Nursing Assistant Program
38. Medicine Aide—Scope of Responsibility
39. Medicine Aide Course Requirements
40. Determination of Conditions Warranting Civil Money Penalty, Procedures for Corrective Actions, Determination of Amount, and Procedures for Hearing and Appeal

3. *Licensure regulations:* These typically protect residents' rights and establish minimum levels of care. These regulations mandate staff training, and education requirements, and may also establish requirements for dining services, record keeping, laundry services, and resident monitoring.

4. *Department of health building standards:* These are intended to establish minimum performance requirements to assure a quality environment both for staff and residents.

5. *Building codes:* These establish minimum life-safety standards for building construction, egress, fire safety, etc. The regulations are typically based on use and include Residential (R), Institutional (I), Business (B), etc. One of the national-based model codes is BOCA (Building Officials and Code Administrators), and the other is the International Building Code.

6. *Independent testing standards (such as the National Fire Protection Association (NFPA) and Underwriters Laboratories (UL):* These are adopted by state and local government agencies to supplement other code requirements for life safety, equipment and fixtures, use of materials, etc.

The intent of all regulations is directed at eight primary issues: life safety, adequate space and equipment for the facilities' programs, health-care provision and overview, appropriate building systems and construction practices, public policy (historic preservation, energy conservation, and accessibility for the disabled), enforcement, and land-use policy.

LIFE SAFETY

The most important issue behind the development of any code is life safety. All state and local codes—as well as enforcement—start with this issue.

Key life-safety considerations built into the codes include: fire-safety and evacuation standards, environmental safety, and elimination of hazards.

Fire Safety

The important issues in fire safety are:

- Regulation of construction materials to reduce the likelihood of fire. For example, wood-frame construction is limited in most states, and restrictions are often placed on the use of flammable interior finishes.

- Reduction of the potential for fire-related structural collapse. While this is more often an issue during fire fighting, many codes require structural assemblies that will withstand some period of exposure to fire or require buildings that are designed to permit collapse of one area of the building during a fire while other areas maintain their structural integrity.

- Early fire detection through smoke and/or heat detectors—particularly in high-hazard spaces such as kitchens and mechanical spaces—is now common.

- Fire and smoke containment through use of compartmentalization and rated assemblies between floors is also common. High hazard areas—including mechanical rooms, storage areas, etc.—are typically to be enclosed with fire-rated walls, floors, and ceilings.

- Fire suppression through mandatory installation of extinguishers, fire-suppression systems in high-hazard spaces such as kitchens, and the growing, often mandatory, use of sprinklers to prevent the spread of fire beyond the room of its origin. As noted by the U.S. Senate Special Committee on Aging, 1976, the NFPA handbook states that there has never been a reported case of multiple deaths due to fire in nursing homes protected by a functioning sprinkler system.

- Evacuation in case of fire or other emergency is the most universal concept built into the codes. Almost all codes require that there be two means of egress from most spaces. The concept of having a choice of evacuation routes—in case one is blocked—is fundamental. Most codes also define the exit widths and aisle or egress width from larger spaces such as the main dining room, large multipurpose room, or other assembly spaces.

- Some codes and/or local and state fire marshals require emergency and fire access to all sides of a senior housing or health-care building. They usually also establish the location of a standpipe, hydrant, or other devices required for fire fighting. Typical requirements call for hydrants to be located such that any fire can be reached with 500 ft of hose and provided with 500 gallons of water per minute.

Typical of the standards applied are those in the International Building Code (IBC) or BOCA (Building Officials and Code Administrators). These codes often, either directly or through state adoption, reference the NFPA Life Safety code or incorporate its requirements. A growing number of states are adopting the IBC.

Environmental Safety

The codes dealing with environmental safety vary from state to state, but some of the most common issues are the following:

- Required ventilation (see Chapter 8) and indoor air quality standards

- Required removal or containment of asbestos

- Required removal or containment of lead-based paint

- Requirements for food-service equipment (stainless steel, easily cleaned, etc.) and food preparation and server spaces

- Requirements for safe drinking water and water fountains

- Minimum lighting standards (see Chapter 13)

Elimination of Hazards

Most state codes and regulations and departments of health also try to minimize potential hazards. Typical cautions or prohibitions in the codes include:

- Use of flooring materials that minimize slipping

- Marking of glazed doors and sidelights

- Use of safety glass or glazing within 18 inches of the floor

- Site designs that minimize pedestrian/vehicular conflicts, with particular emphasis on drop-off and pickup areas

- Physical restrictions on access to high-hazard spaces such boiler rooms, electrical closets, etc.

- Elimination of overhead power lines that cross the property near occupied areas

- Restrictions on the location and use of high-pressure boilers

- A variety of guidelines for natural gas use and distribution

- Protection from resident access to electrical heating devices

- Swimming-pool depth and layout standards

SPACE STANDARDS

Most states establish minimum space standards for resident rooms and program areas in licensed facilities. This subject has been covered in Chapter 1. Unlicensed facilities are typically not covered by code-mandated space standards, but they are subject to requirements in building construction codes.

APPROPRIATE BUILDING SYSTEMS AND CONSTRUCTION PRACTICES

The largest quantity of code material regulates the selection of appropriate building systems and methods of construction. The International Building Code is becoming one of the most widely used building codes. Many state building codes also reference other codes or standards, such as the NEC (National Electrical Code), the ASHRAE (American Society of Heating, Refrigerating, and Air-Conditioning Engineers Inc.) or ANSI (American National Standards Institute). These codes regulate everything from use groups and construction types to energy conservation. Separate codes or sections of the code typically exist for mechanical, electrical, and plumbing systems.

PUBLIC POLICY

As with many other building types, senior housing and care facilities are often subject to laws and codes passed to further some public policy such as historic preservation, energy conservation, and/or accessibility for the handicapped.

Historic Preservation

Preservation regulations vary widely across the United States. In some areas, designation as an architecturally or historically significant building comes with few restrictions. In others, a structure designated as a landmark or historically significant, or even a new structure adjacent to or near a designated landmark, may involve additional public reviews, restrictions on renovations and additions, and/or a prohibition against demolition.

Energy Conservation and Sustainable Design

Most states have an energy code that focuses on the energy performance of the building envelope, with particular emphasis on the performance of exterior walls, windows, and roofs. Many local codes and, increasingly, client sponsors and user groups, have requirements for trash recycling, water conservation, and other conservation practices. Some client sponsors are also looking to incorporate a degree of "green" architecture in their projects (see Chapter 6).

ACCESSIBILITY

One of the most discussed—and often misunderstood—code issues is the Americans with Disabilities Act (ADA). Many people think it is a building code, when it is in fact a civil rights law whose intent has now been built into many existing building codes. The general intent of this important legislation is stated in Title II of the law:

"Subject to the provisions of this subchapter, no qualified individual with a disability shall, by reason of such disability, be excluded from participation in or be denied the benefits of services, programs, or activities of a public entity, or be subjected to discrimination by any such entity."

While the law refers only to a "public entity," ADA's supplemental technical guidelines have been referenced by most building codes so that they apply to virtually all buildings serving the public, including all senior housing and care facilities.

This section of this chapter summarizes some of the guidelines that generally guide the application of this law and the related codes, but these have been subject to myriad local and state variations and interpretations. This discussion should not be considered either legal advice or an interpretation of every accessibility code; it is intended as a framework to help in understanding and interpreting this evolving area of building regulation.

While most people are aware of the need to create accessible routes for the mobility-impaired, ADA also covers other disabilities, including sight, hearing, and other impairments. Some of the items covered include curb ramps, elevators, properly designed ramps, accessible toilet and bathing facilities, telephones, and drinking fountains. Installation of fire and smoke alarms suitable for the hearing- and visually impaired, hardware appropriate for people with hand impairments such as arthritis, and other provisions may be needed as well. The codes in most states establish the minimum standards, but the definitions of disability are still evolving.

One area that is the subject of particular debate is the degree to which design guidelines should be adjusted for the aging. Most code officials do not take into account the specific physical limitations and needs of the aging, who may have, for example, limited upper-body strength and cannot effectively use grab bars located behind water closets.

The main issue facing many owners of existing facilities, of course, is what to do with the barriers in the facilities. The primary issue usually relates to toilet rooms and bathrooms where existing space constraints usually make it difficult or impossible to provide fully accessible facilities. This becomes a critical issue when outmoded plumbing fixtures are replaced and officials require full code compliance as a result.

New buildings built or significantly altered after January 26, 1992, however, are to be designed and built so that they are "readily accessible to and usable by individuals with disabilities." The state codes are now reasonably clear, but the federal government references the Americans with Disabilities Act Accessibility Guidelines for Buildings and Facilities (ADAAG), published as 59 Fed. Reg. 31,676 (1994). Some state codes reference the CABO (Council of American Building Officials)/ANSI (American National Standards Institute) Standards, CABO/ANSI A117.1-1992 and A17.1-1987.

In addition to the accessibility codes listed in the previous paragraph, multi-family dwellings must comply with the U.S. Department of Housing and Urban Development Fair Housing Accessibility Guidelines.

Among the special issues of accessibility for the aging are the following:

- Provision of grab bars at water closets. Codes provide for water closets to be placed 18 inches from a sidewall with a grab bar and a second grab bar located behind the water closet. These provisions respond to the needs of young adults with good upper-body strength who are wheelchair bound. It is widely believed by experts that, for the aging, two grab bars (usually flip down from the wall behind the water closet) would provide better support—like two armrests in a chair—and respond to the possibility that the user might be right- or left-arm strong. Also, to reduce staff back injuries occurring from lifting of the user who requires assistance in transferring to the water closet, the water closet is better located 24 inches from the sidewall to allow two staff persons to assist in the transfer.

- Ramps are best avoided. While ramps are permitted if they meet prescribed design criteria, seniors have difficulty maintaining balance on ramps because their center of gravity shifts as they lean forward or backward. Ramps can also be difficult to negotiate for persons using walkers or wheelchairs.

- Falls and injuries that result from falls are one of the greatest concerns for aging persons, some of whom have serious vision or balance problems. A large number of falls occur due to tripping at changes in flooring material. Further, while most accessibility codes and guidelines permit a ½-inch-high transition strip between flooring materials, the transition strip becomes a barrier for a person using a walker or a wheelchair.

- Vision impairments are common among the aging. Such impairments limit independence and accessibility in ways that may include everything from difficulty in using a key to unlock one's apartment door to reading notices, menus, and the like. In addition to compensating with higher light levels, particularly at critical places like entrance doors, senior housing facilities may use a number of electronic options, like proximity card readers, to ease access for residents.

ENFORCEMENT

Most codes also outline the enforcement procedures that will be used. However, code officials may have subjective and varying interpretations of the statutes in force. These can vary from city to city as well as from state to state. They are often based on how a particular code official interprets the same regulation. Experience shows that such varying interpretations are not easily appealed. It is therefore important to review design assumptions—especially related to life-safety issues, construction type, and fire access—with code officials early in the design process.

FISCAL AND BIDDING CONTROLS

When a senior housing or care facility is built with public funds, state laws and other regulations may govern the purchase of design services, construction, equipment, and furnishings. While most states permit qualification-based selection of professional services, construction equipment and furnishings are typically purchased via a competitive bidding process. Though the competitive bidding process can be conducted by a construc-

tion manager selected on the basis of qualifications, most other construction, furnishings, and equipment must be purchased through competitive bidding.

LAND USE POLICY

While land-use regulation is typically a local issue (supplemented by some state and federal codes), most new senior housing and care facilities may be subject to some or all of the following:

- Planning and/or zoning board review, which typically focuses on issues such as vehicular access, storm water, landscape, and other site-planning considerations, such as availability of water and sewer, as well as compliance with the height, setback, lot coverage, parking, building use, and other provisions of local zoning

- Coastal zone, state historic preservation office, wetlands, and other reviews, which typically deal with one of the public policy issues noted earlier in the chapter

- Board of architectural review, which typically focuses on the materials and aesthetics of the proposed design

- State or local department of transportation, which often governs the road improvements, curb cuts, and other actions necessary for vehicular access

- Environmental impact review, which is often mandated by the expenditure of significant public monies, size of the proposed facility, or location on an environmentally sensitive site

OBTAINING WAIVERS FROM EXISTING CODES

Many of the more innovative senior housing and care facilities have features that do not comply with one or more of the

Typical Environmental Impact Statement Issues

1. Land use, public policy, and zoning
2. Natural resources
   Soils, geology, and topography
   Groundwater and surface water
   Ecology
   Air quality
   Noise
3. Hazardous materials
4. Utilities
   Water supply
   Sanitary sewer
   Storm-water management
5. Visual and cultural resources
   Historic structures
   Visual impacts
6. Archaeological resources
7. Traffic and transportation
8. Community services and facilities
   Police
   Fire protection
   Solid waste
   Open space and recreational facilities
   Schools

codes. Most codes provide for an appeals process that can lead to relief from a particular code provision. Some of the more common subjects of appeals in senior housing and care have been the following:

- Areas, such as lounges, dining rooms, and country kitchens, opening directly onto corridors in jurisdictions that treat the senior living facility as a residential structure

- Provision of Dutch doors for dementia-care residential units when a fire-rated partition is required

- Design of a country kitchen as a resident activity space (i.e., not a commercial kitchen) open to surrounding areas and not within a fire-rated enclosure.

- Delayed or controlled unlocking of egress doors in dementia-care facilities to provide for the security of the residents

- Accessibility waivers for water closets and grab bars as discussed above.

- Provision of adaptable provisions in lieu of accessible provisions

- Ability to serve food from bulk deliveries and provide dishwashing within country kitchens accessed by residents

Standard code-compliance procedures do not, unfortunately, lend themselves to the testing of alternative approaches. Therefore, promising new solutions are often not formally recognized and tested. Waivers, when granted, are isolated and approved on a case-by-case basis. Thus, they rarely become the basis for future policy or code reform.

CONCLUSION

Navigating the increasingly complex code and public-approval system has become a major task for most senior living facilities and their planning and design teams. It is not unusual for the various reviews to add 6–18 months to the normal time required to plan, design, and start construction of a senior housing or care facility.

CHAPTER 6

ENERGY/ENVIRONMENTAL CHALLENGES

There are signs of a strong trend toward sustainable design in senior housing and care facilities. This chapter examines how current advances in energy conservation, environmental protection, and sustainable design are being incorporated into environments for older adults.

More sponsors are asking their design teams to incorporate sustainable-design concepts into their projects. Some ask that the design qualify for the U.S. Green Building Council's "Leadership in Energy and Environmental Design (LEED) Certified" status. Certified projects must demonstrate performance beyond accepted standards in six areas:

1. Sustainable sites

2. Water efficiency

3. Energy and atmosphere

4. Materials and resources

5. Environmental quality

6. Innovation and design process

CODES

Designing senior living environments involves an understanding of the complex web of national, state, and local energy and environmental regulations (see Chapter 5).

Among the codes most relevant to sustainable design are those governing energy performance, indoor air quality, removal of toxic materials, and water usage.

ENERGY CONSERVATION

Energy required for the operation of senior living environments consists primarily of lighting, heating, ventilation, air-conditioning, and water management. Secondarily, energy is also used for vertical

transportation, food service, laundry, and power for other equipment.

Total energy budgets vary considerably by project type, climatic region, and local utility infrastructure. Energy-conservation approaches in senior living environments vary considerably depending on who is responsible for paying utility costs: the residents or the operator. This is in turn dependent on the balance between private and public space, the cognitive capabilities of the residents, and the level of care being given. Independent and congregate living projects devote the bulk of the building area to private resident space, often giving residents both control over the conditioning of their environment and the responsibility for utility bills that comes with it. In skilled nursing and dementia environments, the preponderance of public space, when combined with consideration for the limited capabilities of residents, typically results in centralized HVAC systems and utility bills apportioned to residents as part of the monthly fees.

When day-to-day energy usage is largely controlled by residents, conservation strategies need to address motivation, ease of operation, and comfort. The elderly population today is more likely than the general population to have a resource-conserving lifestyle. Residents should be informed about the cost of the energy they are using (for example, how much of their monthly bill comes from air-conditioning) and the benefits to themselves and their environment of even modest conservation measures. These measures can be facilitated by designing the environment to facilitate residents' energy management, such as installing windows that are easier to open for a person of limited strength and providing easy-to-read thermostats with simple programming options. It is unrealistic to expect residents to reduce their energy usage to the point of discomfort. Comfortable low-energy alternatives need to be provided. Alternatives to air-conditioning can provide valuable yet comfortable energy savings. Rooms with cross-ventilation and high ceilings take advantage of natural cooling. Ceiling paddle fans are often a cost-effective alternative that some residents will choose over constant use of air-conditioning.

When the management of energy is more the responsibility of the facility operator, the design of centralized building systems and controls has a far greater impact on conservation. Since there is generally a financial incentive to reducing the use of energy, the issue is to find ways to conserve without compromising quality of life offered to the residents. Overall building HVAC zoning anticipates both the natural exterior rhythms and the patterns of interior usage.

Lighting

High-efficiency lighting fixtures may offer dramatic conservation gains, especially considering the higher lumen levels and glare-free spaces required by older adults. Senior living sponsors have followed the lead of hotel operators in replacing incandescent downlights with compact fluorescent fixtures. Even in spaces such as offices, where fluorescent lights have been standard, switching from the older T-12 to newer T-8 lamps can reduce costs as much as 20 percent. Fluorescents have also replaced incandescent bulbs in decorative ceiling pendants,

wall sconces, and table lamps. Thanks to the development of warmer color-corrected fluorescent lamps, the energy savings can be gained without sacrificing residential ambiance. Bulb-substitution programs can result in a 30–40 percent reduction in energy costs with annual savings exceeding $6–20 per bulb, in addition to reduced maintenance costs related to lamp life.

Further incremental reductions in lighting costs are being achieved through the following:

- The use of occupancy sensors in bathrooms, offices, and other periodic-use areas to turn off lights when neither residents nor staff members are present.

- Using multiple circuiting, time-clock switching, and centralized panels to control light levels by time of day and projected occupancy of spaces. Unless staff is conscientious in turning off lights, centralized control is particularly important for table and floor lamps, which can be connected through switchable electric outlets.

- Designing public spaces to maximize daylighting. Proper daylighting design, including glare control, can eliminate the need for artificial lighting in public spaces during the most active periods of day. Care should be given to orientation of glazing. Perimeter design should incorporate drapery or blind pockets inside and shading by landscape elements outside.

- Use of photocell-controlled lighting is a natural complement to daylighting design, and can be used both inside the building and for site lighting, entry canopies, and parking areas.

- Low-energy fixtures are appropriate for some uses, such as light-emitting diode (LED) exit lights and high-pressure sodium lamps for parking lots. LED fixtures have long expected life, and sodium vapor lighting produces twice as much light per watt as mercury vapor lighting and five times as much per watt as incandescent fixtures. The location, mounting height, and orientation of sodium lamps must be carefully controlled to avoid light spill onto neighboring property or glare back into resident rooms.

Heating, Ventilation, and Air-Conditioning

HVAC-related costs can be the biggest component of total energy use. In response to stricter energy codes and higher operating costs, plans to limit HVAC costs include more compact floor plans, greater insulation, more efficient heating and cooling equipment, more localized system controls, and dual-pane glazing. Many sponsors have been able to implement measures that have dramatically reduced energy costs by 30 percent or more for an investment that is paid for by the savings in a few years.

Some of these strategies include:

- Tightening the building envelope, with emphasis on continuous vapor barriers and upgrading insulation levels beyond code standards, especially for roof areas. However, this needs to be done in a way that does not compromise air quality due to reduced ventilation.

- Improving the performance of glazing systems, including a switch toward "low-e" dual-pane glazing. This advanced coating improves window thermal performance and solar shading, permitting the use of larger windows that provide natural light without subjecting residents to drafts and the discomfort of large cold surfaces.

- Increasing personal control of heating and air-conditioning systems, often with the incentive of direct impact on monthly utility costs. This can be done through individual metering of water, gas, and electric usage, as is frequently done in independent living settings, or through flow meters on both domestic hot-water and HVAC piping.

- Increasing localized zoning and control of heating and air-conditioning within centralized systems. This is especially important for "two-pipe" systems, most frequently specified for public areas. Zoning perimeter areas by solar orientation and locating thermostats where they can accurately respond to fluctuations in solar load will increase resident comfort while reducing complaints and energy costs.

- Specifying more efficient boiler systems, which can save energy through flue gas heat recovery, flue dampers, and dual-fuel combustion. Boilers should be selected and sized to operate at high efficiency throughout the year. Two or three smaller boilers instead of one larger one, although more expensive initially, are better able to keep energy consumption down even during the "shoulder season" and reduced demand periods.

- Using separate systems for kitchens, wellness centers, laundries, auditoriums, or other spaces that have unique utility requirements. Some sponsors outsource food service, which creates an additional incentive to separate the kitchen's energy use from the whole. Wellness centers, especially those with large pools or gymnasiums, have energy demand "spikes" that can be efficiently handled by separate equipment but that inefficiently inflate the size of centralized equipment. In addition to the energy savings gained, it is advisable to separate systems for pools from those for other areas to limit the potentially adverse impact of humidity and chlorine.

- Reducing energy consumption of fans, which are often the major energy user in an air-conditioning system. Using high-efficiency variable-speed air supply and ventilation fans as well as variable-volume fans for ducted conditioning areas is a common strategy.

- Incorporating heat-recovery or heat-exchanger systems to transfer the heat from exhaust air or return piping to supply air in winter or, reciprocally, transfer in the reverse direction during summer.

- Analyzing the feasibility of alternative energy sources. In some regions, photovoltaic cells for electric panels and solar panels for hot water and heating can be cost-effective.

- For larger projects, installing cogeneration systems can reduce energy costs significantly over the typical useful life of the equipment.

- Reevaluating design temperature for the thermal comfort of the residents. The mechanical engineer can establish a baseline cooling temperature that deviates from the 68–70 degree norm to 74–75 degrees and therefore results in the design of more appropriately sized systems.

Energy Management and Control Systems

Sophisticated energy management and control systems (EMCS) are used in some newer and larger facilities, but many facilities for the aging do not have the sophisticated personnel required to operate and maintain some of the more complex EMCS options.

Water Supply and Sewage/Waste Treatment

Senior housing and care facilities can be major consumers of water. Where water is expensive or scarce, conservation has become increasingly important. Conservation measures vary somewhat by locality but can include the following:

- Reducing water waste due to leaking faucets and other plumbing-line connections. Although this sounds minor, it is often a major source of waste, especially when all aspects of the plumbing and HVAC systems are considered.

- Installing low-flow devices for showers and sinks and low-water-use toilet fixtures.

- Using high-efficiency domestic hot-water heaters for resident areas, allowing larger boilers to be either shut off or eliminated entirely.

- Operating with lower hot-water temperatures (120° F vs. 140° F). This is a natural for senior living communities, where residents' reduced skin thickness can make them more sensitive to temperature extremes.

- Designing low-water-use landscaping, whatever the climate. Especially for communities on large suburban sites, water use in landscaping can become a significant cost. At the Felician Sisters in western Pennsylvania, the redevelopment plan included replacing six acres of lawn with natural meadow vegetation, thereby significantly reducing yearly water use, eliminating the need for herbicides, and eliminating the need for summertime lawn-maintenance staff positions.

- Applying rainwater or other "gray water" to various tasks. These might include landscape irrigation, use in heating and air-conditioning systems, or even for flushing toilets. The actual potential of this option varies by region.

- Using well water. Where underlying soil, water table, and regulations permit, the use of well water can reduce the cost of municipal water. Some facilities have used well water (after filtration and treatment) for cooling and toilet flushing.

Calculating the Costs and Benefits of Energy Conservation

The two most common methods for calculating the costs and benefits of energy-conservation strategies are the "years-to-payback" and "life-cycle cost" methods. For-profit sponsors are likely to focus on the former; not-for-profit sponsors can be more easily persuaded to consider the latter.

The "years-to-payback" method allows simple one-item-at-a-time comparisons of an energy-saving alternative. First, the alternative's projected additional first cost (for example, changing from clear to "low-e" glazing) is estimated. At the same time, the annual energy savings in gas, oil, and/or electricity consumption are converted to a dollar value. The cost of the alternative is then divided by the annual savings to yield a payback period,

expressed as the number of years required to recover the capital cost of the alternative through money saved from lower operating costs. The shorter the payback period, the more attractive the alternative. While each sponsor is different, energy-saving alternatives with payback periods of less than seven years are often considered worthwhile investments.

The "life-cycle cost" method is used for more complicated comparisons. Some comparisons require consideration of more than first cost and annual utility savings. In the life-cycle method other factors—such as the difference in the life expectancy of the equipment, the time required to maintain the system, and other variables—are considered. The different annual costs of the alternatives are made comparable using "present value" techniques. Typical of such calculations in senior living is the comparison of less efficient, shorter-lived, through-the-wall air-conditioning with a central system. In these cases, the services of an energy-conservation professional are recommended.

ENVIRONMENTAL PROTECTION

Environmental protection embraces the impact of a project both on the environment around it and on its own residents, staff, and visitors. Some key issues, and how senior living communities are facing them, are listed below.

Water and Soil Run-off

Water/soil runoff and water-table retention are usually addressed during site design. The desire to balance all cut-and-fill on-site and to minimize grading can often run counter to providing the easily traversed, barrier-free environment older adults require. In one creative approach to barrier-free circulation on steep sites,

▲ *This retirement community on a steep site used bridges to create a common level. Kendal on Hudson, Sleepy Hollow, New York. Perkins Eastman Architects PC.*

individual buildings were tucked into existing grades and connected by a series of bridges at a single "commons" level. The result is both better for the environment and more convenient for the residents.

Solid Waste Management

Solid waste management has risen significantly in importance in the last ten years. Its importance will continue to climb, as recycling requirements increase in specificity and multiply in category. This requires larger "recycling" rooms closer to resident areas as well as space-programming changes for clean supply rooms, soiled holding areas, and trash handling.

Construction-Period Disruption

Construction-period disruption, especially dust, noise, and traffic, is a major environmental issue as more projects involve renovations or extensions to existing buildings. Older residents are particularly sensitive to these problems, and strict controls are typically demanded by the department of health and the municipality.

Air Quality

Measurement and consideration of interior, exterior, and off-site air quality

have become much more sophisticated in the last ten years. Interior air quality is particularly important for frail seniors, who tend to spend greater periods of the day indoors. Most senior living communities now receive low off-gas paint, wall covering, and carpet finishes. One common challenge for designers is the need to balance direct outside ventilation (e.g., operable windows) with energy efficiency.

Toxic Materials

The dangers, difficulties, and costs of dealing with toxic materials apply to all project types (see Chapter 16).

Traffic and Parking

Traffic and parking are major issues for senior living projects. Environmentally sensitive site design can reduce on-site impacts, such as the use of water-permeable paving, placing parking under buildings to reduce site disturbance, or tandem and/or valet parking to reduce the total hard surface area per car. Most zoning codes require more parking than is needed during a typical day at a senior living facility. As noted in Chapter 4, an effective land-use approval strategy has been to offer a landscaped reserve area and commitment to additional parking if and when actual usage demonstrates need.

Most senior living communities operate a shuttle bus service for residents to take them to outside activities, doctor's appointments, or shopping. If a transit station (bus, trolley, train) is nearby, sponsors should consider methods to encourage employee usage. If explored at the planning stage, this can assist in reducing employee parking requirements.

SUSTAINABLE DESIGN

In addition to energy conservation and environmental protection, sustainable design highlights site selection and design, alternative energy sources, and resource-efficient building materials and operations. Detailed discussion of the entire "green building" concept can be found in the U.S. Green Building Council's LEED Reference Guide Version 2.0,

June 2001 edition. Below are some examples of how designers are incorporating sustainability into successful senior living projects.

Site Selection

The Weinberg Terrace Assisted Living project is an example of an "urban infill" development that takes advantage of and reinforces an existing neighborhood.

◀ Assisted living can be developed on small urban lots. Weinberg Terrace, Squirrel Hill, Pennsylvania. Perkins Eastman Architects PC.

This assisted living project was built over a community-center parking garage on a small urban lot. Adjacency to neighborhood shopping and public transit benefits both residents and staff, and allows the building to tap into the existing road and utility infrastructure. By combining community recreational, cultural, and social service uses together with the housing component, the sponsor was able to increase the relative density of the development and make it easier for residents to travel between services.

Adaptive Reuse

Many obsolete schools have been converted into senior housing. A typical former classroom is an appropriate size for an independent living apartment. This typical adaptive reuse is a frequently cited example of good sustainable-design practice.

Alternative Energy Sources

Solar energy, photovoltaic cells, passive heating and cooling, geothermal systems, and wind power are some of the alternative energy sources that may be possible depending on a project's location and size. Passive solar heating and cooling is potentially feasible for many projects if considered early in the design.

Recycled Materials

A growing number of projects are using recycled materials for major portions of floor and wall finishes, as well as other parts of the building. For new construction, recycled drywall, flooring, and wall-covering materials continue to increase in quantity and quality. For sustainability, preference is given toward materials that are:

- Produced locally
- Developed from sustainable or renewable resources
- Salvageable if the structure is later demolished
- Manufactured in a way that produces no toxic by-products
- Installed in a way that eliminates off-gassing

Of course, all of these concerns must be balanced against the material's relative performance, aesthetics, cost, code acceptability, and availability.

CHAPTER 7
STRUCTURAL SYSTEMS

Senior housing and care facilities have used virtually every structural system normally employed in relatively simple structures: wood frame, masonry bearing wall and concrete plank, structural metal stud, steel, precast concrete, poured-in-place concrete, and so on. The selection of the appropriate system or combination of systems is usually the result of an evaluation of at least 12 factors.

CONSIDERATIONS

This chapter reviews these 12 factors and how they can lead to the choice of a system. This section is followed by a review of typical issues faced when using the most common structural systems.

Soil Conditions

Poor soil conditions can have a major impact. A site requiring expensive piles may choose a system such as steel that has longer spans and requires fewer footings and supporting piles. Unstable or variable soils, subject to differential settlement, may preclude less flexible systems, such as bearing walls. In addition, the presence of a high water table may preclude the inclusion of a basement, especially for buildings over four stories. If poor soil found on a site dictates that it must be removed prior to construction, the inclusion of a basement may be more economical because soil must be removed anyway. Some soil types, when located in zones subject to seismic activity, can dictate much of the structure. As these examples indicate, it is advisable to have some basic geotechnical data prior to making the selection of a structural system or the decision to include a basement.

Conditions in selection of structural systems
1. Soil conditions
2. The program and concept
3. Applicable codes
4. Potential code changes
5. Flexibility
6. Impact on finished-ceiling and building height
7. Material delivery and construction timing
8. Local construction capabilities and preferences
9. Ease of construction and schedule
10. Cost of the selected system
11. Cost impact on other systems
12. Appearance and aesthetic potential

The Program and Concept

The program of uses and whether they will be directly above or below one another from floor to floor is also a major factor. A building that contains only nursing units or apartments can select from the simplest systems because the required spans are short. Spaces such as major dining or multipurpose rooms need longer spans and are likely to be reconfigured over time, and mid- or high-rise stacking of program is likely to require more complex systems.

Applicable Codes

At least three code issues directly impact the choice of a system: the required loads and subsurface soil conditions, the building code use group and related permitted construction type, and special structural requirements to deal with extraordinary conditions such as a hurricane or earthquake. In addition, the choice of floor systems can be influenced by fire-rating requirements, the ability to run mechanical systems and sprinkler lines, and the assembly thickness when overall building height is an issue. The typical design live loads are 40 pounds per sq ft (psf) for residential units and 100 psf for common spaces.

If unusually heavy loading is required in some areas to account for special radiology equipment, compact files, rooftop mechanical equipment, or swimming pools located above grade within the building structure, the added dead load for these items for that part of the structure can be in the range of 100 psf for mechanical systems to up to 300 psf for some compact file systems. If known in advance, these loads can be supported by most systems.

More prescriptive are the use groups and construction types incorporated in most codes. Some states define assisted living, the housing parts of a CCRC, congregate living, and other senior living options as multifamily housing. In many states, housing can be wood-frame up to four stories. In others, wood-frame senior housing is permitted but restricted to one or two stories.

In addition, a growing number of state and local codes mandate structures that can withstand extreme stresses or loads, such as those generated by hurricanes or earthquakes. In most cases, these requirements point the design team toward the more complex and often more costly systems, such as steel or concrete in multistory construction.

Potential Code Changes

The codes governing senior housing and care facilities are all subject to change, and some of these changes can influence the selection of a structural system. For example, the International Building Code, which many states are now adopting—in whole or with modifications—as their state building codes, has the potential to alter the system choice. In this code, assisted living facilities with more than 16 units are defined as use group I-1, and combustible structural frames, such as wood, are permitted for structures up to four stories high.

In general, there has been a trend toward more code restrictions on the use of combustible structures for frail or confused populations that are hard to evacuate. Some experts argue that the addition of sprinklers as well as smoke and fire protection is far more important than the relative combustibility of the structure, but this argument is not necessarily prevailing.

In general, it is good practice to design to meet any likely future code requirements. This avoids the need for future waivers or upgrades in other systems (such as sprinklers).

Flexibility

Most successful buildings have to accommodate some growth and change. Over the last 20–30 years, senior living environments have had to accommodate more change than many other building types. For example, the increased frailty of many occupants, the desire for more space and privacy, and other factors have required many sponsors to reconfigure the basic building blocks of their facilities: resident rooms, nursing units, or apartment units. Some structural systems, such as the use of bearing walls between units (vs. exterior walls and one corridor wall) can be very inflexible. The altering of concrete planks may also be problematic if the desire is to cut through the floor, as structural strands generally cannot be cut. Wood-frame and larger span structures tend to be more accommodating of change.

Impact on Finished-Ceiling and Building Height

Some structural systems, such as two-way (flat-plate) concrete slabs or bearing walls and concrete plank, allow the design team to minimize floor-to-floor height. The structure is only 7–9 in. thick and can double as the finished ceiling. Other systems, such as trusses or structural steel beams, are often 10–15 in. deeper, and usually need to be covered by a hung ceiling that adds 14–18 in. more than flat-plate or concrete plank floors to the overall floor-to-floor height.

Material Delivery and Construction Timing

The choice of a system can have a significant impact on the project schedule. Some structural materials, such as wood, concrete blocks, poured-in-place concrete, and structural studs, are readily available. Others, such as structural steel, can have long lead times. Careful planning can reduce the schedule impact, but delivery time can still influence the choice of systems.

Local Construction Industry Preferences and Capabilities

Virtually all local construction markets have preferred systems, as well as systems that are rarely used. For some areas, pre-stressed or post-tensioned concrete, for example, is rarely used. Local preferences and familiarity typically result in lower costs.

Ease of Construction and Schedule

In addition to local preferences, some systems are selected due to their ease of construction (particularly wood or metal-stud framed buildings) and the construction schedule, to diminish the impact of severe winter weather conditions. If the construction schedule is such that concrete would be placed or masonry bearing walls constructed during winter months, the steel-frame or structural-stud building system is often selected to avoid the necessity of heating and protecting the structure while concrete or mortar cures.

Cost of the Selected System

Because of the economics of most senior living projects, first cost is always a major factor.

Cost Impact on Other Systems

What has been less well understood by many owners and their design teams is the structural system's cost impact on other building systems. For example:

- The systems that add to floor-to-floor height can add significantly to the costs of interior partitions, exterior skin, and other systems.

- When systems must be covered, at least part of the cost of the dropped ceiling and soffits should be considered in the structural cost

- Some systems, such as wood roof trusses in some states, require additional sprinklers and fire protection.

- Some systems, such as bearing walls and structural steel, can complicate (and increase the cost of) the distribution of ducts, conduits, and other systems.

▶ Trusses at the Weinberg Village Winter Garden are both structurally functional and aesthetically important. Weinberg Village, Pittsburgh, Pennsylvania. Perkins Eastman Architects PC. Photograph by Jim Schafer.

CHARACTERISTICS OF STRUCTURAL SYSTEMS

	Spans appropriate for resident units	Spans appropriate for large spaces	Flexibility	First cost	Impact on other system costs	Appearance	Material delivery and construction timing	Impact on interior space and building height	Responds to current and future codes	Familiar to local construction industry	Impacted by soil conditions
Wood Frame	O	⊘	O	O	O	O	O	O	⊘	O	O
Structural stud	O	⊘	O	O	O	O	O	O	O	⊘	O
Bearing wall and concrete plank	O	X	X	O	⊘	⊘	⊘	O	O	O	⊘
Steel and concrete plank	O	O	O	⊘	⊘	⊘	⊘	X	O	O	O
Steel and poured concrete deck	O	O	O	⊘	⊘	O	⊘	X	O	O	O
Precast concrete	O	O	⊘	⊘	⊘	O	⊘	⊘	O	⊘	O
"Beam & Slab" poured in place concrete	O	O	O	⊘	O	⊘	O	O	O	O	O
"Flat plate" poured in place concrete	O	⊘	⊘	⊘	O	O	O	O	O	O	O
Prestressed/post-tensioned concrete	O	O	⊘	X	O	O	O	O	O	X	O

O Not often a significant issue
⊘ May be a problem or issue
X Often a significant problem or issue

Source: Perkins Eastman Architects PC.

Appearance and Aesthetics

It is uncommon for the structure to be expressed in most senior living environments, but when it is, its appearance can be important. For example, some design teams dislike the joints inherent in the plank system. Others find the running electrical services and sprinkler lines on the ceilings created by flat plate concrete slabs to be a significant aesthetic problem, and therefore place these utilities in walls. There are, however, some opportunities to expose the structural system as an important part of the project's design vocabulary.

STRUCTURAL SYSTEM TYPES

Based on the factors discussed above, there are some issues that come up fre-quently in the review of options. The following is a brief summary of the discussion surrounding nine of the most common structural systems.

Wood-Frame

With the exception of buildings in some urban areas, senior housing is predominantly wood-frame. This system is typically inexpensive, it can be implemented by a wide variety of contractors, it is fast, and it can be flexible. The span limitations can be overcome with trusses, laminated beams, heavy timber, or mixing with steel or other systems in larger spaces. The most common reason for not using wood is current or probable future code restrictions on combustible structural systems.

Another potential disadvantage is that the flooring surface can feel bouncy underfoot in high traffic areas.

Structural Stud

The use of steel studs instead of wood is common. It often has a slightly higher material cost, but it is noncombustible. Its other advantages and limitations are similar to those of wood-frame construction, yet an additional problem can occur especially in exterior walls. Water damage or moisture problems can lead to a loss of structural integrity, even if the steel is galvanized.

Bearing Wall and Concrete Plank

A third frequently used option is a combination of masonry bearing walls and precast concrete plank. Again it is a simple method, familiar to many contractors, relatively low in cost, and relatively quick to implement. The span limitations can be overcome by mixing it with other systems for larger spaces. The major problems with this system are its relative lack of flexibility; performance on unstable soil; height limitations (50–70 ft in most construction markets); impact on the distribution of mechanical, electrical, plumbing, and fire-protection systems; and the occasional shortages of masons and/or precast companies. Senior housing projects often have large quantities of open dining and common space on ground-level floors, which become difficult to achieve with this system. In addition, many design teams object to using the underside of the planks as the ceiling for the space below. When this objection leads to having a hung acoustical tile or sheetrock ceiling to cover mechanical/electrical distribution systems and the uneven joints between planks, some of the cost advantages of this system are eroded.

Steel and Concrete Plank

The fourth option eliminates some, but not all, of the objections to bearing wall and plank. This option has minimal height limitations (as long as the beams are in the same plane as the walls), is quite flexible, performs adequately on unstable soil, and rarely suffers from a lack of skilled manpower. On the other hand, steel requires fire-proofing, hung ceilings are almost always required, steel can have long delivery times, and the floor-to-floor heights are greater.

Steel and Poured-Concrete Deck

This option has somewhat the same characteristics as the steel and plank system, except that it is more costly and the depth of the system is greater than that for steel and concrete plank, due to the inclusion of intermediate beams.

Precast Concrete

Precast concrete can be used for more than exterior wall systems. It is also used in some locations for the columns, beams, and bearing walls. It is also a common structural choice for garages, site bridges, and other simple long-span, heavy-load structures. Some areas, however, are not served by a nearby sophisticated precast company. Moreover, many senior living facilities do not have the scale and degree of repetitiveness necessary for precast to be cost effective.

"Beam-and-Slab" Poured-in-Place Concrete

Concrete is commonly used in many parts of the country. It is a particularly common choice for projects that must have a noncombustible structure or must withstand significant lateral loads, such as those produced by hurricanes. It is also relatively easy to build in most local construction markets, and it can produce a relatively flexible building. Poured-in-place, however, tends to be relatively expensive and often has greater thickness than steel-and-concrete plank.

"Flat-Slab" Poured-in-Place Concrete

A two-way, flat-slab concrete structure is a common choice for taller residential buildings since it minimizes floor-to-floor height, is fast to build, creates a finished ceiling with the underside of the slab, permits flexible column placement, and is relatively easy to brace or stiffen for lateral loads. This option, however, requires substantial reuse of forms (usually created by a mid- to high-rise program) and an experienced structural concrete subcontractor to make the cost acceptable. Even when these conditions are met, flat-plate structures are usually substantially more expensive than some of the other options.

Prestressed and Post-Tensioned Concrete

These two options have some of the same advantages and disadvantages of flat-plate, but are less frequently used. The systems can be thinner than flat-plate but are also more costly. In addition, there is less flexibility in cutting the concrete in future modifications, due to the locations of structural steel tendons embedded in the concrete. The construction industry in many parts of the country does not have the experience to implement these systems.

As a final point, it is common to employ two or more systems in a single project. In some CCRCs, for example, poured-in-place has been used for the foundations, precast in the garages, structural stud for residential wings, and structural steel for the common areas. Overall, the selection and design of a structural system, or combination of systems, is an issue with significant cost, aesthetic, and functional implications.

CHAPTER 8
MECHANICAL/PLUMBING/ FIRE-PROTECTION SYSTEMS

This chapter discusses three systems:

1. Mechanical systems, specifically heating, ventilation, and air-conditioning (HVAC). Within the building shell defined by structure, floor systems, and exterior enclosure, HVAC systems condition the space, including temperature, humidity and draft control.

2. Plumbing.

3. Fire-protection systems. In this chapter, the focus is on sprinklers and other fire-suppression systems.

These systems, although relatively simple in most cases, account for significant parts of both the construction and operating costs of senior housing and care facilities. Moreover, their design should be carefully focused on the typical needs of older adults.

NEEDS AND REQUIREMENTS OF OLDER ADULTS
Mechanical/HVAC

Perceptions of what is comfortable can be quite different for the aging, as they are more sensitive to changes in temperature, drafts, and extreme cold or heat. This sensitivity is partially related to loss of strength and to cardiovascular strain. In addition, the brain reflex that controls perspiration does not function as well in the aging, making them less able to adapt to extreme temperatures. An older person can perceive even the movement of warm air as cold. Therefore, a controlled interior temperature that is higher than the norm for younger people is appropriate for this population.

The perception of temperature can also be influenced by variables such as the activity level of the individual, type of clothing worn, effects of medications, and the subjective comfort that one feels relative to the use of colors and textures in the environment. The history of where the older resident has lived or visited may also affect relative tolerance of temperature extremes.

Additionally, one's activity can influence the perception of temperature. For example, older persons in the act of assisted bathing will often complain of being cold, despite the use of heat lamps and other augmented heating devices. This may in part be due to the use of tubs that require the older bather to sit while the tub fills, but it is also possible that compromises in one's privacy and control over an activity as intimate as bathing may lead to complaints about the temperature.

Noise generated by the mechanical system can also be an issue. As discussed in Chapter 12, a system that generates significant background noise can cause problems for older residents with hearing loss. Finally, there are safety issues. Heating sources should be protected so that confused residents cannot burn themselves, and mechanical rooms should be accessible only to facility staff.

Plumbing

Anatomical changes in older adults significantly influence the design and specification of plumbing fixtures. Reduced body height and upper-body mobility as well as loss of dexterity due to arthritis or stroke influence the specifications of faucets, switches, and toilet and bath/shower controls. (See also Chapters 1, 5, and 10.)

Fire Protection

Virtually all professionals in the field strongly advocate the use of sprinklers, heat-detection, and smoke-detection systems in all senior housing and care facilities. Rapid evacuation is not feasible, so early detection and suppression is essential.

CODES AND LOCAL REQUIREMENTS
Mechanical/HVAC

Depending on jurisdiction, the design of mechanical and plumbing systems is governed by several overlapping sets of codes (see Chapter 5). For an overall introduction to HVAC systems, the American Society of Heating, Refrigerating and Air-Conditioning Engineers (ASHRAE) is probably the best general source. The 1999 ASHRAE Handbook (ASHRAE, Atlanta, 1999) provides an introduction to the major issues.

Plumbing

Plumbing system design begins with the National Plumbing Code, the AIA publication "Guidelines for Design and Construction of Hospital and Health Care Facilities" and ADA guidelines. Additional local clarifications usually specify the types of materials usable in different piping situations.

Hospital and Health Care Facilities Guidelines Nursing Facilities Section, Table 8.3, "Hot Water Use—Nursing Facilities" lists recommended temperatures and hot-water consumption for resident-care areas, dietary services, and laundry.

Fire Protection

The National Fire Protection Association (NFPA) 101 is the primary basis for fire-protection system design, but local codes may vary significantly in their requirements for fire-resistive walls and doors, allowable compartment sizes, and sprinkler head location and coverage. Local fire departments have a strong influence, and it is essential for design professionals to meet with them early and often throughout the course of a project.

Electrical

Consult the following codes: NFPA 10 (NEC) and NFPA 110, Emergency Systems.

KEY ISSUES AND TRENDS
Flexibility

Most facilities want a system that can provide either heating or cooling whenever required, but few can afford the systems that do this. Therefore, a major task for the design team is to select a system that approximates this at a more modest cost.

Individual Comfort Control

In HVAC there is a trend toward increased space-by-space control, and direct allocation of utility costs.

Noise and Vibration

The noise and vibration produced by mechanical systems must be controlled (see Chapter 12).

Ventilation, Sick Buildings, and Infection Control

Mechanical ventilation is required by code in virtually every senior housing facility. The ASHRAE Handbook recommends ventilation rates for different spaces.

ASHRAE Standard 62.1 (latest version) is more current, with addenda, and is often the basis for the ratios in codes.

Many sponsors want their residents to feel they have control over their own unit's heating and cooling. Safety, operational efficiency, and the capabilities of the typical resident put limits on how close they come to this goal.

MECHANICAL/HVAC SYSTEM OPTIONS

HVAC systems in most senior housing and care projects are not very complex. Most consist of only a few basic components:

- A central heating and cooling plant serving the entire complex, including boilers, chillers, cooling towers, and pumps that supply hot and chilled water to resident rooms and common areas

- Decentralized HVAC systems, including supplemental heating, for resident rooms

- Air-handling systems to provide ventilation and conditioning for common and service areas, including large rooftop-mounted units

- Specialized and/or independent HVAC systems for commercial kitchens, fitness areas, pools, and other spaces with unique occupancy needs

- Automated temperature control systems for equipment monitoring and control, which are often integrated with life-safety, security, and telecommunications networks

As with all building types, there is significant variation among regions, but the outline above covers the majority of the projects discussed in this book.

OPTIONS FOR SINGLE-RESIDENT ROOMS

Maintaining resident comfort and control are key criteria in the selection of resident room HVAC systems. While most systems permit a certain level of resident comfort control in heating and/or air-conditioning, the majority of systems do not offer simultaneous heating and cooling year round. Some have limited or no heating in the summer, and others offer limited or no cooling in the winter.

The following are options for decentralized systems that may be selected to serve residential facilities:

1. Often the lowest first-cost option is a through-the-wall air-conditioning unit and hot-water (or electric) baseboard radiation. The drawbacks of this option are the appearance of the large grill or louver on the facade, the relatively short life of the air-conditioning equipment, higher maintenance costs, higher noise levels, and relatively high operating costs. Architecturally, careful design of the exterior louver can minimize the aesthetic problem associated with this option.

2. A second low first-cost option is a gas-fired package unit that provides a high degree of individual control and the ability to individually meter energy use. In comparison to electric utility rates, equipment utilizing gas fuel will usually provide lower operating costs. The most prominent downside is its typical installation. The equipment is usually installed in an exterior closet-size room with a large louver on the outside. Most architects have found it very difficult to make this

▲ *This affordable assisted living residence uses packaged terminal air-conditioning units that also heat from a central circulating hot-water source. Carnegie East Assisted Living, New York City. Perkins Eastman Architects PC. Photograph by Kyo-Young Jin.*

feature attractive, but careful design can reduce the unsightly look.

3. Another option is to use fan coil units for cooling combined with baseboard radiation heating. The fan coil typically has an electric coil to provide some heat if required during the cooling season. This system is simple and relatively inexpensive to operate. The major operating costs are associated with a central cooling and heating plant that serves the individual fan coil units.

Fan coils may be installed either below a window or vertically in the corner of a room. In the vertical configuration, one unit may be located in the wall between two adjacent rooms to serve both rooms. In order to be less obtrusive, the unit may be located over the bathroom or in an entry vestibule. Typically, if outdoor air is introduced through the wall, a small brick vent is required. However, an alternate option would be to accommodate ventilation requirements by means of a central air-handling unit in lieu of a through-the-wall vent. The latter scheme would obviously

increase first cost, due to the additional ductwork and added equipment.

In comparison with self-contained systems, the two-pipe fan coil unit scheme will have lower operating and maintenance costs.

4. The fourth common option is the heat pump, which provides both heating and cooling year-round. This unit is often mounted in the same locations as a fan coil. Although a heat-pump unit provides independent control capability, the disadvantages of a heat pump system are operating and maintenance costs and higher noise levels. Generally, these systems operate inefficiently during cold climate conditions. Either electric or hot-water coils are generally required to supplement the heat under some conditions.

5. Another option is a system that introduces the concept of radiant heating and/or cooling. Radiant heating is usually installed within the floor construction. If heating is combined with cooling, the equipment is typically located in ceiling panels. This system is common in Europe and eliminates the drafts associated with mechanical-ventilation equipment. However, outdoor ventilation requirements still need to be addressed. When selecting a radiant cooling system, the system needs to be engineered correctly, to avoid potential condensation that results from a cold panel surface interacting with uncontrolled humidity. In addition, the system can take longer to condition a space. Consequently, the combination of radiant heating/cooling sys-

tems has not been widely accepted in the United States so far.

6. Many owners consider a four-pipe system that circulates both hot and chilled water. Although few facilities can afford the higher first cost associated with this option, this scheme provides inherently lower operating and maintenance costs, as well as providing the capability for independent comfort control.

Not all of the systems listed above are equally appropriate to all senior living program types. While the option of using gas-fired package units may be attractive for independent living apartments, their large equipment size, capacity, and high first cost make them inappropriate for use in smaller rooms that are common in skilled-nursing or dementia care settings. Anecdotal evidence suggests that some male residents with dementia sometimes confuse under-the-window or baseboard HVAC equipment with toilet fixtures, so it may not be advisable to install these types of systems in dementia care rooms. Because of differences in climate, performance criteria, first cost, local construction industry preference, operating cost, and owner/resident preferences, it is unlikely that any one of the above systems will become the primary HVAC solution for all senior living project types.

CONSTRUCTION AND OPERATING COST IMPACTS
Life-cycle Cost Analyses

Since most senior living environments are occupied 24 hours a day, life-cycle cost analysis needs to be performed to select the system with the greatest economic payback. However, due to con-

▲ Integrating low-cost gas-fired package units into an attractive facade requires design skill. Turtle Creek, Dallas, Texas. Courtesy of First Operation LP. Photograph by Dennis Strini.

cerns of high first cost, many owners select systems with unnecessarily high operating and maintenance costs.

First Cost

As with all building systems, construction or first cost is almost always a major issue. Mechanical systems typically make up at least 7–12 percent of total construction costs. The percentage of total cost varies by program type, with slightly lower percentages in the less complicated congregate and independent living settings. Plumbing systems make up 5–8 percent of total construction costs. Fire-protection systems usually make up approximately 2–4 percent of total construction costs.

INFLUENCE ON PROGRAMMING AND DESIGN
Program Area

The space required for central mechanical systems varies widely due to project location, site size, sponsor preference, and local construction practices. Enclosing all equipment within the building reduces MEP system costs but enlarges the total project size, which may result in a larger total project cost. Although most boilers, chillers, cooling towers, pumps, exhaust fans, and electrical switch gears are available in exterior-located versions, extreme climates or the need to control noise emissions may preclude their use.

The size of central mechanical plants also varies by program type. Primarily residential settings, such as congregate care and independent living, tend to have very limited central services, while settings for skilled-nursing or continuing-care communities generally have larger central plants. When a central system requiring mechanical rooms is selected, the normal allocation varies from 2–4 percent of total area for independent living to about 5–7 percent for a CCRC with a full complement of social, dining, and sports/activities spaces.

In addition to the central plant area, additional shaft spaces are required for vertical piping, plumbing, cabling, and duct distribution. Additional floor space may also be required for local mechanical rooms housing air-handling units. The amount of area required will vary considerably depending on the number of floors and the complexity of the program.

The area required for residential space HVAC systems varies by system selected. Package units and individual hot-water heaters appropriate for large independent living apartments may require a closet of 8–10 sq ft per unit. In-the-ceiling fan coils, used for dementia and skilled nursing, may require no floor space at all. No matter what system is selected, developers tend to include these mechanical spaces within the area of the apartment, thereby avoiding any loss in overall area efficiency.

Impact of Horizontal Distribution on Ceiling Space and Floor-to-Floor Height

Designers should have a clear understanding of all of the MEP systems that may be located above various types of spaces before setting floor-to-floor heights. The need to coordinate the overlap and interpenetration of structural, HVAC piping and ducting, potential transfer of plumbing risers from above, electrical cabling, and sprinkler mains will dictate requirements for ceiling spaces. While ceiling spaces can often be eliminated above the main portions of individual resident rooms, several vertical feet are often required to accommodate HVAC piping and ducting above main public spaces, such as dining, service areas, and kitchens.

CHAPTER 9
ELECTRICAL AND COMMUNICATIONS SYSTEMS

Electrical and communications systems are playing an ever-increasing role in settings for older adults. Advances in wireless technology, phone systems, and automated reporting are facilitating operations, enabling staff to spend more of their time in direct contact with residents, and allowing detailed record keeping, thus minimizing liability problems. Many of the early low-voltage systems were developed from the technology used in security systems. These simple stand-alone systems for nurse call, emergency call, fire-alarm, and building perimeter control are being replaced by integrated networks whose capabilities increase every year. Resident expectations, especially in independent and assisted living settings, have increased with the spread of the Internet, and high-bandwidth connectivity is rapidly becoming a standard feature in apartment design. This chapter takes up the traditional electrical system requirements for power as well as rapidly developing communications and information technology (IT) options. For discussion of other technologies and equipment, see Chapter 10; for discussion of lighting, see Chapter 13.

Electrical and communications systems have become common in senior housing and care environments in recent years. The reasons for this expansion include the following:

- Marketplace expectations for technology are increasing because residents and sponsors have become more sophisticated about the available options. This plays an important part in marketing and competition among facilities.

- Economic pressures have led to the adoption of technologies that reduce overall costs by increasing efficiency. These technologies allow for the following:

  1. The provision of more services to more residents with lower staff costs

  2. Better business analysis through information gathering and study; for example, tracking consumables and intelligent purchasing

  3. More efficient building management and thus lower operating costs

  4. "Just-in-time" (JIT) or stockless inventory, (arrangement of supply deliveries so that materials needed for one day's work arrive at the start of the day and are consumed during the day, effectively reducing/eliminating inventory). JIT may be especially useful for larger facilities, which will need less staff and space to accommodate inventory.

- Security concerns have increased.

- Sponsors and care providers have an increasing need for record keeping to protect themselves from accusations of malpractice and substantiate compliance with practice standards. Record-keeping systems help staff keep track of services provided; wandering systems help monitor cognitively disabled residents.

- Increasing numbers of the very old and frail require a continued emphasis on user-friendly equipment; communication devices support resident autonomy despite physical limitations.

- Technology must address the needs of the full range of individuals involved with the aging:

  1. Volunteers

  2. Potential residents

  3. Potential staff: recruiting

  4. Existing staff, support: continuing education, staff retention

  5. Users of home health: logging on to change schedule of home health aids, access billing and medical information

  6. Resident families: access to resident information such as bills or medical records (especially helpful for out-of-town families), and other building amenities, such as cooking equipment, through use of a proximity card

  7. Caregivers: medical referral and information

  8. Residents: access to religious and other organizations, research on genealogy, and distant friends and relatives for support and socialization

ELECTRICAL ISSUES FOR SENIOR HOUSING

Before elaborating on a discussion of communications systems, it is important to recognize some basic electrical issues related to senior housing.

Power-Supply Distribution

- The utility supplying power to the site will have specific requirements for the arrangement of the incoming service, transformer, and metering. In most cases, the utility will provide the primary cable (within length limits) and transformer, and the customer will be responsible for conduit and transformer pads.

- It is important to establish early contact with the serving utility to determine guidelines, location of incoming supply, rate schedule, and service date. All are important in facility design and critical to proper electrical system selection and life-cycle analysis.

- Primary supply voltage is usually high, with the transformer supplying secondary voltage to the facility at 480/277V. A secondary voltage of 208/120V may be available on request, and should be considered for smaller facilities, particularly where mechanical cooling/heating is not powered by electricity. In larger facilities, the cost/space increases for its larger feeders offset the benefits, and 480/777V is the voltage of choice. A brief comparative analysis can be performed at the schematic design level once electrical system selection has been made, the facility general layouts established, and utility rates identified.

Power Quality

- With the proliferation of technology in senior housing, the quality of utility power becomes increasingly critical. The typical measure of power quality is the amount and duration of voltage variation outside a standard value. Most utilities offer a +/- 10 percent variance from nominal supply voltage as their standard. All equipment planned for the facility must be able to regularly operate within this range or be provided with voltage-regulation equipment. Conditions commonly referenced as "brownouts" are actually 5–8 percent reductions from nominal voltage.

- Power outages may cause equipment shutdown, immediate equipment damage, or long-term degradation if frequent. Historical data for the area will help determine what protective measures are appropriate.

- With the proliferation of electronic equipment, a problem common among commercial facilities is surfacing in senior facilities. All present technology equipment utilizes switch-mode power supplies. These generate feedback into the input conductors, which causes an increased current on the neutral conductor. In large facilities with substantial technology equipment, care must be taken that neutral conductors are properly sized. In some applications, the neutral must be double the capacity of the phase conductor. This is of particular concern where electrical codes permit neutral size reductions in residential applications.

Metering

- Most facilities have a single utility meter for all electrical energy consumed. Rate analysis identifies demand and energy costs, seasonal variations, daily on/off peak variations, and any penalty for power factor. This important information is needed to project overall energy cost for the facility and is a major component in the decisions leading to HVAC system selection.

- Individual metering of the resident units is an option to be evaluated at the initial stages of the project, since

it will impact HVAC system selections as well as the electrical distribution system arrangement. Individual metering is best suited to independent living facilities, where resident energy use is significant and varies among occupants.

- Some jurisdictions have regulatory restrictions, which should be checked before implementing any metering arrangements.

Emergency Power

- An emergency power-supply generator may be needed, depending on the nature of the facility and the local authority having jurisdiction. Independent living facilities are less likely and skilled care is more likely to have such requirements. Where facility is multiuse, the more stringent requirement will apply.

- At minimum, egress and exit lighting and fire-alarm systems will require an emergency power source. Where generators are not mandated, battery-supported equipment can be used.

- Battery equipment, where used, must consider the increased illumination and longer egress time needs of seniors. Typical emergency lighting fixtures have a 90-minute capacity with degrading performance over the period. When applied as supplemental "battery packs" on normal lighting fixtures, the initial illumination is about 40 percent of the normal fixture output, with degradation similar to separate battery fixtures.

- A generator with capacity beyond code requirements may be considered where there is a history of frequent or long utility interruptions.

Alternate Energy Sources

As technologies mature, there is an increasing interest in alternate energy sources to augment or replace utility supplies (see Chapter 6).

COMMUNICATIONS SYSTEM ROLE AND OBJECTIVES

Communications systems play important roles in supporting the lifestyle, safety, and security of residents in senior living settings. In addition, a well-designed electrical and communications system will assist staff in providing a variety of hospitality services as well as simplify program and building management.

Emergency Response/Nurse Call

Early technology included wired pull chords in toilets and adjacent to beds in skilled-care environments. At one time wired systems at these locations were mandated by most codes. Recently, several states have adopted the 1996–97 *AIA Guidelines for Design and Construction of Hospital and Health Care Facilities*. This standard allows the use of radio-frequency systems for nurse call. Governing bodies are becoming increasingly open to using radio-frequency systems because of the resident-beneficial features they can provide. While newer devices allow for greater flexibility in call locations and staff communication, not all new equipment is UL-rated, a requirement in most jurisdictions.

- Desired features include voice-to-voice communication between staff and residents, and flexibility in call locations. Remote-control access to call stations is a recently developed feature.

- Fall/movement alarms indicate whether someone has fallen or monitor whether a resident is active. They can take the form of infrared monitoring of a space, a mat positioned next to the bed to indicate motion, or devices attached to furniture or a wheelchair.

- Pocket paging devices and handsets, rather than speaker systems, allow for staff mobility and a quieter environment. The ability for staff to communicate from multiple locations aids in the assessment of the emergency and helps to direct treatment.

Phone

One of the main issues is whether phone service should be set up and managed by the sponsor or by a telephone company. A sponsor-initiated service may become an income source for the facility.

- Phone equipment may respond to aging users, with features such as enlarged and color-contrasted buttons with enlarged numbers, enhanced speakers (potential for hands-free use) for auditory clarity, and handset/cradle design for ease of use by those with compromised mobility.

- Service may be integrated with voice mail, Internet, etc.

- Phone-switch software may be used to track and report important calls and billing information.

Cable TV

A significant issue is the length of time a sponsor maintains a contract with a cable provider whose system may not be compatible with other equipment.

- Cable service may be linked with building and site security and tied to the computer system. A dedicated channel may allow each resident to view the building entry from his or her unit.

- The sponsor may have a dedicated channel, allowing for broadcast of entertainment, events calendar, and more.

Security

- Emergency call and elopement systems have been based on security technology; thus this system can often be integrated with other systems. Simple security systems often provide superior elopement control at lower costs than resident wander-protection systems.
- Features may include voice and face recognition, key-card access, contact alarms, and infrared motion detection.
- Incidences of costly facility rekeying and/or time-wasting twice-daily rounds by staff to unlock and lock doors often convince senior living community management to install a security system.

Fire Alarm

The ability to link with the fire-alarm system is important, though such systems have traditionally been proprietary because of liability issues. The security system must link with the fire-alarm system so that locked elopement doors will open automatically in a power outage. This is a standard of most regulatory agencies.

When possible, links with computer systems allow for wireless notification of municipalities, administrators, and facility managers.

Elopement Prevention

Staff and designers can help prevent the hazards associated with the wandering and elopement behavior of dementia care residents by addressing not only the individual needs of the resident but by carefully designing the building plan and program to suit their needs (see Chapter

1). One of the many responses to this behavior has been the development of elopement-prevention systems that keep staff informed about the location of each resident. Technology should not be used as the main corrective measure, however.

- The function may be a modified version of emergency call systems, with provisions including a bracelet, pendant, notification of door opening, or delayed egress response.
- The function indicating that a resident has left the building may be as simple as a light illuminating at designated locations, or as complex as a computer screen or PDA (personal digital assistant) carried by staff showing the location and a complete resident profile.

Internet Access

- For the resident, access to the Internet is a means to stay connected with friends and family. Visiting physicians will be able to access resident medical records via the Internet.
- For a sponsor, Internet access can aid with education, referral, and other support services.

Intranet Data Network/Building Management Systems

Intranet systems link the various aspects of senior care environment, including purchasing, medical records, social-service records, staff support, and education. They can also monitor building systems such as lighting, heating, ventilating, and air-conditioning.

Point-of-Sale System

Similar to the use of a banking card, a point-of-sale system may be used by staff to record and track resident care or to

APPLICATIONS OF SYSTEMS TO SENIOR LIVING ENVIRONMENTS					
	Emergency Response	Phone	Cable TV	Security/Fire Alarm	Elopement Prevention
Geriatric Clinic	X	X	X	X	X
Adult Day Care	X	X	X	Liability	Dependant upon client population
Long-Term Care Residents	Fall/motion alarms	User-friendly equipment	X	Least mobile residents	X
Assisted Living Residences	X	X	Can be coupled with security	X	X
Alzheimer's Residents	Less effective	Used less frequently, although still a familiar activity	Usually not used in resident units	Guided more by staff	As an accessory to planning
Independent/ Residential Living Apartments	Devices must be most mobile/flexible; not a code requirement	X	Can be coupled with security	X	O
Caregivers/ Families	Expected response time. Record-keeping expectations.	Portable/wireless	Potential for communication from family to resident	Security/liability	Security /liability
Administration/ Staff	Staff communication	Portable/wireless	Activities broadcast	Portable communication	Staff communi- cation
Community/ Public	Connection to hospitals/other professionals	O	O	Code	May allay neighbor concerns

X indicates that the technology applies to a particular environment or service; a description indicates a more specific application; O indicates that the technology is less influential.

Internet Access	Intranet Data Network	Point of-Sale-System	Audio Visual	Building Management System
X	Support and connection to sponsor	Potential to record services rendered/record keeping	O	Dependent upon tie with larger facility
X	Support and connection to sponsor	O	X	Dependent upon tie with larger facility
Growing interest & participation	Pharmacy/medical care	Credit purchases at residence café/gift shop	X	Record keeping
X	Communication; information/referral	Credit purchases at residence café/gift shop	X	X
Memory enhancement with staff/family assistance	Support and information for families	O	Used less frequently	X
Offered in units and commons	Communication; information/referral	Credit purchases at residence café/gift shop	X	X
X	Communication with residents; access to residents records	Use of country kitchen appliances; other amenities	O	O
Information and referral	Training and staff retention	Record care delivery	User-friendly equipment	User-friendly equipment
X	Marketing/support	Clinic Services	O	O

allow residents to charge purchases made at a gift shop or café within the facility. Many facility managers are requesting that residents have a single card for access control, point of sale, and keyless entry to their units.

Audiovisual

Many newer residences have incorporated movie theaters as an addition to the traditional multipurpose room. Systems that are sensitive to the visual and aural changes that occur with aging can help to offset the difficulties that can occur in larger spaces (see Chapters 1 and 12).

CODES AND LOCAL CONDITIONS

The national electric code typically governs the design of these systems. With the introduction of the International Building Code, regions that once had their own electrical codes have begun to adopt the national code. NFPA 101 has additional restrictions related to fire alarm and suppression systems, which will influence system design. It is wise to verify with local cable and Internet service providers any requirements that may be imposed by the FCC. Underwriters Laboratories (UL) typically governs the specification and availability of electrical fixtures and appliances. The result of these overlapping sets of regulations can at times be confusing, especially where it applies to communications, but by and large it has not prevented innovation.

CONSTRUCTION AND OPERATING COSTS

Life-cycle costs for electrical and communications systems include both initial construction costs and ongoing running and maintenance outlays. Although initial construction costs are almost always entirely born by the project sponsor, ongoing utilities costs may be assigned to individual residents, depending on project type. In higher-care settings, individual resident consumption is usually averaged over the entire community, but in active adult, congregate, and independent living settings, electric meters are often installed at resident apartments.

Electrical systems typically make up 8–12 percent of total construction costs. This includes power supply, switch gears, meters, main distribution, lighting fixtures, controls, and outlet hardware. The percentage of total cost varies by setting, with slightly higher percentages in the less-complicated congregate and independent living settings.

Communications systems typically make up about 2 percent of total construction costs, up to double the percentage required a decade ago. This includes conduit and wiring for telephone, computer, cable TV, Internet, intercom, perimeter control, security and fire-alarm systems. These costs do not include computer systems and equipment or phone equipment including PBX switches.

Cabling, switch gear, meters and main distribution have relatively long useful lives compared with mechanical equipment. And although conduit and wiring for communication systems is also quite durable, the control systems and software have been developing so rapidly that near-term obsolescence can be a real concern. This is one advantage of wireless systems, as they can require less initial cost and intrude less into the main construction effort. As "add-ons," wireless solutions offer the possibility to upgrade and integrate without costly renovation.

SYSTEM RECOMMENDATIONS

Tier 1[1]	Tier 2[2]	Tier 3[3]
EMERGENCY CALL SYSTEMS		

Unit Apartment

Tier 1[1]	Tier 2[2]	Tier 3[3]
• Resident activates wireless alarm device from any location in apartment through a personal device, which is worn or affixed to surfaces in locations chosen by staff and resident. • Activation of alarm device sends wireless signal to device, which is attached to resident's personal phone in bedroom location (typical). • Device "dials" resident's phone to reach communication receiver carried by staff. • If staff carry voice communication receiver, then device opens its "speaker" feature for two-way communication. • Staff receiver device displays resident unit #, name, and related essential information.	• Resident activates wireless alarm device from any location in apartment through a personal device that is worn or affixed to surfaces in locations chosen by staff and resident. • Activation of alarm device sends wireless signal to communication receiver carried by staff. • Staff communication receiver device displays resident name and zone from which signal was sent (e.g., third floor west, etc.).	• Resident activates wall-mounted hardwired alarm by pulling chord or pushing button located in multiple locations in apartment (bedroom and bathroom typical). • Activation of alarm sends signal to communication receiver carried by staff and central station. • Staff receiver device displays resident unit #, name, and related essential information.

Common Areas

Tier 1[1]	Tier 2[2]	Tier 3[3]
• Resident activates wireless alarm device, which is worn or activates (push-button) wireless alarm device conveniently located in all common resident use areas and bathrooms. • Activation of either wireless alarm device sends signal to communication receiver carried by staff. • Staff receiver device displays resident's name and location of nearest device registering signal (e.g., "library," "dining room," "unit 234, third floor west corridor," etc.).	• Resident activates wireless alarm device, which is worn. • Activation of wireless alarm device sends signal through transmitters to communication receiver carried by staff. • Staff receiver displays resident's name and zone from which signal was sent (e.g., first floor east, dining room/living room area).	• Resident activates wall-mounted wireless device pull alarm chord station located in strategic "risk" areas such as bathrooms, dining room, and exercise room. • Activation of alarm sends signal to communication receiver carried by staff. • Staff receiver device displays location of alarm device (e.g., main dining room, men's restroom first floor, etc.) • Resident activates hard-wired pull alarm chord station located in strategic "risk" areas such as bathrooms, dining room, and exercise room. (Note: resident wireless device will not activate alarm.) • Activation of alarm sends signal to communication receiver carried by staff. • Staff receiver device displays location of alarm device (e.g., main dining room, men's restroom first floor, etc.)

[1]*Typically considered to be the ultimate system to flexibly meet all needs, but may not meet local codes (nursing home) or resident needs where cognitive ability may limit resident operation (assisted living dementia).*
[2]*Typically a minimum baseline system that responds to budget considerations while maximizing flexibility.*
[3]*Typically a system that has limited flexibility but is based on proven technology and meets most state codes, if there is a requirement.*

continues

SYSTEM RECOMMENDATIONS (continued)		
Tier 1	**Tier 2**	**Tier 3**
Building Exterior Campus Areas		
• Resident activates wireless alarm device, which is worn. • Activation of wireless alarm device sends signal through transmitters to communication receiver carried by staff. • Staff receiver device displays zone from which signal was sent.	• Resident activates wireless device that is worn. • Transmitters located only at strategic site locations, e.g., walking path, pool, gazebo, etc.) • Activation of wireless alarm device sends signal through transmitters to communication receiver carried by staff. • Staff receiver device displays zone from which signal was sent.	• Same as Tier 1 but coverage is only from transmitters affixed to building, which defines a zone of "x" feet from the building.
STAFF COMMUNICATION DEVICES		
Resident Emergency Call Systems Communication Receiver		
• Wireless phone with sufficient display to identify resident apartment unit/name or common area/zone name.	• Wireless pager with sufficient display to identify resident apartment unit/name or common area/zone name.	• Central station reporting with 24-hour coverage/supervision.
Staff-to-Staff Communication		
• Wireless phone communication to locate other staff or page "all staff" in emergency situation.	• Wireless pager to locate other staff or page "all staff" in emergency situation.	• Standard wired phone system.
BUILDING SECURITY		
• Door alarms (stair doors and exit doors) are connected to staff communication receivers to notify that door has been violated (operated at a time when door control system indicates "locked" or "secured" status for that location). • Staff communication receiver device receives door alarm signal and displays name and location (e.g., stair #1, floor #3).	• Door alarms report to a single staffed security station with 24-hour coverage.	• Local, audible alarm. • Ability to receive notification of doorbell activation at main entrance or delivery entrance. If voice communication is a staff feature, then communicate to speaker at a door location.
INTERNET CONNECTIVITY		
• Each apartment wired for high-speed connectivity through campus-wide network.	• Each apartment provided with two phone lines and assigned two phone numbers for resident-arranged Internet service.	• Each apartment provided with standard phone line and connection to jack locations for possible computer connectivity.

[1]In Tier 1, facility becomes provider of Internet service and can charge monthly fee in addition or as part of monthly rent/service fee.

PHONE SERVICE

- Facility provides "dial tone" service to all residents for both local and long-distance service.
- Resident receives consolidated monthly bill for local and long-distance service.

- Facility provides dial-tone to all residents for local service only.
- Resident arranges own long-distance service and receives two monthly bills (facility for local and long-distance carrier).

- Resident units are prewired for phone service, but each resident arranges privately for local and long-distance service.

OTHER POSSIBLE FEATURES/REQUIREMENTS/OPTIONS

Emergency Systems
- Connection of apartment unit smoke detector to activate alarm device and send signal to staff communication receiver.
- Daily "check-in" button on resident apartment device. Allows resident to send "ok" signal by the same time each day.
- Standard resident service package may include a pendant or "watch" device, which can be worn, and one remote device for each bathroom or bedroom in the apartment (which can be attached at any location in apartment). Residents can purchase additional devices or rent on a monthly basis. Units must be waterproof with minimum battery life of two years and low battery signal.
- Phone ajar sends signal to staff communication device.
- Activation of wireless alarm device overrides phone use and sends signal to staff communication device.
- Battery backup for resident unit device that is attached to resident phone.
- Maintenance/backup
  - Staff "in-service" training of minimum of 20 hours offered at up to three different dates over a maximum of six months.
  - 24/7 service calls with a maximum 2-hour response time to the site.
  - One-year guarantee from time of written acceptance of the system by the owner.
  - Annual maintenance agreement after first year with guaranteed rate for years two, three, and four.

Resident Call Receiver
- Ability to flexibly program calls to different and/or simultaneous staff communication receivers.
- Ability to flexibly establish protocol for response backup with up to three successive phone numbers if call is not answered (e.g., facility can have calls forwarded to various devices after "x" seconds without response).
- Ability for facility to decide how to complete response to alarm (e.g., deactivate only at alarm source or remote deactivation).
- Ability to receive notification of outside calls to facility (particularly for night shift).
- Ability to receive notification of security device activation (door alarms).
- Provide one staff communication receiver with voice (wireless telephone) for each 40–50 apartments in independent and congregate living and one for each 20–30 assisted living units.
- Provide one staff communication receiver without voice (pager) for each 20–25 apartments in independent living and congregate living, one for each 10–15 assisted living units, and one for each eight nursing beds.

continues

SYSTEM RECOMMENDATIONS (continued)

Staff-to-Staff Communication
- Interface with house phones available throughout facility for staff not carrying communication devices.
- Computer logging of time of all calls received and time of response on a network-able PC-based operation by facility staff.
- Wireless phone or beeper staff communication receivers must be planned/engineered by system provider to guarantee no dead zones within building envelop and no false readings by floor (e.g., 2nd floor signal read as 3rd floor.
- Options if integrated with dial tone service:
  - Integration with fire alarm, building/energy management systems and security systems.
  - I4-digit dialing.
  - 911 notification (if 911 is dialed from anywhere in facility it is automatically routed to staff communication receiver).
  - Voice mail.

Phone Service
- Facility provides telephone"switch" and wiring in Tier 1 and 2
- Facility can leave phone-system switch and wiring in Tier 1 and 2 and explore revenue-generated payback period.

SYSTEM RECOMMENDATIONS

The table on pages 185–188 gives baseline recommendations for the operations of emergency call systems, staff communication, and building security. Clients must view their operational approach, staffing level, building design, and building location as a unique set of circumstances from which to develop a system that responds to resident and staff needs. Each tier represents a conceptual grouping of services. The tiers are arranged in complexity, from the most complex to the simplest.

INFLUENCE ON DESIGN OF OTHER SYSTEMS

Compared to HVAC or plumbing, electrical and communication systems have relatively low technical impact on the design of other components of senior living settings. Main conduits and cables can usually be routed through the floor slabs and through beams without impacting component sizes. Care must be given to integrating wiring and convenience outlets with partitions to maintain required fire or sound transmission ratings. Rooms containing primary communications equipment like phone switches and TV head end should not be located below rooms, such as kitchens and bathrooms, with plumbing fixtures due to potential water leaks. Lower temperatures may be required for rooms incorporating servers or other communications equipment, often necessitating independent temperature monitoring and air-conditioning supply. Depending on local regulations or client preference, communications and computer equipment may require non-water-sprinkler-type special fire-suppression systems such as Halon gas.

INFLUENCE ON PROGRAMMING AND ARCHITECTURAL DESIGN

On the other hand, communications systems can have a tremendous impact on programming and design. Despite miniaturization, sophisticated computers and telephone systems demand expanded electrical/computer rooms. As the examples listed above demonstrate, wireless and portable communication systems can influence the location, configuration, and equipment required for nurse stations and care staff. Corridor ceiling design can be affected by requirements for "sight lines" to nurse call antennas, call lights, or numerical displays.

Communication system advances will impact resident spaces as well. Ceiling-mounted "rhythm sensors" with adjustable time sensitivity are already widespread in retirement communities in Asia. Connected to monitoring panels within administration, these sensors provide nonintrusive monitoring of resident status and alert staff if movement is not detected within the prescribed time span. Some facilities are also experimenting with systems that track the location of staff. Both residents and staff may find increasing applications for touch-screen terminals located either near the entry or at bedside, depending on program type. Sensors coupled to call systems for early detection and responses to resident falls are being developed, and prototype systems may reach the market in the next few years. If economical, these systems may have a substantial impact on room layout or finish materials.

INFLUENCE ON OPERATIONS

Recruiting, training, staffing, and quality assurance are all shaped by advances in communications systems. Computer-literate staff and specialized IT personnel have become important parts of the staffing plans for senior living communities. Even for entry-level care staff, basic computer skills can be essential to properly operate touch screens, bar-code readers, and swipe cards; therefore, communities are investing more time and resources in training. Increased job skill requirements place upward pressure on salaries as well. Wireless technologies have encouraged a shift from centralized to decentralized staffing, presenting new challenges for care staff supervision and service quality control.

Automated systems that automatically document resident calls, waiting time, and staff response have helped control quality of care and liability issues in skilled-nursing settings, allowing families access to records of services and delivery of care. Such systems are likely to spread to assisted living in the near future.

TRENDS/KEY ISSUES/OTHER FACTORS

Although Europe and large parts of Asia do not share it, the U.S. point-of-use standard of 110V and 60 cycles is likely to continue for the foreseeable future. Within that system, however, the spread of low-voltage technologies has enabled power and energy savings in increasing numbers of electrical appliances. Current trends in electrical and communications systems design fall into two broad areas: expansion of services available to residents, and rapid development of staff-focused communications systems.

As a result of the spread of high-speed Internet and "smart house" systems into senior housing, power requirements, wiring density, and therefore construction costs of resident units continues to increase. A typical one-bedroom independent living apartment built in 1990 might have required a single 20-amp incoming electrical circuit. This would have been sufficient to power the refrigerator and stove, general lighting, one telephone, and one TV outlet in each room and outlets spaced every 15 ft along the walls. The same apartment built for occupancy in 2005 will require 60 amps of incoming service. The increased power will accom-

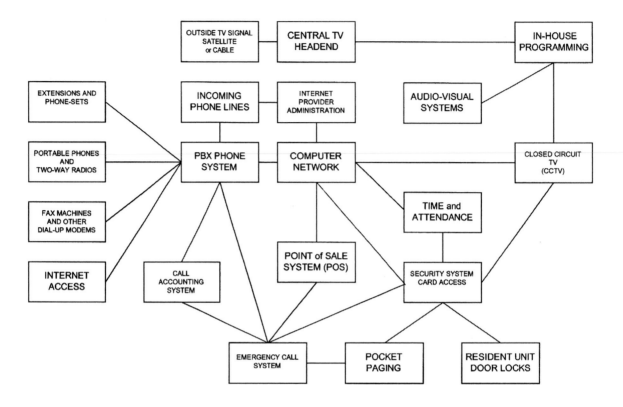

modate a dishwasher and microwave added in the kitchen, twice the number of electrical outlets previously planned. Final installation will include multioutlet boxes that combine telephone, cable TV, high-speed Internet, separate fax line, and accessory power.

Improvements in hardwired and wireless communications technologies are changing staffing patterns, location of support spaces, and management policies and procedures. Weinberg Terrace is an example of how communications technology advances have supported the development of new approaches to senior living. During the planning for this 60-unit, four-story assisted living project in Pittsburgh, Pennsylvania, the client and

architect both realized that traditional approaches to locating care substations would result in inefficient staffing and long customer response times. The project team sponsored the development of an affordable wireless nurse/emergency call response system that enables care staff to "float" freely, remaining available to receive and respond to customer calls anywhere in the building. Such emergency/nurse call systems can help staff to respond quickly in emergency situations and help residents feel more comfortable being alone.

At the Manor at Yorktown, voice-activated, face-recognition, and swipe-card technologies installed on specialized computer touch-screen terminals were placed in each apartment and at strategic locations throughout the facility to coordinate security, access control, billing for care and miscellaneous charges, and automated reporting of staff response to resident calls. The result is a system that reduces clerical staff, increases staff direct-connect time with residents, and improves "capture" of miscellaneous à la carte charges for resident-requested discretionary services that have a strong positive effect on the bottom line.

How to respond to these changes in technology? Consider the following:

• Where possible, use standards-based products and systems. Systems that are based on "open" (nonproprietary) languages are more readily interconnect-ed. The most common language is Internet Protocol (IP), which is the language of the Internet. Any system that uses the IP language is more likely to be easily interfaced with other systems.

• Recognize that technology has a short life cycle:

infrastructure (equipment buried in walls, wiring, etc.): 15 years

central telephone equipment: 10–15 years

hardware (5 years)

software (3 years)

What is considered "state-of-the-art" will change at least twice during a typical project's five-year development/construction period.

CHAPTER 10

SPECIAL EQUIPMENT AND TECHNOLOGIES

SPECIAL EQUIPMENT SYSTEM ROLE AND OBJECTIVES

Special equipment and technologies encompass a broad range of tools, including equipment, innovative care and daily living practices, and services whose primary objectives are assisting in prolonging resident independence and in supporting resident dignity. Please see Chapter 1 for a discussion of the aging process and how it affects mobility and Chapter 15 for a discussion of wayfinding, the means by which a person finds direction and orientation within an environment. In any living or care environment, the ability of staff, residents, and families to generate novel and useful ideas and solutions to everyday problems is often more important than the possession of a high-technology gadget. Nevertheless, new technological solutions are steadily improving the lives of older adults. The following are examples of both equipment and innovative strategies.

LOW-VOLTAGE AND COMMUNICATIONS TECHNOLOGIES

See Chapter 9 for full descriptions. Low voltage and communications technologies may include computers/personal data assistants, teleconferencing to family members for care planning, hands-free communication, wireless connectivity, handheld digital resident records, automatic billing and reordering at "point of utilization," robotic nursing, time released medication dispensers, financial and information management systems, and resident and staff computer resource centers. In addition, voice-recognition technology continues to be better integrated. Such systems allow for speech-powered computer software, voice-activated phone and emergency call systems, security and access systems, and mobile communications systems.

FINISHES AND FURNISHINGS

See chapters 13 and 14. The compositions of finishes and the dimensional/er-

> "The engine of real economic growth is not technology but innovation."
> Hector de J. Ruiz, CEO of Advanced Micro Devices

◄ Access to the Internet is becoming a basic service in senior housing and care. Photograph by Judith Perkins.

◄◄ Wireless technologies are minimizing the impact of hearing loss and other effects of aging. Photograph by Bradford Perkins.

gonomic characteristics of furnishings respond to age-related sensory changes, support life-safety issues, and prolong independence and mobility. The shape and height of a handrail, careful attention to flooring transitions, and the appropriate placement of signage, accessories, and assistance devices all become the long-term measure of a senior environment's success from the resident's perspective. The ease of maintenance, the freshness of the appearance, and the residential qualities of the setting all become important measures of success for the sponsor. Continued research, testing, and listening to clients and users all assure continuing development of these technologies.

▼ Careful detailing is particularly important in the design of bathrooms for the frail elderly. Universal Design Room, Kohler Design Center, Kohler, Wisconsin Photo courtesy of Kohler Co., and Cynthia Leibrock, ASID, Hon. IIDA.

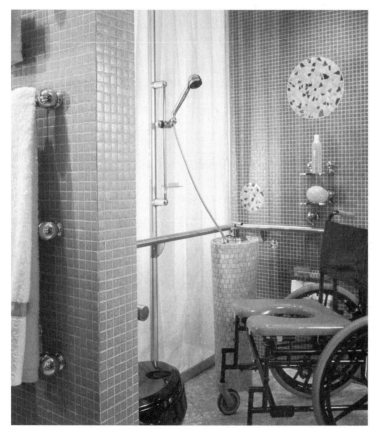

DESIGNING SPACES FOR OPERATIONAL SUCCESS

See Chapter 1 for descriptions of resident spaces for particular living and care environments, and Chapter 15 for a description of wayfinding devices. The room layout, adjacency of furnishings and equipment, and even wall geometries can contribute to the efficiency and ease of use of any space.

MEDICAL EQUIPMENT

As this is a book emphasizing residential environments, medical equipment is not the focus here. Nonetheless, advances in exam equipment and in services related to prescription dispensing are important to the support system. Again, what is important is that staff is comfortable and knowledgeable about the use of equipment. During the next decades, one technological focus will be on reducing injury and death due to medical error, which is estimated to contribute to 44,000–100,000 deaths annually.

ACCESSORIES OF UNIVERSAL DESIGN

Please see Chapter 5 on codes and accessibility. Many products, including door and window hardware, kitchen and laundry appliances, cabinets, bathroom fixtures, climate and lighting control, and stairway lifts and elevators, as well as gardening tools, tableware, and kitchenware are designed to serve the entire population, regardless of age, stature, size, or physical ability. Most universal products are modifications of designs that were originally created to help people with physical limitations to live more comfortably.

For example, grab bars that were once commonly found in a stainless-steel finish in mostly institutional settings have been created from many materials, including colorful plastics and wood moldings that resemble a component of millwork. Realizing that many residents make use of towel bars for support, one option is to utilize decorative grab bars in place of towel bars, so as to prevent the collapse of a towel bar that was not originally designed to support the weight.

Two helpful resources for universal design accessories are the "Directory of Accessible Building Products," sponsored by the National Association of Home Builders Research Center, and Lighthouse International, a center for education, research, and product recommendations/sales for persons with vision impairment.

MOBILITY DEVICES

For the senior population in residential environments, walkers, canes, and motorized carts are used more frequently than wheelchairs. As accessibility codes have traditionally been written based upon the needs of wheelchair users with some upper-body strength, the mobility variations within the aging population and the space needs for their mobility devices warrant special consideration. Please see Chapter 5 on accessibility issues. Considerations include corridor width (for passage as well as parking), storage and battery-charging space for carts, and areas adjacent to dining and other activity rooms for cart parking.

FOOD SERVICE OPTIONS

Across the various senior living environments, meal delivery has evolved from the traditional hospital models to residential and hospitality models. The designers of dining spaces have been more attentive to issues of acoustics, furnish-

◄▲ *Innovative mobility devices are becoming increasingly available and affordable. Courtesy of Sunrise Medical.*

ing comfort, lighting, room size, and quality and character of finishes (see Chapters 1 and 14 for descriptions of dining spaces and interior effects), and food-service delivery has emphasized food quality/texture and temperature control, as well as promoting a congenial atmosphere for dining. Dining is perhaps one of the most important activities of the day, and is under the scrutiny of prospective families and residents alike. How food-service delivery impacts the various senior living environments is described below. Note that some concepts, such as the "country kitchen" or family-style model, can be used to create a more familiar setting in many of the senior living environments.

Adult Day Care

Food delivery is dependent upon whether the facility is stand-alone or connected to a larger campus. Facilities may use any of the systems listed below, depending upon the type of client served.

Long-Term Care

Most long-term care residences are still largely reliant upon tray service, but a growing number are opting for country kitchen or family-style models, as described below in the section on dining for assisted living. For long-term care residents, restrictive diets and the need for greater assistance with eating are major considerations. Following are advances to enhance traditional tray service. Please see Chapter 14 for a description of furnishings appropriate to this setting.

- Bulk delivery: Some facilities deliver food in bulk to a nursing unit and then plate it individually for the residents. This tends to keep food at the

appropriate temperatures and provides a more residential-style food service. The pantries, however, add space, equipment, and cost.

- "Mixed Meals" concept: This Canadian concept has been introduced in the United States, France, Belgium, and Spain. Each food item is mixed then reconstituted in its original form, preserving most of its natural flavor and appearance. The intention is to make dining easier and more pleasurable for people who have trouble swallowing.

- Cook-chill: Still a tray-based method, this is used in environments where meals must be served in large quantities or where meals are distributed from a kitchen remote from the dining room. The advantage of this system is higher food quality, the result of a process by which food is prepared, rapidly chilled for safety and quality control, and then reheated or restored to the proper heated temperature as needed. Conduction and convection "retherm" (reheating) systems provide computerized control of temperature and time, with automatic scheduling for the reheating of food. This system has a high first cost, but in some places this can be balanced by lower labor costs, since all three meals can be prepared during one shift. Its critics refer to it as the "airline food" approach.

Assisted Living

- Main dining: In some independent and assisted living residences, the hospitality/restaurant concept has turned mealtime into show time. Every day, the chef, dressed in full costume, fixes a meal in front of residents. Equipment includes a presentation area with sink, warming devices, and meat-carving area. The event is designed to appeal to the senses, provide entertainment, and encourage dialogue by bringing kitchen teams into the dining rooms. This has been found to improve both residents' appetites and relations between residents and food service staff.

- Decentralized dining—country kitchen/family-style models: Features include a residentially appointed warming pantry, from which food is plated from either a hot/cold cart transported from the main kitchen or from built-in food wells, which have received food in bulk from the main kitchen. This enhances the experience of the various aromas of the meal, as well as providing a more residential atmosphere. Some facilities serve a hot breakfast in decentralized spaces within each resident cluster, while lunch and dinner are provided in the main dining room.

Independent Living

Many residences offer both formal and informal options for dining, with the less formal option gaining popularity. Features of an informal setting include a salad bar or even a cafeteria tray line. Café or bistro environments have also been integrated into the social atmosphere of the lobby setting. Equipment for these settings might include a bar/sink, espresso maker, ice-cream cooler, or blender. Formal settings may include the equipment necessary for presentations by a chef or for meat carving within the dining space.

Special Care/Dementia

Please see Chapter 1 on special considerations for special care and dementia patients. Features include:

- Irregular schedule: Not all residents will necessarily eat at once, so provision for keeping food appropriately cold or warm is recommended. Depending upon health department regulations, some meal preparation may occur adjacent to the dining room, remote from the main kitchen. This may be especially important for foods such as eggs or toast, which need to maintain textural quality. See the section on assisted living, above, as the country kitchen/family-style dining model is especially applicable to this setting.

- Smaller group size: Groups of no more than 10–14 are recommended.

Kosher Preparation

Jewish clients and the local rabbinical council have requirements for maintaining a kosher kitchen; specific requirements may vary. This typically results in a main kitchen that is at least ⅔ larger in size than a nonkosher kitchen, for the following reasons:

- Separate preparation, storage, and cleaning areas for meat and dairy food as well as storage space for separate equipment and utensils.

- Dedicated Passover storage and/or preparation space.

BATHING EQUIPMENT

See Chapters 1 and 14 for descriptions of bathing spaces and their finishes. Although bathing equipment has become

▲ *Many sponsors and their design teams seek to move away from institutional bathing settings by creating spalike settings. Foulkeways at Gwynedd, Gwynedd, Pennsylvania Reese, Lower, Patrick & Scott Ltd. Photograph by Larry Lefever Photography.*

space for the tub; decorative light fixtures, shower curtains, draperies, artwork, or limited use of mosaic tile. Practice includes the use of thick heated towels, choices in beverage, music, or scents, and special or familiar soaps. Additional services might include massage, pedicure, or selected beauty services that occur separately from the facility's barber/beauty parlor. Depending on the lighting levels and bathing products used, the experience could move from relaxing to invigorating. For example, the textures of a back brush, loofah sponge, or differently textured or colored towels affect resident perception of the experience. Equipment might include an electric towel warmer, whirlpool tub, piped-in music, or a device for aromatherapy.

Tubs

Of all environmental features, tubs are likely to be one of the strongest influences on resident and caregiver satisfaction with the activities of personal hygiene. The more familiar the tub and its use in comparison with the resident's memory, the less likely it is to cause agitation. The tubs and bathing equipment typically found in institutional environments is unfamiliar-looking to most residents, and some equipment has often been likened to a space ship.

Frequently cited tub problems include:

- Slow-filling tubs chill residents.
- Complex controls make operation or control of spray strength or temperature difficult.
- Unfamiliar, oversize, institutional equipment upsets many residents, as does noisy equipment and the sound of high water pressure flowing through pipes.

easier to use and more familiar looking, the floor-plan configurations and care practices typically found in traditional long-term care settings have tended to focus on hygiene rather than on life-enhancing experiences. Depending upon individual preferences and customs, the bathing experience may be about a calming retreat at the end of the day, a vigorous shower after exercise, or a romantic occasion; not simply a scheduled cleansing service. In addition, an individual's lifelong preference may be a shower over a bath or vice versa, making a mandatory experience elsewhere uncomfortable and unfamiliar.

One model of bathing is that of the spa. Environmental applications include recessing a therapeutic whirlpool tub into an archway or creating a defined

- Lifts, transfer devices, and moving tubs can be a source of anxiety and disorientation.

Like furniture or clothing, there doesn't appear to be one tub that fits all, and it is recommended that facilities provide more than one type of tub, if feasible. However, the following are features found to be desirable:

- Nonslip floors and temperature-control systems that prevent scalding are important.

- Tubs for assisted living residents or those in early and midstage dementia should allow for independent entry and for bathing in the sitting position, while tubs for long-term care residents or those with advanced dementia need to accommodate a sitting or reclining position, providing ready access for the caregiver to all body areas.

- Some models offer a feature with jets of warm air for resident comfort while the tub fills. Many residents perceive the movement of air as a cold draft. An integrally heated sitting surface, similar to heated seats in luxury cars, might be a solution to mitigate the problems potentially created by moving air.

- Some models now provide a water reservoir that can deliver warm water gradually once the resident has been seated.

Showers

Showers seem to be preferred over tubs by many residents and staff, but this may be due in part to a lack of satisfaction with bathing equipment.

Frequently cited shower problems include:

- Slipping is a common hazard in shower areas.

▲ New tubs such as this one with a pull-up side and a built-in seat facilitate entry and exit for the frail elderly. Courtesy of Arjo Inc.

- Negotiation of a shower threshold can be difficult; residents of one facility had difficulty negotiating a 3" curb, so they began to resort to extending the handheld shower wand into the bathroom area with a floor drain, where they could shower more easily.

- Integrally molded seats and fold-down seats are not recommended, unless required by federal or local codes, as these seats are often small, sometimes difficult to fold up and down, are far from controls, and make it difficult for staff to assist in reaching all parts of the body.

Desirable features include:

- An adjustable handheld shower nozzle improves cleansing flexibility, avoids a

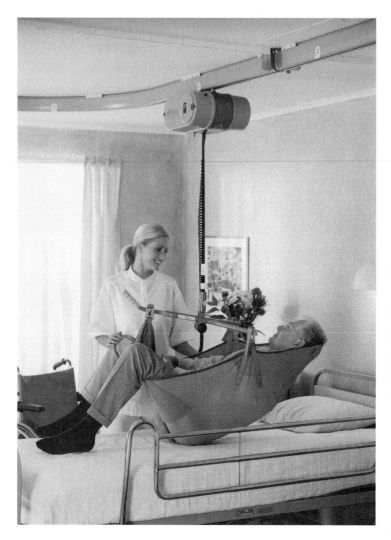

▲ For residents who are completely immobile, ceiling-mounted lifts are used increasingly in acute-care services. Courtesy of Arjo Inc.

- A freestanding plastic shower chair is an inexpensive option that adds flexibility and can be safer than an integral seat.

- ANSI standards, upon which most accessibility codes are based, designate clear inside dimensions of 36" × 36" for a transfer-type shower stall and 30" × 60" for a roll-in type shower stall. Experience suggests that to comfortably assist a resident, shower depth of at least 36" and a width of at least 48" are desirable.

Features important to both tubs and showers include adequate space for toiletries, robes, and clothing adjacent to the fixtures. This helps to shorten the time the resident must wait to dry off or cover up just after bathing, as well as supporting resident independence and privacy during the process. A shelf within the bathing enclosure should be large enough to hold several bottles and soaps, with a continuous surface rather than open slats, so that contents remain stable.

Showers and baths are not the only means of attending to resident hygiene. Cleansing with a washcloth is sometimes the only option for residents who are unable or unwilling to sit in a tub.

EMPLOYEE LEARNING AND TRAINING

Facilities should provide a comprehensive employee educational and wellness program. Internet and online programs can provide continuing education and training.

Equipment should be well-designed, functional, and staff-friendly. Equipment that is easy to use and maintain will be used more safely and effectively, increasing staff efficiency and reducing the incidence of injury to staff and residents.

harsh or noisy shower spray, and supports resident autonomy.

- Although a raised threshold does not always meet accessibility requirements, the threshold can help to maintain water within the shower area. Shower thresholds that collapse when stepped upon or rolled upon with a wheelchair are a newer means for providing accessibility and for containing water within the shower.

THE FUTURE

Technology is also beginning to address a number of other key issues in design for aging. As discussed in Chapter 9, computers tied to telecommunications are providing vital-signs monitoring and medication-reminder services. New mobility aids are being developed, and robots are being tested to perform routine support tasks. The Robotics Institute at Carnegie Mellon's School of Computer Science is an example of a center that has already begun to study the use of robots in senior care settings.

All experts in the field anticipate the expansion of technological innovation.

◀ *The Massachusetts Institute of Technology is developing a "smart walker," which can potentially be programmed to respond to the needs and habits of a specific resident. Courtesy of Professor Dubowsky and the MIT Field and Space Robotics Laboratory. Photograph by Matthew Spenko*

CHAPTER 11
MATERIALS AND PRODUCTS

INTRODUCTION
In selecting materials and products for senior housing, special care must be taken to create surroundings that will be comfortable for residents, minimize barriers for the aging, allow for unobtrusive maintenance, and facilitate efficient operations.

MATERIAL SELECTION CRITERIA AND CHOICES
Most senior housing and care facilities are very budget sensitive, as entry fees and monthly fees are high and competitive among facilities. As capital costs often represent at least 30 percent of a facility's operating budget, it is important that materials incorporated into the building be selected with care. First cost and life-cycle cost are both important.

Foundations
See Chapter 7.

Superstructure
See Chapter 7.

Roofing
Sloped roofs are often selected for senior housing and care facilities, for residential character and image in addition to excellent watershedding characteristics. To keep costs down as well as to avoid potential leaks, complex pitches and excessive dormers and penetrations should be avoided. Common surfacing materials for sloped roofs on senior housing and care facilities include all of the typical choices found in residential buildings: asphalt and fiberglass shingles, wood shingles,

metal roofing, clay and concrete tiles, single-ply membrane, and built-up roofs.

When flat roofs are used in the building design, they can be surfaced with a number of materials.

- Single-ply membranes, which are the most popular on flat roof surfaces (typically EPDM, synthetic rubber), are joined by modified bitumen and thermoplastic membranes.
- Built-up roofs consist of roofing applied in overlapping layers or plies, generally utilizing an asphalt-based embedding material between coats.

Exterior Envelope
Options for exterior wall finishes also include the full range of materials commonly used in residential construction: shingles, siding, stucco, masonry and so on. Building-code restrictions, however, mandate that many facilities use noncombustible materials, such as cementitious boards for siding.

Windows and Curtain Walls
By building code, most sleeping and other habitable rooms require operable windows. Most facilities use the typical residential choices—casement, double- or single-hung, slider, awning, or hopper windows—in part to break down the building scale and for a more residential appearance. Low first cost and maintenance requirements often lead to the selection of windows made of wood, aluminum- or vinyl-clad wood, or vinyl or aluminum with a long-life finish. The selection should also accommodate the

requirement for ease of use by residents. Few have sufficient arm strength to open heavy double-hung or slider windows, and casements with small opening mechanisms may be hard for an arthritic hand to use.

INTERIOR MATERIALS

When considering interior product selection, the following are important:

- Durability and appropriateness for specific use: For example, while some residential products can be used, most often commercial-grade products, with a residential appearance, are most appropriate for senior living environments.

- Maintenance: Most products provide specific maintenance guides, which need to be followed to assure longevity of material.

- Life-cycle costs: Initial cost, maintenance cost, and operating cost over the useful life of the material.

- Appropriateness for a senior population: See Chapter 14.

Flooring

Soft finishes and carpets

Usually, the first interior product addressed when designing the interior of a senior housing facility is flooring. Due to market competition and the desire to create a hospitable residential environment, carpet is being used more frequently in all living settings for seniors. This is primarily because of recent developments in carpet construction, including advances in fiber type with soil repellant treatment, very effective antimicrobial treatments, and improved backing systems. These backing systems increase the tuft bind rating of loop carpet, so that pulling on a single loop does cause the carpet to "zipper" or unravel, as well as providing a moisture barrier against spills and incontinence. Dense loop carpet is ideal for senior living facilities because it provides the best walking surface for the frailer population; it allows sufficient friction to prevent slipping and provides a soft yet firm surface for shuffling feet without impeding the use of wheelchairs or walkers by those with compromised mobility or balance. It is recommended to use a minimum of 4,500 (density) for high-traffic areas, and a loop face weight of 26–32 oz. For further information about matching carpets to specific locations, consult the Carpet and Rug Institute or individual manufacturers.

Carpet considerations

- Carpet construction: Designers must be aware of the types of backings, fibers, types of pile (loop or cut), and weight of the carpet they are going to install, and be sure that they are specifying the appropriate carpet for each space.

- Slab treatment: Carpet with moisture-barrier backing is recommended for senior facilities because of the risk of spills and incontinence. It should be noted, however, that the backing might require special installation and a compatible adhesive. Gypsum sealant products, for example, absorb moisture that is locked between the slab and the waterproof carpet, causing the sealant to degrade and crack. New Gypsum products are being developed to avoid these problems.

- VOC (Volatile Organic Compound-Free) adhesives: Minimize the use of products that produce off-gassing, as frail seniors are particularly susceptible to airborne contaminants, which may cause irritation to eyes and respiratory systems.

- Installation guidelines: If proper installation procedures are not followed, manufacturers' warrantees may be voided. For example, some moisture-barrier carpeting is perforated for easier rolling and shipping, and must be resealed when installed with a special adhesive. Failure to use the appropriate adhesive voids the warranty and renders the moisture barrier ineffectual.

- Cost: Product selection should be tailored to work within the project budget. There are often ways to maintain desired aesthetics even within a limited budget, such as reducing the face weight of carpet, selecting all products from one mill to increase buying power, and understanding mill minimum yardage requirements to provide the client with the advantage of a custom-colored carpet without spending significantly more than you would for a standard color.

- Broadloom versus carpet tile: For some spaces, carpet tile might be worth the extra cost. In others, it is superfluous and broadloom carpet is sufficient or even preferable. Use of carpet tile is an advantage on floors that conceal computer raceways or equipment below, or where incontinence or spilling will require tiles to be removed for cleaning or replacement. Some facilities find that the machines used to clean a heavily soiled carpet in place are too disturbing for seniors, especially those with dementia, and thus carpet tile is

preferable because it can be temporarily replaced and cleaned off-site.

Hard finishes

Although carpet is being increasingly used in senior housing, where environments require frequent cleaning or are in frequent contact with water, hard finishes are still utilized. New products that are easier to maintain, more hygienic, and less institutional in appearance continue to be introduced.

Sheet vinyl/vinylized wood

Resilient flooring materials are ideal for use in wet areas or areas of high maintenance, such as utility and bathing areas. In addition, some sponsors of long-term care facilities, concerned with incontinence and maintenance issues associated with carpeting, prefer resilient flooring in resident rooms and other areas. The disadvantage of these materials is that they require frequent buffing and cleaning by specialized machines that may cause significant disturbance and noise.

Resilient flooring issues

- Glare: Often staff and sponsors view high sheen as signifying cleanliness. However, by definition high-sheen flooring materials produce significant glare and are thus not appropriate for senior housing facilities. Instead, there are low-luster finish products available, which reduce glare and often increase traction to prevent slipping.

- Cost: Cost usually drives the selection of the product. Vinyl composition tile (VCT) has the lowest first cost of the available options. However, VCT requires frequent and serious cleaning and buffing, giving it a high life-cycle cost. Other types of resilient flooring

▲ Transitions between flooring materials, such as this one from vinyl to carpet, should minimize tripping hazards. Sun City Takatsuki, Takatsuki, Japan. Perkins Eastman Architects PC. Photograph by Chuck Choi.

a slip-resistant coefficient (relevant codes include the Static Coefficient of Friction Guidelines of the Americans with Disabilities Act, and the Occupational Safety and Health Administration (OSHA)). Slip-resistant products require more maintenance because their rough surfaces are more susceptible to dirt collection and are more difficult to clean.

- Slab treatment: See above section about moisture-barrier carpet.

- Seaming: Heat and chemical seals may be used for sheet goods, depending upon the product.

- Transitions: Transitions between flooring materials are very important because they help keep the edges of the material in place and prevent the loose edges that can cause tripping. Designers are encouraged to use vinyl transition materials that create a smooth, gradual transition appropriate for wheeled traffic. In addition, it is very important that flooring materials are carefully cut and adhered, and that transitions are properly installed.

- Base materials: In areas where sheet goods are selected due to water use and high maintenance requirements, it is recommended to install a flash-coved base. This base is integral with the floor, avoiding a seam between wall and floor. If a flash-cove base is not used, a resilient base composed of rubber, vinyl, or a combination can be utilized. The recommended minimum is a ⅛" thick base, to avoid telegraphing irregularities in wall surfaces. (See Chapter 14 for discussion of contrast between floor and wall surfaces.) Vinyl base should be selected in continuous rolls, because vinyl shrinks and seamed

can be as much as three times the first cost of VCT, but require less maintenance.

- Pattern/visual perception: See Chapter 14 on interior design.

- Color trends: See Chapter 14 on interior design. Consider color longevity in use of materials and avoid colors that may become dated.

- Slip- and water-resistant options: In wet areas, use flooring materials with

lengths will eventually separate, leaving gaps between pieces. The traditional approach is to use flat resilient base with carpet. However, the irregularities of gypsum board partitions and the difficulty of cutting carpet make it virtually impossible to match the edge of the carpet with the base along its entire length. When using a higher pile carpet, the carpet itself obscures gaps between the carpet edge and base. However, with lower face-weight and tight loop construction, gaps will be obvious, and thus a vinyl cove base should be considered. If a cove base is ruled out for aesthetic reasons, there is another option: a base product that is tapered, giving the look of a flat base while still covering potential irregularities between carpet and wall.

- Maintenance: As mentioned above, VCT requires high maintenance because it is more porous (a result of the high volume of "composition" relative to the volume of vinyl in the product). Products that feature a solid vinyl wear layer are more scratch-resistant, less porous, and require less sealing and buffing. Thus, these products have lower maintenance costs and are ultimately less disruptive to residents.

Stone/wood

Stone and wood are appealing options for senior housing facilities because they help create a residential atmosphere. However, both have their drawbacks, and designers should be careful when specifying these materials. Although stone floors are generally slippery and thus not recommended for senior housing facilities, a sealer can be applied to meet slip-resistant coefficient requirements. However, some stone products can still appear slippery

and inhibit residents from using those spaces. Thus, such materials should be used sparingly and limited to such areas as prominent entries or a fireplace hearth. Wood, though not necessarily slippery, has a high first cost and requires significant maintenance. The inherent flammability of wood may also be a code issue. Because of its thick construction, transitions between wood and other flooring material can be problematic, and may require a slab depression, which adds additional cost. Instead, consider using sheet vinyl goods that provide a wood look, cost less, require less maintenance, and are easier to transition.

Ceramic

In senior housing, ceramic flooring can be used for commercial kitchens, as decorative entry features, or as a mosaic theme in a café or ice-cream parlor. Although it may also be used in bathrooms, many designers are choosing to substitute vinyl flooring because it is more hygienic, provides a softer surface, and is less cold to the touch.

Ceramic flooring considerations

- Grout color and treatment options: Because grout is porous, it readily absorbs urine. To overcome this, use grout with additives to make it less porous. Epoxy grout, though more expensive, is another option. Grout color selected for floor installations should be darker in value, so as to avoid showing soil and traffic patterns.
- Slope and size: In floor areas with drains, be sure to use tiles that can accommodate floor slope. To accommodate the slope in shower stalls, 2" × 2" tile works best, while kitchen floors can accommodate larger tiles due to their more gradual slope.

- Slip resistance and product selection: For entryways and showers, attend to slip-resistance information provided by manufacturers. For example, tile should have a minimum slip-resistance coefficient of friction of 0.06.

- Slab treatment: If ceramic tile is to be used in a shower or wet area, a waterproof membrane should be installed in accordance with the Tile Council of America guidelines.

Wall Coverings

Vinyl wall covering

Vinyl wall covering is relatively resistant to stains and abrasion, and is durable (depending upon the weight). Fabric-backed vinyl (as opposed to paper-backed vinyl and vinyl-coated paper) coverings are recommended for senior housing facilities because they are more durable and stain-resistant, and more stable since the fabric effectively adheres to the hanging surface. The fabric backing increases the abrasive strength as well.

There are three types of vinyl wall covering on the market:

- Type I, or light-duty wall covering (7–13 ounces per square yard) is typically used for residential applications. When the wall covering is located above a chair rail, so that it is not exposed to rubbing by cart or wheelchair traffic, this lighter-weight material can be used.

- Type II, or medium-duty wall covering (13–22 ounces per square yard) is specified primarily for commercial areas. This weight is the most commonly used when there will be high cart traffic or wheelchair use.

- Type III, or heavy-duty wall covering (22+ ounces per square yard) is re-

served for use in high-traffic areas such as public spaces and food-service areas. This material weight is rarely used since its cost is higher. For high-traffic areas, such as a loading or service area, crash rails would be used to protect the walls.

The trend in recent years toward more residential environments has encouraged designers to specify wall coverings in lieu of a solid-colored paint. Wall covering patterns can bring texture and detail to spaces and make them feel more comfortable, especially when used in rooms where one would expect to find wallpaper in a home, such as kitchens, bathrooms, living rooms, and bedrooms.

Because residential-character wall coverings are generally offered only in Type I material, designers often specify these patterns in places that should really receive Type II or III covering. One solution to this problem has been the development of protective acrylic finishes, which help resist staining and contain antimicrobial additives to protect against bacteria, fungi, and molds. There are many such finishes on the market, which differ in terms of how long they resist staining and what solvents or detergents may be used to clean them.

Vinyl wall covering considerations

- Environmental issues: Despite their wide use in senior housing and care facilities, environmental impact is a concern. Vinyl (or PVC) production produces potentially dangerous inhalants. There are also problems with disposal. Chemicals may leach into landfills after disposal, polluting nearby water sources. If it is incinerated (or catches fire unintentionally), chemicals are released that pose a risk to firefighters and incineration-plant workers. Though PVC is recyclable, very little of what is produced actually gets recycled. Manufacturers of vinyl wall covering are beginning to explore more environmentally friendly means of creating the product. The durability and affordability of vinyl continue to make it a top choice for most projects. (See Chapter 6 for more information about sustainable design.)

- Proper wall prep for future removal: It is imperative that walls be properly prepared to receive vinyl wall covering. With such preparation it can be easily removed for future renovation; improper installation makes removal difficult. For information about locating qualified wallcovering installers, consult the National Guild of Paperhangers (NGPP) or the Better Business Bureau (for general contractors).

- Maintenance: Vinyl is often chosen specifically because it is easy to clean and requires little maintenance. Because different coverings and finishes are compatible with different cleaning products, it is important to consult the manufacturers' cleaning suggestions.

- Cost: Prices range dramatically. Cost per square yard might be as little as $7 or as much as $35 depending on quality of pattern and weight. Some manufacturers offer protective coatings free of charge. Vinyl can be a very effective and low-maintenance option if evaluated on a life-cycle cost basis.

- Color trends: Although colored and patterned vinyls are increasingly popular with senior housing designers, be wary of trendy colors or patterns, which may become quickly dated.

- Customized vinyl wall covering: This includes custom-designed patterns or colors. Due to the large quantities required by most manufacturers, this is rarely an option, unless, for example, the pattern is used throughout all corridors.

Paint

Paint continues to be a popular wall finish for senior housing and care facilities. Like vinyl, paint can be durable and low-maintenance, but it is important to use the appropriate type of paint for the correct area. For example, the wrong paint used in bathing and shower rooms or kitchens can lead to cracking, flaking, chipping, and fading because of the high levels of heat, humidity, expansion, and contraction of surfaces.

Paint is made up of three basic ingredients that influence its performance:

- Binder: suspended particles that give paint its ability to form a finishing film; affects durability, adhesion, and color retention

- Pigment: suspended particles that give paint color and body

- Solvent: the liquid component in which the other two components are suspended; makes paint spreadable

As a general rule, the higher the proportion of solid components, the more expensive the paint, because of superior durability and color retention.

Paint considerations

- Environmental concerns: It must be VOC free.

- Color: It is desireable to have a value difference in relationship to flooring.

- Types and proper location: The choice

of paint finishes is dependent on application. As noted above, the conditions in bathrooms mandate a more washable paint surface. However, the benefits of increased durability and stain resistance offered by higher-gloss paints are balanced by the increased glare, which can be hard on aging eyes. Thus, eggshell finishes are often recommended for most walls in senior housing.

- Latex vs. Alkyd: There are two types of wall-covering paint: latex (water-based) and alkyd (oil-based). Latex paint, because of its vinyl acrylic binders, is more durable. It also dries faster, is easier to clean (requires no special cleaning products), is smoother, and is easier to apply.

- Surface preparation: Although paints differ in quality, an improperly prepared surface can shorten the life of even the most expensive and highest-quality paints. The surface to be painted should be smooth, clean, dry, and stain- and mildew-free. Primer should be used to render the wall surfaces consistent.

- Colors: See Chapter 14.

Fabric wall covering

The use of fabric wall covering is usually limited, due to budget constraints, maintenance issues, seaming difficulty, and time needed for wall preparation. As noted under durability and maintenance, if the process of cleaning the special wall covering is too complicated, it will very often not be maintained. Olefin, a fabric with a durable fiber, first introduced in the late 1980s, was difficult to clean. Today's fabrics have soil-repellant treatment, but their use is still limited.

The inherent acoustic property of fabric is a positive aspect of the material. Fabric can be wrapped and glued to rigid panels and hung with Z-clips to improve the acoustic characteristics of a space. Another method, though higher in cost, is to stretch the fabric over soft or rigid acoustic material on a track system that permits easy replacement. The recommended fabric is one such as polyester, which does not absorb moisture and therefore will not sag over time.

Ceramic tile

Ceramic tile provides a washable surface; however, the somewhat porous grout joints can be a maintenance problem and have a tendency to absorb liquids and odors. It is recommended that grout be sealed around toilets and urinals. The use of larger-size tiles helps to reduce the amount of grout. In lieu of ceramic tile floors in bathing and toilet areas, seamless sheet vinyl flooring with an integral cove base is a common alternative.

Ceramic wall tile considerations

- Pattern: benefits for balance and defining horizontal and vertical planes
- Cost and size
- Transitions with other materials

Wood trim

The use of wood in senior housing facilities supports a residential atmosphere. Wood can be used for standing and running trim, such as moldings, baseboards handrails, and window trim, as paneling, or for cabinetry and millwork.

Wood considerations

- Cost: Wood is generally a higher-cost

option for wall covering, though its cost varies greatly depending on regional availability, species, grade, and the way in which it is cut and joined. Standard profiles in standing and running trim are less expensive than custom cuts.

- Finishes: painting, staining, and varnish techniques
- Flammability

Wall Protection

As a final note on wall materials, corner guards and rub/crash rails are important details in some areas. They are installed to protect against damage by carts and delivery in service areas and to protect against damage from wheelchairs in resident areas.

Corner guards come in several materials appropriate to each use:

- Clear Lexan
- PVC bumper: PVC bumpers are sheet goods. Their mounting height should be based on the use of the carts or equipment, but generally corners will be protected with a height of 12–18" from finished floor.
- Steel: Steel protection devices are typi-

cally most appropriate in areas where there is significant cart traffic or where residents' wheelchairs cause frequent damage. For example, resident doors typically have a plate or steel material to protect them from damage caused by wheelchair foot-rests.

Windows and Window Coverings

Daylight contributes to the quality of spaces and to the general connection to the outdoors. Window treatments are an important part of controlling glare and amount of light. In addition, decorative window treatments can change the feel of a room. Depending on the desired result, they may help to create a residential or hospitality environment. (For further information about this topic, refer to Chapter 14.)

REGIONAL ISSUES

In addition to the installation, maintenance, and durability of materials as discussed above, designers should keep in mind that the selection of each material can reflect the region in which the building is located, further supporting the image of a familiar, residential environment.

GERIATRIC HEALTH CLINIC

*Donald W. Reynolds Center on Aging,
University of Arkansas, Little Rock, Arkansas.
Perkins Eastman Architects PC with Polk
Stanley Yeary Architects, Ltd.
Photograph by Timothy Hursley.*

◀▲ *Copper Ridge, Sykesville, Maryland. Perkins Eastman Architects PC. Photograph by Curtis Martin.*

▶ *Woodside Place Alzheimer's Residence, Oakmont, Pennsylvania. Perkins Eastman Architects. Photograph by Robert Ruschak.*

▶ *Meadows Mennonite, Chenoa, Illinois. OWP&P. Photograph by Hedrich Blessing.*

▼ *Waveny Care Center, New Canaan, Connecticut. Reese, Lower, Patrick & Scott Ltd. Photograph by Larry Lefever Photography.*

SKILLED NURSING FACILITIES

▲ Miami Jewish Home & Hospital for the Aged, Florida. Perkins Eastman Architects PC.

◀ Jewish Home & Hospital–Bronx Campus, Bronx, New York. Perkins Eastman Architects PC. Photograph by Chuck Choi.

▼ Teresian House, Albany, New York. The Architectural Team Inc. Photograph by Stephen Sette-Ducati.

◀ *Joseph L. Morse Geriatric Center, West Palm Beach, Florida. Perkins Eastman Architects PC.*

▼▼ *Weinberg Village, Pittsburgh, Pennsylvania. Perkins Eastman Architects PC. Photograph by Jim Schafer.*

▼ *Montefiore Home, Beachwood, Ohio. Perkins Eastman Architects PC.*

ASSISTED LIVING FACILITIES

▶ *Sunrise of Bellevue, Bellevue, Washington. Mithun Inc. Photograph by Robert Pisano.*

▼ *The Laurels, Wellsboro, Pennsylvania. Wallace Roberts & Todd LLC. Photograph by John Reis*

ASSISTED LIVING FACILITIES

◄ *Weinberg Terrace, Squirrel Hill, Pennsylvania. Perkins Eastman Architects PC and Urban Design Associates.*

▲ *Job Haines Home Expansion, Bloomfield, New Jersey. Wallace Roberts & Todd LLC. Photograph by Jon Reis Photography.*

◄ *Seabrook Village, Tinton Falls, New Jersey. Wallace Roberts & Todd LLC.*

◀ ▼ *Gurwin Jewish Geriatric Center, Commack, New York. Perkins Eastman Architects PC. Photography by Chuck Choi.*

▲ ▶ *Masonic Village, Sewickley, Pennsylvania. Perkins Eastman Architects PC. Photography by Edward Massery.*

CONTINUING CARE RETIREMENT COMMUNITIES

Sun City Takatsuki, Takatsuki, Japan. Perkins Eastman Architects PC. Photograph by Chuck Choi.

Sun City Takatsuki, Takatsuki, Japan. Perkins Eastman Architects PC. Photograph by Chuck Choi.

▲ *River Woods at Exeter, Exeter, New Hampshire. EGA Architects PC. Photograph by Assassi Productions.*

◀ *The Summit at First Hill, Seattle, Washington. Mithun, Inc. Photograph by Lara Swimmer Photography.*

▶ *La Posada at Park Centre, Tuscon, Arizona. EGA Architects PC. Photograph by Assassi Productions.*

▼ *Mountain Meadows, Ashland, Oregon. Mithun, Inc. Photograph by Robert Pisano.*

▼ Buckingham's Choice, Adamstown, Maryland. Perkins Eastman Architects PC.

▲ ▼ Glenmeadow Retirement Community, Longmeadow, Massachusetts. Perkins Eastman Architects PC.

▲ *Villages at Collington, Mitchellville, Maryland. Perkins Eastman Architects, PC. Photograph by Edward Massery.*

◄ *The Osborn, Rye, New York. Perkins Eastman Architects PC. Photograph by David Lamb.*

▼ *Mary's Woods at Marylhurst, Lake Oswego, Oregon. Mithun Inc. Photograph by Eckert & Eckert.*

▲ *Hunterbrook at Fieldhome,*
Yorktown Heights, New York.
Perkins Eastman Architects PC.
Photograph by Chuck Choi.

CHAPTER 12
ACOUSTIC CONTROL

INTRODUCTION

As discussed in Chapter 1, hearing loss is an important factor in the aging process. The National Institute on Aging reported that "about one-third of Americans between age 65 and 74, and one-half of those age 85 and older have hearing problems." Poor acoustical design in a senior living facility can make it difficult for residents to hear and be heard, and may cause them social discomfort, contributing to fear, embarrassment, depression, or isolation. Even those with hearing aids are affected by background noise. Although new developments in hearing-assistance technology have helped to minimize this problem, some older hearing aid models still may amplify background noises along with messages, making it difficult for hearing-assisted individuals to distinguish the message addressed to them. It is therefore vital that senior living spaces be designed to deal with the way sound will travel in interior spaces to accommodate hard-of-hearing and hearing-assisted residents.

Acoustical design of a space involves the attenuation of unwanted and disturbing sounds, and the enhancement of desired sounds to the point where they can be heard properly. Some factors—for example, a rise in exterior noise levels due to a change in nearby noise sources—are beyond the control of the design professional. Architects and other design professionals practice simple acoustical design procedures in specifying floor, wall, and ceiling finishes in most areas of the facility. For the more demanding design and engineering of multipurpose, dining, or other large high-occupancy spaces, or for the analysis of exterior mechanical equipment to meet the code requirements for noise reduction, it is often recommended that an acoustician be retained. Several software programs model the acoustical performance of spaces before they are built. In addition, criteria for the acoustical design of spaces are widely available in textbooks and technical publications such as *Architectural Acoustics,* by M. David Egan.

COMMON ACOUSTICAL CONSIDERATIONS

Key acoustical considerations include:

- Excessive noise levels
- Transmission of noise from one space to another
- Privacy of individual spaces
- Intelligibility of speech against background noise

Three issues shape how effectively an individual can hear and understand in a given space. These are distance from the source of the sound, the level of background noise, and the effects of reverberation. Designers can improve signal-to-noise ratio and thus increase speech intelligibility by controlling background noise levels and reverberation time.

Background noise from HVAC systems, conversations, telephones, paging devices, kitchen equipment, and many other sources interferes with effective listening because it competes with the spoken message. Louder speech signals are required to overcome high background noise values across the frequencies of

Definitions

- **Sound absorption:** The process of removing sound energy, or the ability of materials, objects, and structures (e.g., a room) to absorb energy.

- **Reverberation:** The persistence of sound after the cause of sound has stopped, or the ear's reaction to echoes in an enclosed space, giving an impression of "liveness" or "deadness."

- **Noise criteria (NC) curves:** A set of spectral curves used to obtain a single number rating describing the "noisiness" of environments for a variety of uses, and generally used to describe the maximum allowable continuous background noise. NC curves plot sound levels across the frequencies between 63 and 8,000 Hz, the speech perception range.

- **Room criteria (RC) curves:** Developed to measure background noise from HVAC systems. RC curves are adjusted at very low and very high frequencies to avoid annoying mechanical sounds.

- **Noise reduction (NR):** Either the reduction in sound-pressure level caused by making some alteration to a sound source, or the difference in sound-pressure level between two adjacent rooms caused by the transmission loss of the intervening wall (in other words, the difference in background sound level between a source on one side of a wall and a receiver on the other).

- **Noise reduction coefficient (NRC):** A single-number rating of the sound absorption of a material equal to the arithmetic mean of the sound-absorption coefficients in the 250, 500, 1,000, and 2,000 Hz octave frequency bands rounded to the nearest multiple of 0.05.

- **Sound transmission loss (STL):** The decrease or attenuation in sound energy of airborne sound as it passes through a building construction. Generally, STL increases with frequency.

- **Sound transmission class (STC):** A single-number wall or other assembly rating describing the sound-insulating properties in the 100–4,000 Hz range, mainly to assess speech transmission through a structure.

Definitions are taken from: William J. McGuinness, Benjamin Stein, and John S. Reynolds Mechanical and Electrical Equipment for Buildings (New York: John Wiley and Sons, 1980); Charles M. Salter, Acoustics: Architecture, Engineering, the Environment (San Francisco: William Stout Publishers, 1998); Federal Register 36 CFR Chapter XI, "Architectural and Transportation Barriers Compliance Board: Petition for Rulemaking; Request for Information on Acoustics."

speech (500–2000 Hz). Background noise (or ambient noise) design criteria are typically expressed as a range between two noise criteria (NC) curves, which plot sound levels across eight standard frequencies. A sound meter can be used to test sound levels at these frequencies in existing spaces. The NC rating for a room is typically between 5 and 10 points below the dBA reading. Design engineers can specify HVAC equipment with low noise ratings and limit sound generated by system operation in a variety of ways. Rooms and space can be protected from unwanted exterior sound by mass, insulation, and isolation in wall and slab construction, and by minimizing (or sound-protecting) openings.

Reverberation—reflected sound that persists within a room or space—also masks the sound of the spoken message and increases background sound levels. Reverberation is expressed in seconds (the time it takes for the sound to decay) and can be controlled by a manipulation of the absorbency surfaces within a space and the proportions and volume of the space. When reverberation time and background noise are controlled, speech effort and sound levels decline, leading to a reduction in room noise.

Noise Reduction Coefficients (NRC)

An NRC rating is a single number indicating the effectiveness of a material in absorbing sound. With a range from 1.00 to .00, an NRC of .99 would indicate almost total absorption; .01 virtually none. The higher the NRC of a particular material, the more effectively it will absorb sound.

Sound Transmission Class (STC) Values

The STC rating of a particular assembly (such as a wall, partition, or screen) is a single number that indicates effectiveness in preventing sound transmission. The higher the STC value, the more effectively the assembly blocks sound transmission.

NOISE REDUCTION COEFFICIENTS (NRC)	
Material	NRC
Bare concrete floor	.05
Tile or linoleum on concrete	.05
Carpet (1/8 " pile)	.15
Carpet (1/4" pile)	.25
Carpet (7/16" plie)	.40
Plaster ceiling	.45
Metal pan acoustic ceiling	.60
Partition system surfaces	.55–.80 (.60 typical)
Carpet over padding	Up to .65
Acoustic ceiling system	Up to .99
Source: Pile 1988, p.484	

SOUND TRANSMISSION CLASS (STC) VALUES	
Material	STC
3/16" plywood	19
Open-plan funiture screen planel (typical)	21
1/4" plexiglas sheet	27
5/8" gypsum wallboard	27
22-gauge steel plate	29
Wood 2"× 4" stud partition	35–39
Staggered stud partition	45
6" concrete block wall	46
Steel-stud partition with two layers of wallboard on each side	55

DESIGN GUIDES AND RECOMMENDATIONS FOR SPECIALIZED SPACES

Dining Areas

Among the largest areas in most residential senior settings, dining spaces produce fairly high noise levels, often making it difficult for hard-of-hearing seniors to converse. Think how difficult it is to hear and be heard in a restaurant with all hard surfaces. By the end of the meal the excess noise can be agitating. Hard surfaces such as tile floors, plaster walls or ceilings, and glass and metal surfaces not only reflect noise, they can also generate noise as feet and chairs scrape on floors or dishes rattle on tabletops.

One solution discussed in Chapter 1 is the creation of smaller dining rooms within the larger eating area. Such smaller spaces allow some separation from background noise without completely isolating those within. The best way to limit excessive ambient noise is to select sound-absorbing materials for walls, floors, ceilings, and even furniture and window treatments. Soft absorbent materials such as carpet, fabric upholstery, and drapery; linens on tabletops; absorbant wall surfaces; and acoustical ceiling tile can help attenuate unwanted noise.

Carpeted floors are now more widely used in dining rooms, even in skilled nursing. If spills are frequent, then carpet tile or a more resilient surface may be required. If one uses hardwood or tile floors, the minimum NRC should be 0.8, and the design team should consider the use of wall hangings or some other absorbent surface to improve the acoustics.

Finally, eating areas should be separated from kitchens and serving areas, and when adjacent to one another, sound-absorbing material or appropriate construction may be used to isolate noise.

Multipurpose Spaces and Auditoriums

Senior housing facilities often incorporate a multipurpose performance space such as an auditorium or a religious sanctuary. The spectrum of sound in these spaces runs from speech at one end to music at the other. Installation of variable acoustics is very expensive and thus impractical for most senior housing. Instead, auditoriums should be designed to the middle of the spectrum with a reverberation time between the optimal times for speech and music. Various factors, including the volume of the room, affect the reverberation time. Elimination of extraneous noise and careful design of the mechanical system serving the space should be important factors in the design.

Once the reverberation time of a room has been established, acoustic materials can be placed in such a way that

▼ *Carpeting and other sound-absorbing materials are important factors in creating a comfortable dining room. Buckingham's Choice, Adamstown, Maryland. Perkins Eastman Architects PC. Photograph by Chuck Choi.*

they achieve the desired reverberation time while providing sufficient reflecting surfaces to project sound and absorbing surfaces to prevent sound reflections.

Sound systems, microphones, loudspeakers, and control locations are required in almost all such spaces in senior environments and should be part of the design of the space from the start.

Bathing Areas and other Hard-Surfaced Spaces

Bathing areas by their nature have surfaces that reflect noise created by running water. One suggestion is to limit the use of ceramic wall tile and use resilient flooring in lieu of ceramic floor tile. Limited use of acoustic ceiling tile designed for high humidity above tub areas can be an additional means of reducing reverberation. This is especially important for residences specializing in the care of persons with Alzheimer's and related dementias.

In addition to surface finshes, there are tubs and whirlpool baths designed especially to reduce noise. Avoid the use of polyvinyl chloride (PVC) pipes and plumbing fittings that create noise when water runs through them (in many cases, the use of PVC piping for interior applications is not code-compliant).

Mechanical and Electrical Systems and Mechanical Rooms

Mechanical rooms adjacent to acoustically sensitive rooms need a minimum structural density in the floor slab so that the slab may act as a barrier to airborne sound and also provide sufficient rigidity to act as a stable platform for operating equipment. If the foundation is not sound, it has a tendency to resonate, and the mountings for equipment will be less effective than specified.

Air-handling systems serving multipurpose spaces require special design, with low-pressure fans, slower-than-average air velocities (less than 1,000 ft per minute), and grilles and diffusers sized at maximum NC20, based on design air quantities.

Noise-producing mechanical rooms should not be placed near residential areas that require quiet. The volume of air circulating in a space can produce noise. Insulation around ducts can be used to help reduce noise levels. In addition, use of insulation and staggering construction of solid walls may help to keep noise levels at a minimum.

Since the human voice lies midrange in the spectrum, drywall construction is preferable to masonry for speech privacy, because it attenuates higher-frequency sounds more effectively. With proper design, almost anything can be programmed over a mechanical space without designing an expensive acoustically isolated structure. However, whenever practicable, it is advisable to avoid direct adjacencies.

▲ *The acoustical characteristics of multipurpose spaces are complicated, because they often have to serve a wide variety of uses, including lectures, musical performances, and religious services. Montefiore Home, Beachwood, Ohio. Perkins Eastman Architects PC. Photograph by Robert Ruschak.*

▲ The hard surfaces of most indoor pools present special acoustical challenges. The Architectural Team Inc. Photograph by Nick Wheeler.

HEARING-IMPAIRMENT GUIDELINES AND CODE REQUIREMENTS

Under the Americans with Disabilities Act (ADA), the Departments of Justice and Transportation are responsible for issuing regulations to implement accessibility standards for newly constructed and altered facilities. These standards must be consistent with the accessibility guidelines issued by the access board. The Department of Justice and the Department of Transportation regulations currently include ADAAG 1-10.

Rules governing the transmission and receipt of acoustic testing are developed and maintained by several private-sector organizations. The acoustical performance of equipment installed in buildings and other facilities is regulated by the American Society of Heating, Refrigeration, and Air-Conditioning Engineers (ASHRAE). The American National Standards Institute (ANSI), in conjunction with the Acoustical Society of America (ASA), has established several protocols for the measurement of room sound levels, including ANSI S12.2 Criteria for Room Noise Measurement. Foreign and international standards also exist. Model codes contain both standards and requirements for sound-rated construction components in multifamily housing and other occupancy types. The developers and operators of medical and housing facilities typically set similar acoustical standards for sound transmission through floors, walls, structure, and HVAC systems.

In addition to mechanical equipment and devices, electrical equipment, such as telephones, paging systems, and office equipment can also generate noise. Wireless communications systems are becoming more prevalent, and their use reduces environmental noise considerably, as well as creating a less institutional setting.

CHAPTER 13

LIGHTING DESIGN

INTRODUCTION

Lighting design can enhance the independence of older residents. Lighting must be responsive to the biological aging process described in Chapter 1. Impaired visual perception can be worsened by improper lighting design, creating hazardous conditions that impede mobility and affect equilibrium. A proper light level can make a space come to life. It helps with color recognition, makes food look more appetizing, and encourages contact by allowing residents to recognize people and see spaces more clearly, making finding one's direction easier.

There is a difference between quantity and quality of illumination. Lighting that is too bright can be as inappropriate as lighting that is too dim. Seniors with cataracts have great difficulty seeing in overly bright spaces. It is vital that the source of light not produce glare; bare bulbs should not be visible and bright spots should not be created. Fluorescent lighting is the lamping of choice. Newer technology offers full-spectrum triphospher lamps, available in many types. The T8 replaces the old workhorse T12; and the newer, sleeker T5 and compact fluorescent double, triple, and quadruple tube offer alternatives. These newer lamps can provide a Color Rendition Index (CRI) of over 80, enabling residents to recognize color more reliably. The designer can be sensitive to energy conservation by selecting higher-wattage fluorescent lamps, as discussed in Chapter 6.

The integration of decorative fixtures not only helps residents find their way, it also adds to the sought-after residential feeling, particularly in long-term care settings. Avoid the shadeless fixtures that use clear candelabra bulbs that create glare. Decorative wall sconces can be used as accent lights but not as the primary source for ambient lighting, since they do not produce sufficient footcandle levels. These fixtures typically produce readings of 5 footcandles (fc) in corridor applications when the recommended minimum level is 20 fc and the ideal is 30. Many times, budget constraints force a reduction in quality of the lighting package. It is important that the designer focus on limiting the cost of the fixture yet not compromise lighting levels as a cost-saving measure. It is better to eliminate wall covering than reduce the quality of lighting when project budgets are being reduced.

LIGHT LEVELS, LIGHT REFLECTANCE VALUES, AND GLARE

Codes for specific facility types as well as recommendations published by such groups as the Illuminating Engineering Society of North America should be considered minimums for the older eye. Light levels need to be increased to compensate for the loss of sight and visual acuity that occurs during the aging process. As previously noted, the footcandle goal for corridors should be a minimum of 20, but the level preferred by residents is generally at least 30 fc. Indirect lighting systems that produce less glare, fewer shadows, and lower footcandle levels will provide adequate illumination for most spaces. When designing

MINIMUM ILLUMINATION LEVELS		
Area	**Ambient Light (fc)**	**Task Light (fc)**
Administrative (active)	30	50
Activity areas (day only)	30	50
Visitor waiting (day)	30	
Visitor waiting (night)	10	
Barber/beautician (day)	50	
Chapel or quiet area (active)	30	
Hallways (active hrs)	30	
Hallways (sleeping hrs)	10	
Dining (active hrs)	50	
Exterior entrance (night)	10	
Interior entry (day)	100	
Interior entry (night)	10	
Exit stairway & landings	30	
Elevator	30	
	30	
Medicine prep	30	100
Nurses station (day)	10	50
Nurses station (night)	30	50
Physical therapy area (active hrs)	30	50
Occupational therapy (active hrs)	30	50
Examination room (dedicated)	30	100
Janitor's closet	30	50
Laundry (active hrs)	30	
Clean/soiled utility	30	
Commercial kitchen	50	100
Food storage (nonrefrig)	30	
Staff toilet area	20	60
Resident room	30	75
Wardrobe	30	
Bathroom entry	30	
Bathroom entry	30	
Makeup/shaving area	30	60
Shower/bathing rooms	30	

Utilization of daylight is encouraged in entryways to provide a transition between outside and interior illumination levels.

Ambient light levels are minimum averages measured at 30" above the floor in a horizontal plane. Task-lighting levels are absolute minimums taken on the visual task. For makeup/shaving the measurement is to be taken on the face in a vertical position.

Lamp color: The lamp shall have a color rendering index (CRI) of 80 or higher. Exam-room lighting shall be 90 CRI or higher.

It should be understood that the values listed are minimums. The optimum solution for task-lighting is to give the user control over the intensity and positioning of the light source to meet his or her individual needs.

Source: Iluminating Engineering Society of North America. From RP-28-96 Recommended Practice for Lighting and the Visual Environment for Senior Living.

light levels, consider the light-reflectance values of the finishes in the room: carpet absorbs more light than resilient flooring; walls and ceilings reflect or absorb light depending on their color. When using indirect lighting, it is important that the ceiling finish be flat white to produce the most efficient light output.

ELECTRIC LIGHTING SYSTEMS
When considering light fixtures during the design process, there are typical spaces that drive the package, including the following:

- Common spaces
- Corridors
- Resident units
- Service areas

Lighting issues for each of these are described below.

The ability to utilize fixtures is based upon price, ceiling height, mechanical ductwork layout, and accessibility requirements—for example, wall sconces mounted under 6'–8' above the floor may not protrude farther than 4" along a corridor or path of egress.

WINDOWS AND DAYLIGHTING
The key to good lighting design is the even distribution of light and the provision of similar light levels from one space to the next. A brightly lit area adjacent to a dimmer area will make the two areas appear darker and lighter than if they were separated. The aging process slows down the eyes' ability to adjust to drastic changes in light levels. The integration of balanced lighting design and natural daylight is important to the health and well-being of the resident. When a naturally lit space during the day is adjacent to a

windowless area, two levels of lighting design are required; one for daylight hours and a lower footcandle level for nighttime—similar to the lighting at the entry of tunnels designed to ease the transition period between very bright sunshine and the darker tunnel. Window coverings are an essential part of controlling light levels and glare.

DESIGN GUIDES AND RECOMMENDATIONS FOR SPECIALIZED SPACES

General Guidelines

The following points are essential to the design of a successful lighting system for any senior space:

- Energy-sensitive design, as noted in Chapter 6

- Even distribution of light levels on the floor surface so as not to create visual barriers of dark and light spots

- Nonglare light sources

- Appropriate light levels for the aging eye—footcandle levels 15–20 percent higher than for younger adults

- Consistent light levels from one area to the next to accommodate the slower adjustment of the older eye to high contrast

- Provision of transition areas to give the eye time to adjust to spaces with different levels of light

Commons

Consider these points:

- It is important to integrate natural and artificial light sources so that the proper footcandle levels are achieved.

- Design should permit a variety of

▲ The use of natural materials and artificial light in areas such as this entry lobby should provide a smooth transition for the aging resident's reduced ability to adjust to changing light levels. Copper Ridge, Sykesville, Maryland. Perkins Eastman Architects PC. Photograph by Curtis Martin.

light levels and flexibility, particularly in the large multipurpose areas. This can be accomplished by using several light sources, such as cove, decorative, and downlighting. Dual switching and dimming capabilities are available for fluorescent light sources, and it is often advisable to mix incandescent lighting in decorative fixtures with more energy-efficient fluorescent fixtures.

- Use lighting to highlight architectural features such as vaulted ceilings, beams, wood ceilings, etc.

- When developing the budget for these spaces, it is important to allocate appropriate funds for decorative light fixtures.

- Dining areas should have light levels as high as 50 fc so the residents will be able to clearly see the color of the food. One of the better light sources is indirect because it minimizes glare and shadows.

- Lounge areas should not rely solely on accessory lighting from table and floor lamps because bulbs are not always replaced swiftly. Accessory lighting should be considered supplemental to general light levels of a minimum of 35 fc.

- Activity rooms: Indirect lighting is the best source for these spaces, because it provides the most even distribution of light on the work surface without glare or shadows, significantly reducing the footcandle levels required to see clearly.

- Library: If there are aisles of shelving, stack lighting is the most efficient way to light the aisles and wash the face of the books. There should be general illumination of approximately 30 fc with directed task-lighting over the table or floor lamps at the proper height next to seating.

- Barber/beauty: While the best light source for general illumination is downlighting, when used in some areas, such as barber/beauty, dining, or an exercise room, downlighting can create unflattering shadows on the face, as well as strong glare while looking up at the ceiling when hair is being washed. In these spaces, indirect lighting with some decorative sconces is recommended. In addition, lighting on both sides of a mirror creates the most even light for viewing the face. Special attention should also be given to the color of the lamps, so as to provide the most flattering quality of light.

- Occupational therapy/physical therapy areas: Indirect is also the preferred type of light source for these areas, because residents often undergo physical therapy on tables looking up toward the ceiling.

Corridors

Points to consider include:

- Code-stated footcandle requirements are minimum goals. As previously noted, some state codes require 20 fc in corridors of long-term care facilities, even though most successful designs (as defined by positive resident feedback) range from 30 to 45 fc.

▼ Indirect lighting is particularly important in therapy areas, where the resident may spend time looking up at the ceiling. Sarah R. Neuman Center for Healthcare and Rehabilitation–Weinberg Pavilion, Mamaroneck, New York. Perkins Eastman Architects PC. Photograph by Chuck Choi.

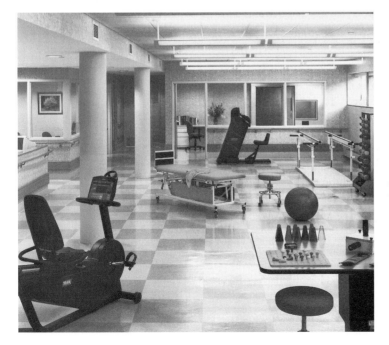

- Variation in light source is a key design element to help visually shorten the length of corridors. The integration of lighting with architectural features creates visual cueing to support wayfinding and areas of interest along the resident's trip down a corridor. To accomplish desirable light levels, recessed downlights should be spaced six feet on center with a minimum of two 26-watt compact fluorescent lamps.

- Decorative sconces placed at unit entries not only serve as wayfinding elements but also provide supplemental lighting for residents to find their keys, read the room number, and locate the keyhole. An alternate way to highlight unit entries is to install a recessed cove over the door, bathing the entry in accent lighting.

Resident Living Spaces

Long-term care resident room
Codes vary from state to state and must be carefully followed. Of the various approaches, not all are code-compliant in all states:

- Ceiling fixture for general lighting with a supplemental light source such as a table lamp on the bedside cabinet.

- Table lamps should have a toggle switch located on the column rather than the customary knob at the bulb. There are table lamps that can be bolted to the bedside cabinet and are offset for mounting at the rear of the cabinet surface to provide a work area and space for personal belongings.

Before (above) and after (below). Lighting can be used to shorten the apparent length of corridors, highlight unit entries and reduce glare. Fairhaven, Sykesville, Maryland. Perkins Eastman Architects PC.

▶ Adjustable table lamps that can be attached to bedside tables are a popular light source. Courtesy of Schumaker Lighting Inc. Photograph by Batemore Productions.

- Night-lights assist the resident in finding the path to the toilet. Their design should properly direct the light to the floor surface, and the cover design should not permit light leaks that could disturb sleep.

- Overbed lighting can incorporate direct and indirect light sources with varied switching options. Nursing units with higher levels of care, bedside treatments, and medical evaluation in the resident's room will require a supplemental light source over the bed or mounted on the wall for exams.

- Ceiling-mounted fixtures that have multifunction light sources to address ambient, reading, examination, and night light are available from several manufacturers. Specular aluminum reflectors allow for precise light control and a glare-free environment, and fixtures may be recessed or surface-mounted.

- The use of floor lamps as a supplemental source is controversial. Many of these fixtures can easily tip

over, so if this lighting option is considered, lamps with weighted bases are essential. Bulbs should be enclosed so that if the lamp tips, the bulb will not shatter.

Assisted Living Residential Unit

The abundance of options makes lighting a highly budget-driven aspect of the design. For example, how many ceiling fixtures should be used? Should they be replaced by a switched outlet? This is a decision that can affect hundreds of fixtures and be a major cost issue. There is also a problem with switched outlets, in that residents will not always understand that the light must be turned off at the wall switch rather than at the lamp. If residents do not understand this, the switched outlets become pointless because the advantage of being able to switch them on upon entry is eliminated.

Other lighting issues in areas within the residential unit include:

- Tea kitchen/entry vestibule: This area is usually provided with a light source upon entry as well as general illumination for the tea kitchen and adjacent closet. Since the light source is overhead for a person standing at the sink counter, shadows will be cast on the work surface. Therefore, it is very important to have undercabinet lighting to enable the resident to see at the sink and counter area. Proper lighting will encourage residents to use their kitchenette.

- Living rooms are very rarely equipped with a ceiling fixture. Instead, a switched outlet is provided. If the resident should turn the lamp off at the source rather than the switch, there usually is sufficient light spillover from the entry area to allow the resident to find a table lamp.

- Bedroom: Some facilities provide a ceiling fixture, but a switched outlet is more typical. However, the bedside lamp that might be plugged into the outlet linked to the switch will always be turned off at bedside, thus eliminating the ability to turn on the light at the doorway. Ceiling fixtures are recommended in this area. More reasonably priced fixtures have a standard incandescent "A" lamp or a less efficient fluorescent circleline. There are other options, such as more efficient fluorescent lamps. If the bedroom is not provided with a ceiling fixture, all closets should have their own light sources.

- Bathroom: Since most accidents occur in this area, the light must be evenly distributed so the resident can clearly see the location of all assistance devices such as grab bars and be able to read the medication labels on items stored in the medicine cabinet. As discussed previously, an indirect light source is the most effective to minimize glare. Fluorescent lamping is the best light source to provide the higher CRI ratings necessary to recognize color and clarity of image, and provides higher light output at lower wattages. Because toilet areas for senior populations are large due to the accessibility guidelines, the light source placed over the vanity may not provide enough light for the bathing area. Thus, the shower/bathing area should have a light as well.

  Supplemental lighting provided by a heat lamp is also desirable. It not only warms the area but also serves as additional task-lighting for drying and dressing. Many times a combination unit is used that includes the exhaust fan if there is no central exhaust system. Codes vary from state to state, but it is good practice to install a night-light to illuminate the path to the bathroom at night.

Independent Living Unit

Independent living units have the same concerns as assisted living units. Lighting upgrades are sometimes offered as options during the sale of the unit. Such upgrades include ceiling fans with lights in the kitchen/dining areas and bedrooms, the addition of dimmers and rocker switches (much easier to use than the standard toggle switch), and motion sensors to activate lights in the toilets upon entry.

CONCLUSION

Keep these six main points in mind when choosing lighting for senior living and care environments:

- Provide lighting that responds to the needs of aging eyes.

- Use energy-efficient lighting products such as fluorescent lamping.

- Provide uniform illumination within spaces.

- Keep adjacent spaces at the same brightness.

- Raise overall light levels only slightly, as overly lit spaces can produce too much glare.

- Incorporate task-lighting without causing too much glare or significantly increasing energy use.

CHAPTER 14

INTERIOR ISSUES

For many older people, the interior design of their home or health-care facility can be more important than any other aspect. As described in earlier chapters, the plan and systems are important, but the interior detailing is critical to a facility's success as an appropriate setting for the aging. For example:

- The wrong mounting height for an appliance or handrail can make it unusable.

- An incorrectly shaped handrail, especially one that is too narrow, can be hard for an arthritic hand to grasp.

- Some floor patterns with strong contrast can be perceived as a hole or step impeding mobility for those with restricted vision.

- A poor selection of lighting fixtures can create glare that can effectively blind residents.

- Many chairs and couches are too deep or do not have arms that permit a frail person to rise from them without assistance.

- The wrong carpet will trap stains and odors created by incontinence.

These are just some of the hundreds of interior design issues that a sensitive, informed interior design can overcome. This chapter introduces some of the most important.

GENERAL ISSUES

The overall goal of interior design for seniors is to provide an environment that does not feel institutional. Even the most acute level of care in a skilled-nursing facility must not feel sterile or hospital-like; it is the resident's home, not a place he or she has gone for a short stay before returning home. The current buzzword is "feeling." Rooms should feel residential, with the style and quality of a hotel and the comforting details of a home. The design must incorporate a variety of spaces that support varying levels of contact, such as large-scale spaces for holidays or special events, and small cozy spaces for family gatherings and quiet times.

▼ Hospitality design concepts are being introduced in senior housing and care. Sun City Takatsuki, Takatsuki, Japan. Perkins Eastman Architects PC. Photograph by Chuck Choi.

Each facility type described in Chapter 1 shares basic quality-of-life goals, but each must address different issues specific to each stage of aging.

Common goals

- A safe, comfortable environment that is supportive of the resident's need to maintain independence

- Design that seamlessly incorporates the necessary support devices (such as grab bars and handrails) in an unobtrusive manner

- An interior environment that avoids the institutional stigma associated with traditional medical and hospital settings

- A design that addresses the six characteristics of aging that have the largest impact on older adults' relationship to their environment (as noted in Chapter 1): loss of balance; cognitive impairment; loss of strength; visual impairment; hearing impairment; and increased sensitivity to cold, drafts, and direct sunlight

As described in this book, there are at least eight different types of living and care environments for the older adult population. Although there are many differences between the types, there are also factors to keep in mind for all interior spaces designed to meet the needs of older populations:

- Install evenly distributed nonglare lighting with appropriate footcandle levels specific to tasks by area (for more information see Chapter 13).

- Provide contrast between the horizontal and vertical planes to provide better visual discrimination that will improve the sense of balance. For example, a corridor whose floor and wall

▼ Creating intimate residential settings for resident and family meetings is an important interior design task in many senior housing and care settings. Hospice LaGrange, West Georgia Medical Center, LaGrange, Georgia. Perkins & Will. Photograph by William Nelson.

finishes were a similar color and value was perceived by the residents of one facility as a "muddy river."

- Be sensitive to acoustics when designing and selecting finishes; choose those that reduce background noise for improved hearing at social gatherings (refer to Chapter 12 for more information).

- Flush transitions from one flooring material to another are vital. Plan for slab recesses to reduce trip hazards.

- Avoid sharp corners or edges in millwork, wood trim, furniture, hardware, and other interior elements.

- Choose flooring products that have patterns without high contrast and with colors close in value. Otherwise there is the potential for vertigo and falls.

- Select textiles and wall coverings with easily recognizable patterns that will not be perceived as objects, faces, or animals.

- Specify colors that are not so dark that they are perceived as black or so subtle that they appear dreary to the aging eye.

- Choose floor finishes that are not slippery or have a high-gloss appearance.

- Install carpets with fiber construction and moisture-barrier backing systems appropriate for the aging population with incontinence, as described in Chapter 1.

- Limit use of mirrors on walls to create the illusion of space, as this can cause confusion and disorientation.

FINISHES

Finishes provide the backdrop for a residential setting, as discussed in previous chapters. Many issues influence the choice of finishes. For designers the aesthetic appearance is a primary consideration; however, cost, appropriate construction for the function of the area, durability, maintenance requirements, visual effects of patterns, and the mobility constraints of the surface must be considered as well. (Refer to Chapter 11 for more detailed information).

Consider that:

- Contrast can improve seniors' ability to locate assistive devices such as grab bars in the shower and doorways. Color is more than a decorating tool; if used properly it can be used as a visual identification system. Too many bathrooms are white on white, making it difficult to clearly see grab bars and the exact location of the toilet or the edge of the shower.

- The transition between different types of flooring must be as close to flush as possible to avoid trip hazards.

- Wall-protection systems, such as corner guards and rub rails, should be strategically integrated into the design of high-traffic areas so they do not detract from the residential feeling of the interior.

- Strong primary colors can be pleasing at first but eventually can become tiring. Strong colors should be used as accents. Too much color can feel just as monochromatic as neutral, similar colors.

The key issue in finish selection is to choose appropriately for each facility type. The chart on page 230 illustrates the basic application of finishes in two facility types providing a higher level of care:

FINISHES						
		Floor	Base	Wainscot	Wall Below Wainscot	Wall Above Ceiling
Long-Term Care						
Resident room	Basic	VCT	VB	P	P	ACT
	Average	VS	VB	P	P & VWC/B	GYP
	Above average	CPT	WD	VWC	VWC	GYP & ACT
Resident bathroom	Basic	VS	VS/B	P	P	ACT
	Above average	CT	CT/B	CT/P	P&VWC/B	GYP
Resident corridor (with handrail)	Basic	VCT/P	VB	P	P	ACT
	Average	CPT	VB	P	P	ACT & GYP
	Above average	CPT	WD	P	VWC	ACT & GYP
Assisted Living						
Resident room	Basic	VCT	VB	P	P	ACT
Tea kitchen	Average	VS	VB	P	P&VWC/B	GYP
	Above average	WD	WD	VWC	VWC	GYP & ACT
Bathroom	Basic	VS	VS/B	P	P	ACT
	Average	CT	CT/B	CT/P	P&VWC/B	GYP
Living area	Basic	CPT	VB	P	P	GYP
	Average	CPT	WD	P	P	GYP

ACT= acoustic ceiling tile P= paint; CPT=carpet; VB=vinyl base; CT=ceramic tile; VS=sheet vinyl; CT/B=ceramic tile base; VS/B= flash cove base (integral with flooring); GYP=gypsum board; VWC=vinyl wall covering;VWC/B=wall-covering border

The choice of finishes for independent living is very much budget-driven, depending upon the location and market demands. Usually, due to financial constraints, prospective renters or buyers are offered a basic level of finish with associated upgrade packages available at additional cost. Many communities allow the residents to do their own upgrades with a clause that the unit must be returned to the original condition at the request of management. The kitchen and bathroom offer the widest range of potential upgrades. Common options for these spaces include the following.

Kitchen

- Cabinets: base—white or natural wood; upgrades—special cabinet wood finishes
- Countertops: base—plastic laminate; upgrades—solid surfacing such as Corian or stone
- Flooring: base—residential grade-sheet vinyl with a no-wax finish; upgrades—vinyl wood-look floor, ceramic tile, wood flooring

Bathroom

- Vanity: white or natural wood that coordinates with kitchen choice

- Vanity top: base—plastic laminate with a rimmed sink or a cultured marble top with integral sink; upgrades—solid surfacing with an integral sink or an under-counter sink, or stone with an under-counter sink.

- Flooring: base—residential sheet vinyl; upgrades—ceramic tile, wood or stone

It is important for living areas to have the proper flooring. The base choice is a cut pile carpet with a face weight of 32 to 36 oz., and upgrades as high as 50 oz. are frequently offered. The cut pile carpet should be dense construction so as to provide a firmer surface for those residents who age in place and require the use of a walker or wheelchair.

FURNITURE
Furniture Selection Should Start in Schematic Design

In the programming and planning phases it is critical during test layouts to use properly dimensioned furniture. The furniture shown in the drawings should reflect the actual items to be used so the area planned is large enough to provide the proper accessibility clearances for wheelchairs or supportive devices such as walkers. The most common mistake is to use the prepackaged furniture templates available in CAD programs, particularly in dining and activity spaces. The chairs typically included in the template are only 18" square, when a chair with arms is at least 22" in width and depth. Multiply this 4" difference by 60 to 80 occupants, and the room becomes too small to accomodate the furniture. Another problem with the typical CAD templates

▲ *Granite countertops, copper-topped tables, woven chairs, and patterned ceramic tile flooring are used to create the image of a garden bistro. Pine Cove at Bay Shore Assisted Living, Bay Shore, New York Perkins Eastman Architects PC. Photograph by Chuck Choi.*

is the size of a table for four. Many times it is only 36" square. Depending on the type of facility, tables as large as 48" square are required if meals will be served on trays. When planning the dining areas, it is crucial to understand the food-delivery system to be used, since it directly affects the size of the table needed, and thus the square footage per occupant ratio used for planning purposes.

It is recommended that a variety of seating choices be provided, to accommodate two, four, and six persons. There are furniture options such as tables for four with leaves that flip up to create a round table for six. It is suggested that the table for two have the same dimension in one direction as the table for four, so that they can be joined for flexibility. Review the height of the table to determine if wheelchair accessibility is required. Adjustable-height tables are available, but in most cases the bases are not aesthetically pleasing. Some manufacturers have introduced wooden pedestals that are adjustable.

Dimensions and Construction Are Critical

When selecting furniture for the various types of senior housing and care, the physical frailty of the users must be kept in mind. Although the occupants using each level of housing and care option will vary, it is better to err on the safe side by selecting for the frailest, keeping in mind that aging in place is a common aspect of most facilities. The physical effects of the aging process, as previously described in Chapter 1, can be addressed by selecting furniture that meets the following criteria:

- Proper dimensions: seat height 18–19", seat depth 20" maximum, arm height 25–26"; style of arm: the arms must extend to the front of the seat so that they will support the weight of residents who lean on them in order to stand or sit unassisted.

- Density and firmness: The cushions must be supportive so that the bottom of the seat will not sink much lower than the height of the occupant's knees.

- Upholstery issues: To address incontinence, the current trend in upholstery is a woven material known as Crypton, which is sealed to repel stains and prevent the passage of moisture through to the cushion. This can be an attractive alternative to stiff and sticky vinyl upholstery (see Chapter 11 for more information). There is

upholstery material made out of nylon that has the same protective top layer as the traditional vinyl material but is soft and supple like leather.

- Durability of construction: Although a residential appearance is desirable, the construction must be of commercial quality, with bracing and sturdy joinery. Chairs for dining should have cross support stretchers to prevent the legs from loosening due to the constant pushing and pulling from residents sitting at and rising from the table. Casters can be added to the front legs to reduce the stress on the structure of the frame and assist the resident when pulling up to the table. For safety reasons, however, casters should be placed on the front legs only.

- Appropriate weight: Furniture to be placed in rooms with multiple functions and flexibility, such as stackable chairs, need to be light enough for the occupant to move while still providing a safe stable frame with arms that will not tip over when the seated person tries to rise. Tables that fold need to have mechanisms that lock in place for stability without any sharp edges or movable parts that can cut and pinch when set in place.

- Rockers: Studies have shown that rocking chairs have a positive effect on the well-being of senior populations. There are safety concerns associated with the standard rocking chair, however. They are a trip hazard, and there is the possibility of rocking over someone's foot. The safest way to provide the benefits of the rocking motion is a stable rocker that will not tip forward when the resident uses the arms for support to stand. There are many manufacturers of this type of seating.

- Code: In skilled nursing, state health codes often mandate the minimum furniture to be provided in each resident room: typically a bed, a wardrobe, a chair, a nightstand, and a bulletin board.

FIXTURES

See Chapter 10 for a discussion of toilet and bathing plumbing fixtures.

DETAILS

Some important interior details that should be considered in most facilities include:

- Package/purse shelf: A convenient shelf adjacent to the corridor side of the resident-room door on which to set a small package while looking for the key to the unit; also used to personalize of the unit entry.

- Outboard-mounted sliding doors: Mounting the door on the outside of the wall to eliminate the space that a door swing can take also makes it easier to operate, clean and maintain than a pocket door, which is mounted within the wall.

- Hardware: Size and configuration

▲ A shelf next to the unit entry door, which some residents use to personalize their entry and others use to set down packages while they open the door, is a common detail. Buckingham's Choice, Adamstown, Maryland. Perkins Eastman Architects PC. Photograph by Chuck Choi.

should be carefully chosen so as to make use easier for those with arthritis or other limitations.

- Memory boxes: Provided adjacent to a resident unit entry, to house personal items that are used to aid a resident in recognizing his or her room.

- Plate shelf: a narrow ledge, usually mounted 65–68" from the floor, used to display personal items or memorabilia, create variety, and help a resident to recognize his or her room from the corridor.

CHAPTER 15
WAYFINDING

The wayfinding system in any building can be an important aspect of resident and visitor comfort, especially for those who may feel insecure in their environment. For older persons who are not as agile and are facing a significant change in their lifestyle, it is particularly important that finding their way around their residential or care facility is as effortless as possible. This makes wayfinding an important issue for the aged.

A wayfinding system should go beyond simple signage to become a multilayered system of spatial cues. Multiple wayfinding cues reinforce a sense of security for residents, who might feel intimidated by spaces that they cannot navigate easily.

Wayfinding is not something pulled from a kit and applied. It is the integration of an intelligent plan that coordinates various architectural and interior design tools including lighting, selection of finishes, artwork, floor coverings, shelves, and accent furniture or objects. It is a total system that must be considered as early as the initial planning and design sessions. If residents feel secure and know they will find their way back home, they will venture out of their living quarters more often, gather, and be more physically active.

Begin with the overall layout of the facility. The layout must be organized in a supportive configuration that responds to function, program, and circulation in a logical progression, guiding residents from space to space. If the basic plan is confused—for example, creating a maze of corridors—wayfinding devices cannot operate effectively.

Visual cues are an essential aspect of wayfinding. For example, interior windows and half-height partitions permit residents to see into adjacent spaces. Integration of feature furniture pieces, such as curio cabinets and artwork, with recognizable objects at decision-making intersections, become cues that help to orient the residents.

The type of flooring is another device used to assist residents' ability to find their way. Color schemes developed around the flooring product may be alternated from floor to floor or area to area. The carpet product used in the public common spaces can have a significantly different appearance from the carpet located in the resident wings. Accent colors, artwork, and carpet design features, such as a border around the circumference of the eleva-

◀ *Familiar objects, such as this grandfather clock, can be effective wayfinding landmarks. Copper Ridge, Sykesville, Maryland. Perkins Eastman Architects PC. Photograph by Curtis Martin.*

▶ *Graphics, color, and other ceiling aids are commonly used, but their effectiveness has yet to be confirmed by postoccupancy analysis. Woodside Place Alzheimer's Residence, Oakmont, Pennsylvania. Perkins Eastman Architects PC. Photograph by Robert Ruschak.*

▼ *Memory boxes, such as this one at Mary's Woods at Marylhurst, help residents recognize their room as well as personalize their entry. Mary's Woods at Marylhurst, Lake Oswego, Oregon. Mithun Inc. Photograph by Eckert & Eckert.*

tor lobby, are all part of the multilayered system of wayfinding devices.

Lighting design and wall finishes should also be integrated parts of the wayfinding concept. A decorative sconce at each entry not only provides additional light but also serves to mark the location of each unit. In addition to the sconce, the ceiling design and lighting can create a recognizable event at a cluster of resident entries. Like a change in light, a change in wall finish also signals entry into a new area and becomes another layer of the wayfinding system.

Persons with Alzheimer's benefit from multiple layers or cues that can be accommodated within the wayfinding system. They generally have trouble storing newly acquired information but find it much easier to elicit memories from their past. Thus, residents in special-care units often have difficulty recognizing their units. One solution to this problem is the installation of a memory box or package shelf outside the door to each unit where residents can place personal objects, such as photographs or keepsakes, to trigger recognition. Alternatively, a device as simple as a hook that enables residents to hang an object on the door can serve this purpose. Dutch doors are another useful room-recognition tool; they allow residents to see into their room and recognize their belongings prior to entry. Inside the living quarters, the provision of plate shelves, deep windowsills, and furniture brought from home enable residents to personalize their rooms and provide further opportunities for personalization and recognition.

Researchers are still learning which visual cues are most effective in guiding residents with Alzheimer's back to their house or neighborhood (see Chapter 1). Subtle single-layered cues such as color changes have not worked well. What the current research indicates is that staff stations where familiar caregivers are visible, major landmarks (for example, a grandfather clock), and cues that engage other senses (such as sense of smell) are more effective.

CHAPTER 16
RENOVATION/RESTORATION/ ADAPTIVE REUSE

Many older senior living facilities are outmoded; they do not appropriately support current care programs or they lack the market appeal to keep the facility competitive and financially viable. The types of problems vary with the type of facility. The following are problems commonly faced by existing facilities that may require restoration or renovation.

In long-term care facilities:

- Resident bedrooms are for three, four, or more persons, offering residents very little privacy.

- Resident toilet-rooms are shared by more than two persons (the current standard) and are not handicapped-accessible.

- Support functions, such as clean and soiled utility rooms, are remote from resident rooms, resulting in soiled linen carts standing in corridors and/or long trips for staff.

- Nurse stations are centralized behind bunkerlike counters. Enclosed nurse stations with high partitions separate caregivers and wheelchair-bound residents.

- Insufficient lounge/activity space, resulting in residents lining corridors in their wheelchairs—usually near the nurse station—creating congestion and a depressing environment for residents and visitors.

- Heating, ventilating, and air-conditioning systems are old and function poorly.

- Smoke and fire-alarm systems and emergency call systems are antiquated.

Before (above) and after (below). Redefining the program for underutilized spaces, such as the single central dining room in many older nursing homes, is a common renovation opportunity. Jewish Home & Hospital–Bronx Campus, Bronx, New York. Perkins Eastman Architects PC. Photography by Chuck Choi.

- Environments with vinyl composition tile floors, 2' × 4' acoustic tile suspended ceilings with fluorescent light fixtures, paging systems, little or no natural light in common areas, and the like are often considered institutional and unattractive, and are not appealing for potential residents seeking a new home.

- Congested bathing rooms provide little resident privacy or dignity.

- Centralized dining in large, cafeterialike settings creates noise and requires significant staff time transporting residents to and from dining.

- There is little or no meaningful, easily accessible outdoor sitting or activity space.

In assisted living facilities:

- Small, cell-like resident rooms are not much more than sleeping spaces.

- Toilet and bathing are facilities shared by several residents.

- Bathrooms are not handicapped-accessible.

- Units lack tea kitchens.

- There is little or no resident storage space within residential units or elsewhere.

- There is insufficient lounge and activity space.

- Large, cafeterialike dining rooms create institutional atmosphere.

- Little or no space allocation for caregivers and other staff.

Before (below) and after (right). Many older facilities recapture spaces to accommodate revised programs. In this case, a staff workroom was recycled into a program area for an Alzheimer's unit. Jewish Home for the Elderly of Fairfield County, Fairfield, Connecticut. Perkins Eastman Architects PC. Photography by Chuck Choi.

- Individuals cannot control temperature within residential units.
- There is no meaningful, easily accessible outdoor sitting or activity space.

In independent living or congregate care facilities:
- Small residential units have one bathroom that is not handicapped-accessible.
- Residential units do not have washer/dryers, dishwashers, or adequate closets and storage.
- Residential units are too small to accommodate residents' furniture and are not competitive with nearby, newer facilities.

- There are no activity, fitness, or other facilities expected by the current market.
- Facility entrances are not handicapped-accessible.

At times the right response to these typical problems is merely cosmetic. This is feasible if the basic structure and systems are sound, and the basic spaces (resident rooms, dining areas, bathing areas, etc.) are appropriately sized. In other cases, moderate renovation and expansion can resolve the major issues. But in more and more facilities only a major renovation or complete replacement will resolve the issues.

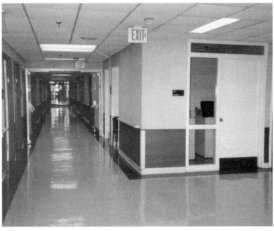

Before (below) and after (left). One of the most common renovation programs is to reposition outdated institutional settings. Hebrew Home of Greater Washington, Rockville, Maryland. Perkins Eastman Architects PC. Photograph by Eric Cohen.

COSMETIC RENOVATION

All heavily used facilities need regular rejuvenation. Hotels typically plan on a major cosmetic upgrade every five to seven years. Senior living and care facilities typically cannot afford such a short cycle, but they begin to show their age within 10 years.

Sometimes modest renovation can achieve a significant new life for an older facility. The most common approaches are to reprogram underutilized spaces, change floor, wall, and ceiling finishes, remove inappropriate existing elements, and upgrade the lighting.

MODERATE RENOVATION

Often, cosmetic changes alone will not address the major issues. Many older facilities were designed for a more alert ambulatory population that had lower expectations of privacy. As a result, for changes to be made to accommodate residents who use assistive walking devices or wheelchairs, create more privacy, and provide more program space nearer to residents' rooms. A typical complication is that the facility must remain fully occupied during renovation. This requires construction of swing beds or units to free up space for phased renovation. Although many older facilities present significant challenges, moderate renovation strategies can result in dramatic improvements.

MAJOR RENOVATION

In many cases, however, only a major reconstruction will reposition the facility to meet current functional, aesthetic, and market expectations. Since major renovation can sometimes cost as much as a new building, there are at least 12 key issues that should be analyzed before committing to this option.

▼ *In some cases, both additions, such as the wing on the left, and extensive renovations are driven by changes in the market. Chestnut Hill Residence, Chestnut Hill, Pennsylvania. Perkins Eastman Architects PC. Photograph by Chuck Choi.*

Twelve Key Questions to Consider

- Will a major renovation or rebuilding trigger a public land-use review process that could be lengthy, expensive, or restrict current rights?

- Will a major renovation trigger mandatory compliance with current codes in a way that will significantly complicate the project or increase costs?

- Are there asbestos, lead paint or other hazardous materials that will add costs or complicate renovation?

- Are the basic building blocks (the resident rooms or units) appropriately sized or can they be expanded to create an attractive, competitive facility?

- When finished, will the project be competitive with or superior to facilities in the same market area?

- Does the reuse of the existing structure cause inefficient layouts, involve extra costs due to too little or too much floor-to-floor height, or be costly because of changes needed to create a barrier-free environment?

- Can enough of the existing structure and systems be reused to represent real savings compared to new construction?

- Has the building envelope been maintained or have there been leaks and other problems that could have created hidden structural problems?

- Will any retained mechanical, electrical, plumbing, or fire-protection systems result in excessive operating, maintenance, or replacement costs?

- Is there a phasing strategy that will permit occupancy to be maintained at economically feasible levels?

- Can the residents' quality of life be maintained during the renovation?

- Will the time saved by reusing the existing facility create significant savings?

The analysis of these and related questions often helps to justify renovation, but owners should not be surprised by an analysis that shows new construction to be more cost-effective in some situations.

ADAPTIVE REUSE

Recycling existing structures into modern senior housing and care facilities is at times an option. Good examples exist of schools, hotels, motels, and many other building types being adapted for the needs of the aging.

To determine the feasibility of an adaptive reuse, it is important to analyze not only the 12 key questions listed above for major renovations but also at least 7 additional issues that arise when changing the use of an existing structure.

Seven Key Questions to Consider

- Is the building structure code-compliant, or can it be upgraded to be code-compliant, with the intended use?

- Will the local land-use and building-code officials support or resist the adaptive reuse for seniors?

- Are the building location and setting appropriate for seniors?

- Is the building's image appropriate or can it be upgraded, made more residential, or otherwise changed to be appropriate?

- Are the building floor plate dimensions appropriate, or are there creative ways to deal with excessive width (such as in a typical office or industrial building) or other floor plate issues?

> The lack of funds is a false barrier in self-evaluation and planning more effective environments for older people. Sponsors sometimes pay dearly for design that does not work, in terms of nonproductive labor, wasted time, turnover, and increased resident dependence. Much can often be done to refurbish a facility without raising rates, increasing reimbursement, or reducing profits.
> *(Hiatt 1991)*

- Will the configuration of the existing structure permit a layout adapted for a particular use, adequate nursing unit size, appropriate adjacencies, and so on, or are there creative ways to overcome inefficiencies?
- Does the existing fenestration (windows or other openings) enable an efficient layout, or can additional openings be created?

If there are acceptable answers to both the original 12 questions on renovations and the 7 questions relevant to adaptive reuse, this option can be a creative way to develop a new environment for seniors.

CHAPTER 17

INTERNATIONAL CHALLENGES

The sociological, political, and economic challenges of an aging society are not confined to the United States. Worldwide, the number of people more than 60 years old is expected to triple to two billion by 2050, making global aging a concern for countries both rich and poor. In fact, the impacts of aging will be more pronounced outside the United States. The U.N. estimates that although the U.S. population's median age is expected to rise from 35.5 today to 40.7 by 2050, Europe's median age may rise to 49.7 and Japan's to 53.1 by that date.

Our planet provides both challenges and opportunities for senior living community design. Although the "old rich" countries of Europe, North America, and Japan have entrenched medical, health, and welfare policies and systems, most of the "new old" countries do not. Therefore, the opportunity exists to help newly emerging "aging societies" create social, political, and economic systems that avoid mistakes made elsewhere. The relative lack of national savings and tax base in these countries suggests that northern European–style state-sponsored social welfare models will be hard to replicate. In these countries, the private sector will probably have to meet more of the needs.

The physical and mental impact of the aging process is universal, as is the need for specialized senior housing. Aging Japanese, for example, develop Alzheimer's, arthritis, and other impairments that make living in a tatami-mat apartment very difficult. Moreover, many have children living far away, and moving to live with them is not feasible. Even Japanese who still expect to care for their aged parents at home can now afford other options. Similar trends are occurring in other traditional societies. As a result, there is a growing interest in facilities for the aging in other developed countries, and potential sponsors are looking to the United States and Canada to learn from our recent experience.

Until recent decades much of the innovation and many of the best models could be found in England and Scandinavia. The relatively small, stable populations in these countries, however, have made many of these models less relevant for some of the larger countries with rapidly growing numbers of people needing senior housing and care options.

How translatable is senior living design expertise to foreign situations? Although the physiological and cognitive changes in older adults are common worldwide, each

> In Europe, countries became rich before they became old. But in the developing world, countries are growing old before they become rich.
>
> *Mohammad Nizamuddin, Director U.N. Population Fund for Asia and the Pacific*

GLOBAL AGING*						
	NUMBER OF RESIDENTS 60+ (in thousands)		PERCENT OF TOTAL POPULATION 60+		PERCENT OF TOTAL POPULATION 80+	
	2002	2050	2002	2050	2002	2050
USA	46,960	106,660	16	27	21	8
China	134,243	436,980	10	30	9	23
India	81,089	324,316	8	21	8	15

Source: United Nations, Population Division, Department of Economic and Social Affairs, Population Aging 2002.

> Today's problems with the oldest old appear to exist in North America, Europe and Japan. However by 2025 China and India will push the U.S. into 3rd place in the 80+ population. (*Regnier 2002, p. 8*)

country develops unique responses to global aging based on local social and political customs, health system economics, the legal/regulatory situation, and family-linked customs and traditions.

Many of the examples cited in this chapter focus on recent experience in Asia, because the wealth and sophistication of a growing number of countries in the region have opened up a potentially large market for experienced North American firms. Europe has its own seasoned firms, but few countries in other regions have the perceived need and wealth to import design expertise for this building type at this time.

When North American design teams do work overseas, they will find that they have to be educators as well as designers. Though the United States has senior living facilities more than 100 years old, and almost all Americans have had a relative or friend who has lived in a long-term care setting of some sort, the same will not be true overseas: the typical resident of the growing number of facilities in Tokyo, Osaka, and Kyoto is the first person in the history of his or her family to move into a senior living community. Education is central to any international design opportunity: educating the client, local opinion leaders, regulators and politicians, staff members, and potential customers and their families.

SERVICE DEVELOPMENT CHALLENGES

The opportunity to work overseas offers a challenge to do something different. Differences in regulatory and reimbursement

environments demand more flexible thinking about what services to provide and how to provide them. The long list of settings for older adults described in Chapter 1 has developed from historical and current U.S. regulations, reimbursement practices, and traditions. Assisted living, for example, became popular as a noninstitutional residential response to the shortcomings and deficiencies in traditional nursing homes. Key to assisted living's rapid development was the private sector's ability to convince potential customers and their adult children that this new approach was kinder and more compassionate, and therefore worth both the increased out-of-pocket expense and abandonment of potential governmental support.

But what if government reimbursement didn't artificially distinguish between independent living, assisted living, dementia care, and skilled nursing, as in Japan? There the *kaigo hoken* system focuses on aging in place, with a "menu" system whereby residents/staff may choose care that responds to individual needs, setting few limits on what services can or cannot be done in any particular place. As a result, the U.S. model, with its typical limitations on what services can be provided in a particular facility, is often inappropriate.

The leading sponsor of new senior living options in Japan has used foreign design teams that have challenged their own "traditions," evolving new service models such as Tokyo's Sun City Chofu. This three-story 118-unit "life care" project combines 94 "independent" and "assisted" living units on the top two floors with 24 beds with 24-hour monitoring for dementia and skilled nursing on the ground floor. The result is a new business

▲ *Many of the overseas retirement communities in South America as well as Europe and Asia have to be developed on small urban sites. This 427,000 sq ft CCRC in Tokyo is being built on a 50,714 sq ft site.*

model where pricing, including entry and monthly fees, is tailored to individual circumstances. Minimum entry ages vary according to the customer's current physical and cognitive situation.

The urban high-rise retirement community, like the fax machine, may be another U.S. invention whose development and perfection will occur overseas. In contrast to the low-rise settings of much of the U.S. senior living product, senior housing in the great cities of Asia, as well as similar projects in large cities elsewhere around the world, call for high-rise solutions. The Ginza East Tower, scheduled to open in 2006, is an early example. The life-care community's 32

◄◄ *Some countries, such as Japan, are building their first retirement communities and exploring the adaptation of international models to their own cultures. Sun City Takatsuki, Takatsuki, Japan. Perkins Eastman Architects PC. Photograph by Chuck Choi.*

floors will include 288 independent living apartments, a 120-bed care center, health club, two restaurants, and other social club and cultural spaces. Security, planning for efficient staffing, and designing for an in-town population likely to be five years older and frailer than the suburban norm were key issues in the design process.

PROGRAMMING AND DESIGN CHALLENGES

How people live, eat, and bathe, as well as their social habits, can make program requirements for international projects quite different from their counterparts in the United States. Sometimes these traditions are at odds with the changing needs of older adults, making the designer's task more difficult. The Japanese traditional lifestyle, for example, where a large proportion of time is spent on tatami-

mat floors, is ill-suited to older adults with declining range of movement, inflexible knee joints, poor balance, and increased susceptibility to drafts. And although Japanese love a deep soaking tub at the end of the day, deteriorating upper-body strength may make it impossible to get back out once in. Before starting any overseas assignment, an architect should spend some time getting to know local lifestyles firsthand, including staying with a family, if possible.

Food is as important overseas as it is in the United States, but the challenges can be different, especially in the kitchen. Variations between cultures will impact space requirements, staffing, operations costs, and development "soft costs." For example, in Japan it is traditional to change dishware with the seasons and holidays, requiring more than twice the dish storage space of an Ameri-

▶ This independent living residence in Japan reflects a regional design vocabulary, using shoji screens as a flexible means of separating the bedroom area from the living room while still allowing for light and openness. Hadano, Kyoto, Japan. BAR Architects. Photograph by Doug Dun.

◀ Northern Europe has developed innovative new environments for the aging. Humanitas-Bergweg, Rotterdam, the Netherlands. EMG Architects.

can community of the same size. Different cookware and utensils are used for fish than for meat and vegetables. Daily deliveries from a large number of suppliers are typical. This reduces long-term stock space but complicates the choreography and staffing for delivery, preparation, service, and trash removal.

Bathing, health, and beauty are closely related in many places around the world. Until recently, cultures and senior communities in both Asia and Scandinavia placed much greater emphasis on bath-related programs than did Americans, although the healthy aging trend is enabling the United States to catch up. Japanese settings for older adults, even at the skilled-nursing level, provide significantly more space for *onsen*-style bathing. This

increases both total space requirements and construction costs. Whereas an American 350-unit CCRC might devote about 10 sq ft per unit to swimming pools, Jacuzzis, exercise areas, and locker rooms. Tokyo's Sun City Kanagawa is typical of an upscale Japanese product in allocating 30–35 sq ft per unit to these uses.

Asian cultures share a variety of beliefs about geomancy or *feng shui,* which can alter room layouts, building-to-building orientation, and even site selection. Despite advances in heating systems, the Japanese and Chinese maintain a strong desire to have all residential units face south. This can lead to inefficient single-loaded corridors, which increase walking distances and promote the construction of narrow and deep apartments.

SERVICE AND SOCIALIZATION

Design concepts can be impacted by differences in values and perceptions of the proper roles of the customer and staff. While many U.S. and European communities allow residents to actively participate in community governance, the current generation of Asian customers may expect more of a "hotel service" concept.

Working overseas is an opportunity to challenge other home truths. Retirement community operators and sales staff often claim that even in a CCRC, independent living customers don't want to see residents of the care center, which is therefore hidden or located out of the way. But the experience of some new senior communities in the United States and overseas has been different. Some operators have followed the philosophy of the Pennsylvania-based Kendal Corporation. In their communities, all residents are part of one community, and all areas and amenities are made available and accessible. The "one community" view seems easier to implant in societies that traditionally respect the aged.

PROCESS CHALLENGES

Client-consultant relationships and communications, project delivery, and economics can vary considerably from the American model. Communication differences are by far the most important, including not only language barriers but those resulting from cultural traditions, government–private sector relations, religion, or family values. Designers contemplating international design opportunities will succeed only if they are committed to meeting clients at least halfway, with staff fluent in the home country language. This is especially important because the designer will be an educator as

well, called upon throughout the design, construction, and start-up process to explain the community's objectives, its design, the details of its program, and the essence of its operation to widening circles of client, staff, politicians, regulators, local architects, contractors, subcontractors, operations staff, and possibly customers and their families.

Whenever possible, communications should be simple, direct, and clear. Use images and charts and keep words to a minimum. Always explain the goals and objectives behind a recommendation, as well as how it fits into the concept of the project as a whole.

European and American concepts of professional training and qualifications are not uniformly held worldwide. In many areas, hierarchical relationships are the norm, which can often put architects at the bottom of the client-designer-builder triumvirate. Designers should research the local situation and the client thoroughly. By and large, U.S. architects have been most successful overseas when contracted directly to the client, and where the U.S. team's responsibilities and authority in relation to both local architects and contractors is clearly delineated. No matter what the client says, the client has enlisted U.S. experts in senior living design because of a lack of similar knowledge locally. This usually translates to the client's expectation that the design, function, quality and image, and sales success of the finished senior living product is the U.S. side's responsibility.

U.S.-style construction documents, bidding, and document-intensive construction administration are rare outside North America. Asian design-build systems shift a large percentage of design detail and construction system definition to the contractor. The result is often local permit documents that are less detailed than the U.S. team's design-development set. This practice tends to create serious design coordination problems among the architects and engineers and to make any early cost estimates less reliable. Successful U.S. designers have had to be more specific than usual in the early stages to provide a clearer and more complete set of design-development drawings and specifications. They also have to plan for considerably more than the usual time for the later phases to react to the frequent phone calls, faxes, and e-mails seeking clarification and coordination.

Project economics will vary considerably with location, local real estate economics, and client motivation. Senior living communities are a balance of housing, hospitality, and health care. As senior living markets evolve, projects will be perceived differently by increasingly sophisticated consumers. Early senior living developments in Taiwan, for example, have been perceived primarily as a special kind of real estate, a sort of serviced apartment for retirees.

For the designer, this means a steady focus on sales-area ratio, and the tendency by developers to ignore universal design in favor of bigger closets or to add units instead of programmable public space. In Japan, life-care communities attract customers interested in purchasing peace of mind in a society whose public welfare health insurance system faces bankruptcy. There, accessible design for all independent living apartments is becoming standard. In a development outside Seoul, Korea, the emphasis on hospitality required regrading the site to incorporate a full-scale health club. With

gymnasium, swimming pool, racquetball courts, and golf practice tees to complement the aerobics rooms, weights, and exercise equipment, the club is available to all residents of Korea's first CCRC as well as families in the adjacent Samsung housing estate.

GLOBAL AGING AT HOME

The next decade will see increased cross-fertilization of new ideas in senior living design between Asia, North America, Europe, and other regions. With less regulation but increasing need, Asian countries in particular will continue to experiment with private-sector communities alongside public-sector service programs. Ten years from now, a list of the most exclusive retirement communities will probably include entrants from Tokyo, Shanghai, Singapore, and Hong Kong. Western Europe will probably expand its existing options while eastern European countries will look for affordable solutions, with a stronger role for the private sector than historically seen in northern Europe. In South America, it is likely that the private sector will have to respond to the limited but growing demand for senior living options for the middle and wealthy classes. Limited public budgets will probably delay response to the need for government-supported programs.

But with one in five Americans now born overseas, part of the international challenge begins at home. Foreign-born residents of American facilities for the aging will stimulate the need for flexible thinking, the ability to design for cultural differences, and the search for more creative programmatic responses to the needs of an increasingly diverse population.

CHAPTER 18

OPERATION AND MAINTENANCE

Over the life of most institutions, the first cost of the building is a small fraction of the total cost of building, maintaining, and operating the facility. In staff-intensive facilities, such as nursing homes, the debt service for the money borrowed to build the facility may be only 20–30 percent of the annual operating budget. Therefore, most experienced sponsors are interested in understanding and minimizing the cost of staffing, operating, and maintaining their facilities.

INTRODUCTION

A well-designed senior living community must be easy to operate and maintain, and require lower than average investments in daily cleaning, operations staff, utilities costs, and routine and long-term maintenance. In addition, well-designed communities will be planned to limit the hospitality and care staff needed to provide the desired level of services to residents. Thus, design for operations and maintenance has three goals: reduce ongoing running costs, maximize durability, and support high-efficiency staffing.

OPERATIONS COSTS OVERVIEW

Depending on resident needs and services offered, real estate, staffing, and operations/maintenance costs could vary considerably. The table on page 252 illustrates a range of costs per occupied unit across all types of units—the respondents are the major for-profit systems that are more independent-program oriented but offer the other levels of care. Operations and maintenance costs are divided into three components: running and maintenance costs, including building operations staff; repair and replacement costs, including phased replacement of both mechanical equipment and finishes; and utilities costs.

In senior living, staffing and real estate costs are inversely related. As the level of service increases, the impact of real estate costs (land, building construction, FFE, financing, and taxes) diminishes. Thus, whereas a 10 percent increase in real estate costs is likely to have a similar impact on total costs in independent living, its impact is only one-third as large in dementia care. On the other hand, a design

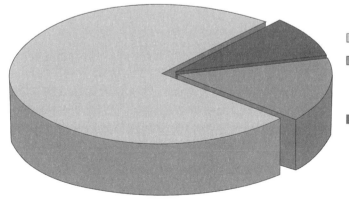

◀ Life-cycle costs projected over 40 years. Perkins Eastman Architects PC.

☐ Labor 77-88%

☐ Energy and Building Maintenance 11-16%

☐ Capital Cost 6-7% Land Acquisition Construction Professional Fees

OPERATIONS AND MAINTENANCE COST				
COST PER OCCUPIED UNIT ($/year)				
Labor Lower Decile	Lower Quartile	Median	Upper Quartile	Upper Decile
Maintenance 435	524	755	951	1,167
Nonlabor				
Utilities 1,007	1,120	1,423	1,806	2,003
Repairs 127	347	525	754	921

Source: The State of Housing 2000, published by American Seniors Housing Associaton

that saves one full-time nursing staff member on each shift can save over $120,000 and cover the debt service on $1.5–2 million of capital cost.

Operations and maintenance costs are influenced primarily by the type of use and building area. Higher-service settings such as nursing homes tend to have less area per resident, which reduces cleaning costs, but have higher densities of sophisticated mechanical and electrical systems, which require more maintenance. In addition, higher-service settings tend to have more cart traffic and more resident mobility aids (wheelchairs, walkers, carts), which inflict more damage on walls and floors.

RUNNING AND MAINTENANCE COSTS

Running and maintenance costs include cleaning, scheduled and routine maintenance costs for building systems, and cost of operations (facility management) personnel. Operations-friendly community design includes locating primary mechanical and electrical equipment in as few easy-access locations as possible and locating all major controls for building equipment, elevators, fire-alarm, emergency/nurse call, and telephone/data systems in one area near administration or nighttime security staffing. Operations-

friendly design also includes providing elevator access to rooftop equipment areas, for ease of parts replacement, and providing access hatches to subfloor pit areas for maintenance of plumbing drains.

Owners and their design teams should be careful not to select overly complex controls and technology, such as advanced facility management systems, which are costly and require sophisticated personnel to operate and maintain. Complicated computer-based management of mechanical systems, for example, may be too complex to be maintained and operated by the routine janitorial staff that operate and maintain most senior housing and care facilities. Sometimes simpler is better.

At a smaller scale, operations-friendly design includes locating light switches in central locations for easier after-hours control, providing switched outlets so that even table and floor lamps can be controlled from central locations, and light fixture specifications that minimize the number of different types of bulbs required. Operations-friendly site design includes providing positive drainage in both paved and landscaped areas, specifying low-maintenance ground cover in place of grass, and installing low-glare site lighting, where bulbs can be changed using a ladder rather than a lift.

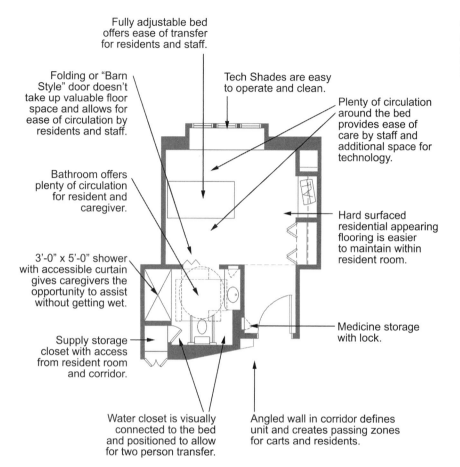

Fully adjustable bed offers ease of transfer for residents and staff.

Folding or "Barn Style" door doesn't take up valuable floor space and allows for ease of circulation by residents and staff.

Tech Shades are easy to operate and clean.

Plenty of circulation around the bed provides ease of care by staff and additional space for technology.

Bathroom offers plenty of circulation for resident and caregiver.

Hard surfaced residential appearing flooring is easier to maintain within resident room.

3'-0" x 5'-0" shower with accessible curtain gives caregivers the opportunity to assist without getting wet.

Supply storage closet with access from resident room and corridor.

Medicine storage with lock.

Water closet is visually connected to the bed and positioned to allow for two person transfer.

Angled wall in corridor defines unit and creates passing zones for carts and residents.

◀ Every interior design detail can make a resident's room easier to use for both residents and staff. Perkins Eastman Architects PC.

Cleaning costs are directly related to materials specifications for floors and walls. While the use of harder materials can reduce cleaning costs, these can be dangerous for residents and can impose liability insurance costs that outweigh first-cost savings. With both carpets and wall coverings, modest first-cost investments in stain-resistant or tear-resistant materials can keep daily maintenance problems from becoming repair and replacement candidates, lengthening useful life by 50–100 percent. A detailed discussion of some of these products appears in Chapter 14.

Cleaning costs for window coverings and upholstery can vary by 100 percent or more according to the type of product and material selected. High-tech fabrics such as Avora are available in a variety of weights and textures, can be printed to look like jacquards or blends, and are machine-washable without shrinkage, saving significantly over traditional fabrics, which require dry cleaning. In hard-use areas, Crypton has become an alternative to both laminated fabrics and vinyl. As an upholstery fabric, it offers the easy cleaning of vinylized fabric but is softer to the touch and much cooler to sit on for long periods.

DURABILITY, USEFUL LIFE, AND REPLACEMENT COSTS

The durability of building products and equipment is directly related to the expenditure of staff maintenance time and the life-cycle costs of the building's systems. The table on pages 255–256 lists the expected useful lives of major building systems as well as recommended cycles for thorough inspection and maintenance.

Some common materials have a wide range of maintenance and replacement cycles. For example, carpets vary extensively in yarn type, pile height and density, weaving technique, and backing, and therefore must be carefully matched to their intended use to balance first cost, maintenance costs, and marketing concerns. Residential areas often get simple low-tech materials due to the marketing advantage of supplying replacement carpet for new long-stay residents. Conversely, dementia or skilled-care settings require high-tech yarns and backings due to the high levels of wear and cleaning these areas must endure.

Lower parts of walls and corners must withstand considerable abuse, requiring special consideration of wall bases, corners, chair rails, and doorframes. Settings where significant cart traffic and wheelchairs are expected should receive a wall base higher than normal. Many providers require a 250–300 mm high base (10"–12"), tall enough to keep wheelchair foot plates from gouging walls. Chair rails, lean rails, and handrails provide a similar protection at 750–850 mm (30"–34") above the floor. Exposed corners often receive corner guards, especially in service areas or where circulation is narrow. Painted metal door frames, a standard in many senior living communities, often receive color-coordinated plastic guards in vulnerable areas. All of these "cart catchers" receive their share of abuse, but they keep problems away from expensive-to-repair walls, reducing maintenance and replacement costs and extending useful life.

Including "attic stock," which is additional product or material, in the construction and furnishings contracts is an easy way to reduce repair and replacement costs in the first few years. Some experienced operators require their contractors to leave on-site, rather than throw away, all carpet remnants larger than six feet long.

DESIGN FOR OPERATIONAL EFFICIENCY

With staffing and operations/maintenance costs contributing up to 75 percent of resident charges, design for operational efficiency is an important part of any senior living community development process. At the broadest level, sizing the project to take maximum advantage of legally mandated highly qualified staff is a given. At the next level, setting the size of units or floors to maximize the utility of day, evening, and night staff is crucial but often overlooked. It is now increasingly common to design facilities so that staff can operate efficiently in smaller groupings of residents during the day, and then supervise and support larger groupings at night. At a detail level, locating clean linen, soiled utility, and charting rooms close to residents can reduce staff walking distances, maximize staff direct contact time with residents, and improve the quality of care.

Staffing levels vary widely due to differences in regulation, sponsor programming, frailty of the residents, and other

EXPECTED LIFE AND RECOMMENDED INSPECTION/MAINTENANCE CYCLES FOR MAJOR SYSTEMS

	Approx. Expected Life Span*	Recommended Inspection/ Maintenance Cycle**
Exterior Envelope		
Foundation		
Block	Indefinite	3 Years
Concrete	Indefinite	5 Years
Structure		
Steel	Indefinite	7 Years
Concrete (poured-in-place or precast)	Indefinite	5 Years
Masonry bearing wall	Indefinite	5 Years
Structural metal stud	Indefinite	If leaks discovered, inspect studs.
Wood	Indefinite	3 Years
Exterior Wall		
Masonry	Indefinite	3 Years
Stucco	40 Years	2 Years
Painted wood	30 Years	3–5 Years
Stained wood & wood shingles	30 Years	3–5 Years
EIFS	20 Years	Annually
Vinyl	20 Years	3–5 Years
Cementitious plank	30 Years	3–5 Years
Windows		
Aluminum/steel windows—long-life finish	40 Years 5-Year Warranty	Annually including weather stops, glass, & hardware lubricator
Aluminum/steel windows—(field) painted finish	40 Years 20 Year Warranty	Annually including weather stops, glass, & hardware lubricator
Aluminum-clad wood	20 Years	Annually
Wood windows	40 Years	Annually including weather stops, glass, & hardware lubricator
Vinyl-clad wood	20 Years	Annually
Roof		
Slate shingles	Indefinite	Annually
Copper roofing	50 Years	Annually
Painted metal	20 Years	Annually
Fiberglass shingle	25–40 Years	Annually
Asphalt or wood shingle	20–25 Years	Annually
Built-up	20+ Years***	Twice Yearly—spring and fall, always after a major storm
Single-ply	20+ Years****	Twice Yearly—spring and fall, always after a major storm
Spray-foam system	15–20 Years	Annually (typically for repair/restoration)

* If properly maintained.

** Greater frequency may be appropriate in climates with extreme heat or cold as well as frequent freeze/thaw cycles.

***10–15–20-year warranty with two-year installer's warranty.

**** 10–15-year warranty with two-year installer's warranty.

continues

OPERATION AND MAINTENANCE

EXPECTED LIFE AND RECOMMENDED INSPECTION/MAINTENANCE CYCLES FOR MAJOR SYSTEMS (continued)		
	Approx. Expected Life Span*	Recommended Inspection/ Maintenance Cycle**
Building Systems		
Mechanical		
Incremental mechanical systems (through-wall air-conditioning units)	15–20 Years	Annually
Exterior mechanical equipment (exposed rooftop heating and air conditioning units)	15–20 Years	Quarterly
Boilers/central mechanical systems with interior mechanical rooms	25–50 Years	Annually
Piping	10–50 Years	Annually (depending on material)
Duct work	20–50 Years	Annually
Electrical	15–20 Years	Annually (limited by tech. upgrades)
Plumbing	20–50 Years	Annually
Fire protection	15–50 Years	Semi-annually
Envelope		
Foundation		
Block	Indefinite	3 Years
Concrete	Indefinite	5 Years
Structure		
Steel	Indefinite	As Required
Concrete (poured-in-place or precast)	Indefinite	As Required
Masonry bearing wall	Indefinite	As Required
Structural metal stud	Indefinite	Unless water damage
Wood	Indefinite	3 Years
Interior Envelope		
Walls		
Paint	2–4 Years	As Required
Painted wood	15–20 Years	As Required
Stained wood	15–20 Years	As Required
Vinyl wall covering	10 Years	As Required
Painted metal frame	2–4 Years	As Required
Floors		
Carpet	10-Year Warranty	Regular
Vinyl composition tile (VCT)	5-Year Warranty	Regular
Sheet vinyl	5-Year Warranty	Regular
Rubber	5–10-Year Warranty	Regular
Ceramic	10–20 Years	As Required
Wood	20–30 Years	Dust mop, broom, or vacuum daily
Stone	30–50 Years	As Required (mild soap and water)
Slate	20–30 Years	As Required (mild soap and water)
Ceilings		
Drywall	Indefinite—dependent upon use and location	Dependent on surface
Acoustic ceiling tile	10–15 Years depending upon how often ceiling is accessed	Remove surface dirt by vacuuming or light brushing

Source: Perkins Eastman Architects.

variables, but it is often important for the architects and planners to know the likely peak staffing level, which typically occurs during the day shift (often 7 A.M. to 3 P.M.). Not only is this figure useful for sizing staff lounge, locker, and related spaces, but it is also a typical question during the land-use approval stage. Most planning and zoning boards want this figure to help them assess parking needs and traffic impacts.

Even though there is great variation in staffing, day-shift staffing levels for facilities run by sponsors offering a high level of care and services are as follows[1]:

Adult day care (40–50 participants/day): 10–12 FTE

Assisted living (80–100 units): 20–25 FTE

Skilled-nursing facility (120 beds): 50–60 FTE

Skilled-nursing facility (280 beds): 100–150 FTE

Small CCRC (120–160 units): 40–50 FTE

Large CCRC (250–300 units): 100–125 FTE

Designs that reduce the required staffing without reducing the quality of service in care are becoming an important goal. It is now common for clients and their design teams to model the staffing required as one of the considerations in arriving at the preferred plan.

Technological advances and the popularity of assisted living have helped wireless communications gain a large share of the senior living market. Staff flexibility has increased, and hardwire costs to run wires from each unit to nurse call/emergency response/fire-alarm/perimeter control panels have reduced. But high-tech does not always mean increased reliability, which poses important challenges for operating costs.

It is clear that the technologies will continue to change, becoming more useful and more elaborate. In specifying these systems, the design team must take care to carefully consider the knowledge and resources of the owner, the size and location of the community where the project is being built, and the availability of backup systems. In some locations, two reliable independent systems, each doing a portion of the nurse/emergency/fire communications work, may actually produce lower long-term operating costs than one integrated system, even if the two overlap and duplicate in some areas.

CLEANLINESS, OPERATIONS QUALITY, AND DESIGN

Senior living communities are service-rich. But unlike the building, the hospitality and care service components are hard for prospective customers to see. Given that situation, families and potential residents often equate cleanliness with quality operation, and quality operation also means compassionate care and high-level hospitality. Thus, design that makes it easy to keep the community looking clean and well cared for sends the message that management provides similar service to residents.

---

[1]Source: Perkins Eastman

CHAPTER 19
COST ISSUES

INTRODUCTION

Cost management is one of the most complex tasks facing the owner and design team. No single chapter can provide a comprehensive review of this topic, but there are several general guidelines that are relevant to the effective cost management of a building program. Specifically, this chapter covers:

- An outline of the basic steps in a cost-management program

- An introduction to the relative costs of typical building systems choices

- A review of some of the nonquantitative factors that can affect the cost of a project

- A discussion of value engineering and life-cycle costing

COST-MANAGEMENT PROCESS

The core of an effective cost-management approach includes setting a realistic budget, developing regular careful cost estimates, and making adjustments to fit the design to the budget. In summary, the key components of a cost-management program are the following:

1. Retain a design team, professional cost estimator, or construction manager with proven cost-estimating and cost-management capabilities. Some owners retain all three.

2. Start the budgeting process during the initial program phase. As discussed in Chapter 2, one of the most common errors is to start a project with an unrealistic budget. An experienced team should be able to translate a space program and evaluation of building conditions into a realistic budget. In well-managed projects, this budget covers not only construction costs but also the many other expenses (fees, financing costs, land, furnishings, marketing, administration, etc.) that make up the total cost of the project.

3. Prepare detailed cost estimates at four points in the design process:
   - The end of schematic design
   - The end of design development
   - The mid-point of the construction document phase
   - The end of the construction document phase

   The earlier estimates tend to be more useful since during these stages it is easier to adjust the design to bring the building program back within budget. The greater detail of the later estimates, however, also helps identify potential budget problems, facilitates final design choices, and helps to keep the project within budget. The detailed estimates also help in the analysis of construction bids or contractor proposals to identify possible problems such as inadequate bidder interest or misunderstanding of the contract documents.

4. Make cost a factor in evaluating major design decisions. Most sophisticated owners and teams evaluate both the first cost and, as is discussed later in this chapter, the life-cycle cost inherent in the design decision.

5. Use value-engineering techniques to achieve the proper balance between cost and quality. Value engineering is often misused for cost cutting. Instead, it should be used to achieve the same program, quality, and design goals at a lower cost.

RELATIVE COSTS

Costs are always a function of local factors (local labor and material costs, contractor availability and interest, building systems required by local climate or site conditions, etc.), as well as regional and national factors. For example, in 2001 a new assisted living residence in an open-shop construction market that permits wood-frame construction could cost less than $100 per square foot, but it could cost over $180 per square foot in some high-cost urban areas with more stringent codes and the need to employ union labor.

Regardless of location, however, the choice of building systems and materials, as well as issues inherent in the site, can have a significant impact on the cost. The chart that follows is a partial comparison illustrating the relative cost of some of the common choices. This chart should be used with great caution, because costs vary significantly over time and between locations. Moreover, the choices listed are far from comprehensive.

OTHER FACTORS THAT IMPACT COSTS

Exact takeoffs of the quantities of each building component and careful unit pricing do not always ensure an accurate construction cost estimate. Care in both areas is essential, but there are many other factors that have significant effects on the final cost of construction.

Some of these factors—for example, the accuracy of the contractors' own estimators—defy prediction. Others, however, can be analyzed and to some extent quantified.

Local Construction Industry Concerns

The first set of factors, including data on population density, proximity to urban centers, and accessibility via major traffic routes, can readily indicate potential problems. The construction industry's capabilities in smaller towns can be strained by the requirements of a large project, so the estimator should take note of the work experience, sophistication, and size of local contracting firms and labor pools. Note, too, the impact of other work in the area as well as other factors, such as strong local unions.

Lack of Bidder Interest Raises Costs

Contractor interest and capabilities are often major cost considerations. Large cost overruns can occur due largely to lack of interest and competition. During an economic recession, project costs often stabilize or go down, suppliers tighten their margins, and labor relaxes overtime policies and other requirements to stay busy. When the economy recovers, however, both contractors and labor are often quick to reinstate their normal markups, overtime requirements, and other costs.

Interest is only one contractor factor; the other is experience. In small cities and rural areas, local contractors may not be able to build a complex project efficiently. Inexperienced contractors facing a complex project or unusual materials and details usually add a significant premium to their bid, if they bid at all.

RELATIVE COSTS

STRUCTURAL

Economic Costs

- Unclassified earth excavation, minimal elevation deviations (contractor takes the risk)
- Stockpiling of excavated material on-site
- Balanced cut-and-fill
- Uniform spread footings
- Continuous wall footings, nonstepped
- Concrete-block or poured-concrete foundation walls
- Concrete slab on grade
- Wood frame with wood roof trusses (if permitted by code)
- Bearing wall and simple joist roof framing

Average Costs

- Unclassified earth excavation, some variance of grade elevations
- Stockpiling of excavated materials on-site
- Balanced cut-and-fill
- Spread footings of generally uniform dimensions with some oddities
- Continuous wall footings, with stepped requirements
- Poured concrete foundation walls
- Concrete slab on grade
- Some interior foundation wall requirements
- Usually uniform baysize layouts for structural system, including variances for special conditions
- Masonry bearing wall and concrete plank construction
- Structural steel frame, with spray-on fire protection with metal deck/concrete or precast plank floors
- Generally more complicated building shape with breaks, corners, and some cantilevers
- Masonry bearing wall and plank structure
- Light-gauge metal roof trusses

Above-Normal Costs

- Classified earth excavation such as hardpan, clay, boulders, rocks, organic matter, etc.
- Great variations in grade
- Dewatering problems
- Required bracing and shoring during construction
- Unbalanced cut-and-fill resulting in need of borrowed or exported material
- Foundation complications requiring footings of varying sizes and shapes; special foundations, such as piles
- Grade-beam requirements more often than typical, continuous wall footings and foundation walls
- Structural slab not on grade
- Water-proofing of basement areas and slab surface water drainage
- Interior requirements for foundation walls and footings
- Varying bay sizes
- Complicated reinforcing concrete frame and slab; structural steel frame encased in concrete fire proofing
- Detailed precast concrete or architectural concrete or cast-stone details
- Generally complicated shaped structure requiring unique structural design solutions or considerations requiring high-caliber contractor
- Design for future expansion

ARCHITECTURAL

Economic Costs

- Simple-shaped building with minimal architectural features
- Clapboard, shingle, or vinyl exterior
- Exterior brick or block with stock window shapes, some stone-work or precast trim, low ratio of windows

Average Costs

- More complex-shaped building expressing architectural features
- Exterior, EIFS, brick, architectural concrete, larger ratio of windows, special-size windows, moderate use of stonework, cast stone, and other special exterior materials
- Use of more expensive interior finishes, such as vinyl wall coverings, especially in public areas

Above-Normal Costs

- Complex-shaped building requiring architectural treatments such as overhangs, setbacks, multilevels, etc.
- Exterior walls expressing and accentuating architectural aesthetics utilizing stonework, complex precast or architectural concrete units, special window shapes and details, high ratio of glasswork, high-quality windows with long-life finishes and low-e glass, greater use of metal alloys for trim and decorative purposes

Source: Bradford Perkins and Douglas King, Perkins Eastman Architects

continues

COST ISSUES

Economic Costs

- Residential-grade windows vinyl or aluminum clad
- Drywall partitions in most areas
- Resilient tile floors, V.C.T., standard carpet predominantly used with vinyl base.
- Suspended ceilings with 2 x 2 or 2 x 4 A.C.T. in corridors and offices
- Utilize standard millwork cabinets
- Simple pitched roofs with residential-grade shingles
- Flat roofs with parapets
- Simple waterproofing requirements
- Limited use of ceramic tile
- Simple program requirements
- Low ratio of interior work
- Wood or hollow metal doors and bucks at normal heights
- Simple stair exiting and fire-protection requirements
- Minimum provision for future flexibility
- Minimum circulation space, double-loaded corridors

Average Costs

- Resilient tile floors, V.C.T., or similar products; some custom carpeting or other more costly finishes; some painted base
- Greater requirement for hung ceilings, simple suspension system and economic use of acoustical tile
- Utilize higher-grade millwork cabinets
- Flat roofs with some setbacks on different levels; pitched roofs with complexities
- More complex waterproofing requirements
- Greater use of ceramic tile on walls and floors in toilet and wet areas
- More complex program requirements, modular design
- Greater density of interior work
- Solid wood doors and metal bucks; heights vary according to need and location
- Greater fire-protection and exiting requirements
- Modest provisions for flexibility
- More circulation space requirements
- Greater need for mechanical equipment space
- Modest use of varied materials for interior finishes
- Limited use of movable partitions

Above-Normal Costs

- Extensive use of vinyl wall coverings; stain-grade trim and base
- Greater use of hung ceilings with dry wall or high-quality 2 x 2 acoustical tile in most areas; architectural ceiling treatments with pop-ups and cove lighting
- Extensive interior custom trim
- Extensive custom millwork and cabinets
- Multilevel roofs, setbacks, penthouses, promenade decks; complicated roof shape such as standing seam roofs
- Complex damp-and-waterproofing requirements
- Ceramic tile or glazed block used on floors and walls in wet areas
- Complex program requirements for multipurpose occupancy
- High-density requirements for interior work; single-loaded enclosed corridors
- Expensive fire-protection requirements, large exiting needs
- Large circulation and public areas, single-loaded corridors
- Need for large mechanical equipment space
- Expensive vertical and horizontal transportation equipment
- Large degree of flexibility inherent in layout and design to accommodate future changes and requirements for mechanical and electrical trades
- Use of large movable partitions

PLUMBING

Economic Costs

- Gravity sanitary and storm system using PVC pipe and fittings when code permits
- Domestic hot and return water systems using submerged tankless coils in boiler

Average Costs

- Gravity sanitary and storm system using cast-iron pipe and fittings
- Sump and ejector pump systems
- Hot-water generator
- Domestic water recirculating system
- Emergency generator gas connections
- Standard plumbing fixtures
- Attic fire sprinklers

Above-Normal Costs

- Sanitary and storm systems using cast iron above and below grade
- Foundation drainage systems
- Preheater for domestic hot water
- Water treatment, if required
- Gas piping for laboratories
- Heavy central commercial kitchen work
- Fire pump

Economic Costs

- Gas-fired, self-contained HVAC units; PTAC units
- Economical toilet layouts,(i.e., typical in-line facilities)
- Fire standpipe system, if required
- Insulation for mains, risers, water lines, and horizontal storm drains in finished areas
- Economic plumbing fixtures
- Fire sprinkler system—occupied areas only

Average Costs

Above-Normal Costs

- Insulation of all domestic water and heating piping
- Luxury plumbing fixtures
- Sprinklers in all concealed spaces
- Piped oxygen and suction

HVAC

Economic Costs

- Low-pressure, one-pipe hot-water system
- Through-the-wall incremental units
- Gas-fired, self-contained HVAC units
- Ventilation of interior areas (toilets)
- Forced-air heat only
- Self-contained boiler rooms
- Limited insulation of piping and supply ductwork

Average Costs

- Central station heating and air-conditioning (single zone)
- Multizone heating and air-conditioning systems with reheat coils
- Fan coil system, two-pipe
- Water-source heat pump
- Kitchen and "simple" exhaust of spaces requiring ventilation
- Mechanical equipment rooms, including converters, chillers
- Acoustic lining
- Pneumatic controls, electronic controls
- Basic rooftop heating/cooling ventilation equipment, limited ducted distribution

Above-Normal Costs

- Four-pipe central HVAC systems
- Variable air-volume system with mixing boxes or terminal reheats
- Humidifier systems
- Dust-collection systems
- Heat reclamation
- Radiant ceilings and floors
- Snow-removal systems
- Water-treatment systems
- Boiler feed system
- Remote power plant installation
- Central station computerized monitoring for automatic temperature controls
- Sound-attenuation systems
- Design requirements for future expansion

ELECTRICAL

Economic Costs

- One main distribution panel serving simple 120/208V
- Feeders: runs feeding one or more panels at a time
- Lighting fixtures: fluorescent and few incandescent fixtures, economy products

Average Costs

- Service and panels: one main distribution board serving light and power panels. Simple 120/208V service
- Feeders: runs feeding one or more panels at a time
- Lighting fixtures: basic 2 x 2 fluorescent fixtures, few incandescent fixtures. Specialty lighting where necessary plus some architectural lighting for aesthetic purposes

Above-Normal Costs

- Service panels: 480/277V service into building, one or more freestanding main distribution board 480/120-208V transformers, subdistribution panels, light and power panels
- Feeders: multiple sets of feeders between main distribution boards and from main distribution boards to subdistribution panels. Single feeder runs from subdistribution panels to light and power panels. Possible use of bus duct for main feeders

continues

COST ISSUES

Economic Costs

- Branch circuit work: use of one light switch per average room, receptacles per code
- Motor work: individually mounted starters furnished by others
- Sound system: master amplifiers with microphone and page common to all speakers
- Emergency lighting: wall-mounted battery units with headlamps
- Security system with local audible alarm
- Hardwired emergency call system
- Central emergency call station
- Internet connection provided through telephone system

Average Cost

- Use of three-way switching. More generous employment of receptacles—both duplex and special
- Motor work: motor control center furnished by electrical contractor
- Sound system: master amplifiers with microphone and page common to all speakers
- Television system: cable or antenna amplifier and receiving outlets
- Emergency lighting system: use emergency generator and autotransfer switch feeding one emergency panel
- Security system with door alarms tied to report at a central security station
- Zone-specific wireless emergency call system
- Central emergency call station plus wireless staff pages/displays
- Dedicated Internet wiring in addition to phone system

Above -Normal Cost

- Lighting fixtures: low-glare and up/down fluorescent and PL fixtures. Specialty lighting where necessary plus some architectural lighting for aesthetic purposes. Some dimming. High-intensity lighting for special areas
- Use of three-way switching. More generous employment of receptacles—both duplex and special
- Motor work: motor control centers plus intricate interlocking and control devices, fan shutdown coupled with fire-alarm system
- Sound system: master system plus subsystems in other facilities interconnected for selective paging
- Television system: cable and/or antennas, amplifiers, and receiving outlets throughout plus program originating and sending facilities. Possible television studio
- Emergency lighting system: emergency generator plus complete system of feeders and panels to all areas
- Telephone system with features (voice mail, etc.): complete system of feeder conduits, terminal cabinets, and outlets
- Intercom telephone system: automatic exchange plus handsets
- Lightning protection
- Security system with door alarms tied to report at a central security station and connected to staff communication receivers and surveillance cameras
- Location-specific wireless emergency call system tied to the telephone system
- Central emergency call station plus wireless staff communicating phones/display
- Building-wide network for high-speed Internet connectivity
- Design for future expansion

Labor Availability and Cost

A major factor in contractor interest and capability is the local labor force. A cost estimator must know the local wage rates, shortages in critical trades, prevailing premiums necessary to obtain local labor or induce migration, trade jurisdictions, work rules with cost implications, and any other factors that can shape costs.

Availability of Materials

On some projects, material supply and cost volatility can be critical. Too often designs include materials that are either unavailable locally or unfamiliar to local contractors. In other cases, too many projects are competing for the same material. As material markets become more national this is becoming less of an issue, but it remains a key factor. In the late 1990s material shortages existed for such basic materials as sheetrock and brick.

If analysis reveals serious problems in any of the above areas, it is possible to save more money by fitting the project to local capabilities and available materials. The difference between an efficient and inefficient design might be less than 15 percent, while market conditions can add far more than that in premiums.

Potential premiums due to a busy local construction industry can also be mitigated. Expedited payment, astute selection of local materials, aggressive bidder solicitation, contractor-orientation meetings, and careful timing of bids, as well as other techniques, are being used more often to solve market problems. The first step, however, is to identify the problems.

VALUE ENGINEERING AND LIFE-CYCLE COST ANALYSIS

As noted earlier, value engineering is often confused with cost cutting. The term was coined, however, to describe a technique for seeking design options that achieve the original design objectives at a lower cost. Some owners and design teams even use a formal process to develop and evaluate value-engineering ideas. At the very least, most owners expect to see construction and operating or life-cycle cost comparisons of the major building system alternatives.

The following questions are well known in the design of facilities for the aging:

- Should the owner use low-maintenance finishes, such as vinyl wall covering, or lower first-cost finishes that require regular maintenance, such as paint?

- Should the owner install long-life light fixtures that have a higher first-cost and bulb-replacement cost to gain the benefits of the lower energy usage, reduced maintenance load, and lesser heat-gain impact on the air-conditioning?

- Will a central mechanical system (vs. a decentralized system of package units) justify a higher first cost with lower replacement, energy, and other costs?

- Should the owner use more durable exterior finishes that require more maintenance such as brick in lieu of wood siding or exterior insulation and finishing systems (EIFS)?

- Should the owner use more expensive clad or aluminum windows with a baked-on long-life finish and high-performance glass, or less expensive wood windows with clear glass that require periodic painting and involve more heating and cooling?

- Should the owner build a new more efficient building or renovate an older, less efficient building?

Finally, with value engineering or cost cutting be sure to update the drawings and recoordinate to confirm that the savings are real. For example, a common value-engineering suggestion is to lower floor-to-floor height. This can result in beam penetrations, soffits, or other measures to permit mechanical, plumbing, and fire-protection distribution that no longer fits in the ceiling plenum.

Cost management is one of the most complex parts of designing a senior housing or care facility. Virtually all projects push the budget envelope, which is almost always tight due to the complex economics of senior housing and care facilities.

CHAPTER 20

FINANCES, FEES, AND FEASIBILITY

It is hard to generalize about the funding of senior housing and care facilities, because virtually every form of financing has been used. Public/private partnerships, philanthropy, publicly offered tax-exempt bonds, and conventional construction loans and mortgages are just some of the many methods employed. Therefore, this chapter focuses on the generic steps in the process, the primary participants, and examples of some of the most common financing approaches for the most common building types.

TEN STEPS TO FINANCING
There are ten important steps that most projects go through. Completing them successfully to secure adequate financial resources to build and open the facility often takes longer than planning, programming, and design and construction documentation.

1. Assembly of core feasibility team and preliminary analysis of market, physical, and financial feasibility

2. Identification of potential sources of equity

3. Identification of potential sources of debt

4. Equity formation through fund-raising, asset allocation, or other means

5. Selection of the financing team and method of financing

6. Detailed financial and market feasibility analyses and other materials required to obtain approval from the sources of financing

7. Selection, if required, of a form of credit enhancement to make the debt saleable

8. Completion of the actions and materials required for financing

9. Closing of construction-phase financing

10. Replacement of construction-phase financing, if any, with long-term permanent financing

1. Preliminary Feasibility Analysis
The first step has already been covered in Chapter 2. It is usually a first test of the viability of a potential new facility: is there a suitable site, is there a real market, can it be financed, is it self-supporting, and so on? A feasibility consultant as well as investment bankers, a legal counselor, and an architect/planner usually assist the sponsor with this first hurdle.

2. Identification of Sources of Equity
Virtually all projects require the sponsor to commit some cash, other tangible assets, or guarantees to the financing package. The amount required varies widely based upon such variables as:

- How conservative (relatively low debt) the sponsor is

- Conditions in and perceptions of the financial markets

- The apparent feasibility of the project, including the reliability of the project's projected income

3. Identification of Potential Sources of Debt
In many states, tax-exempt bonds for senior housing can be issued by counties, cities, and municipalities. Many states and municipalities have also created entities

that can issue tax-exempt debt for senior housing and care projects, including state and local housing agencies and authorities, and industrial development bond programs. Many sponsors, both for-profit and not-for-profit, also look to traditional financing sources: banks, insurance companies, pension funds, and so on.

Each of these sources has different lending requirements. It is important to determine which ones are appropriate for the proposed project and whether their requirements (required percentage of equity, debt-coverage ratios, time to close, credit enhancement or guarantees, restrictions on admissions, rental or entry fee, etc.) are acceptable. Going too far down the road with an inappropriate source can seriously delay a project. If they have not already assembled a core financing team (see step 1), many sponsors retain investment bankers, or other financial advisers with a specialized background in senior living finance, to guide them in this step.

4. Equity Formation

The sponsor can develop very few projects without some tangible investment. This can come from an infusion of cash from the sponsor's endowment or corporate resources, limited or full guarantees of the project debt, the contribution of land, public grants, fund-raising, or some other source. The amount required varies significantly, based on the variables described in step 3 and lending requirements.

Of the sources of equity, fund-raising is one of the most complex. If the amount to be raised requires a formal campaign, professional advice should be retained. Fund-raising consultants do not raise the money; they help plan and guide the process. Many formal campaigns follow four steps:

1. A preliminary analysis to determine the fund-raising potential of the supporters of the sponsoring entity

2. Preparation of the fund-raising materials, which often include plans, renderings, cost estimates, and the answers to potential donors' questions about the need and the project itself

3. A quiet campaign among a limited list of the largest potential donors (This quiet campaign usually must raise at least a third of the project's total).

4. A full campaign to the rest of the potential donor list

5. Selection of the Financing Team and Method

Often simultaneously with the equity formation effort, the sponsor will expand the team who will guide the financing of the project. When tax-exempt bonds are used, this team can consist of a bond counsel, borrowers counsel, a financial feasibility consultant or specialist accountant, a financial adviser, the investment bank or underwriter, the underwriter's counsel, and an issuing municipality or agency for the debt. Together this team guides the sponsor through the steps and prepares the documents necessary to obtain project financing.

6. Preliminary Approval by Financing Sources

The financial team usually begins by helping direct the preparation and submission of the materials necessary to obtain a preliminary or conditional commitment from the source of financing and/or credit enhancement. Typically, a feasibility study, cost estimates, and projections that the project can achieve 95% occupancy in an acceptable period (often two years or less) generate enough cash flow to safely cover projected operating costs and debt service, and maintain adequate cash balances.

7. Credit Enhancement

Many projects financed with tax-exempt bonds are required to have credit enhancement, which is a guarantee from a government agency or financial institution that improves the credit status and saleability of the bonds. Sometimes this is accomplished by a letter of credit issued by a bank or another financial institution that guarantees the debt. In other cases, the guarantee is provided by a government entity. HUD's FHA232 mortgage insurance program is one such form of credit enhancement. The program provides credit enhancement for as much as 90–95 percent of the project value. Bank letters of credit typically provide credit enhancement for as much as 80 percent of the project value.

8. Preparing for Closing

Following preliminary approval, most sources of financing require the project team to assemble a number of items prior to closing the financing. These typically include the following:

- Complete plans and specifications

- A lump sum or guaranteed maximum construction price contract from a contractor with a performance bond

- Loan agreements, mortgages, and other financing documents that provide security to the financing source (lender or investor) and specify the terms of repayment

- When tax-exempt bonds are the source of financing, bond-offering documents for bond sales to investors

9. Closing

Once the lender's requirements have been met and documents are final, and in the case of bond financing, the bonds have been sold, the entire project team meets so that the documents can be executed and the financing can be funded.

10. Permanent Financing

If the financing is for the construction phase only and is not long-term debt, following project completion the construction financing must be replaced with long-term bonds, a mortgage, or other permanent funding. Tax-exempt bond financings often provide construction and permanent financing at the same time.

FINANCING VARIATIONS FOR SENIOR SETTINGS

As noted at the beginning of this chapter, there are many variations on the steps summarized above, and many sponsors have found unique ways to fund their building programs. Nevertheless, there are typical approaches relevant to some of the more common building types. Among these are the following:

1. Assisted Living

Many of the for-profit chains have arranged conventional financing for their building programs. In some cases they use this credit to build and operate until profitability is achieved, and then the completed project is sold to an investor group, real estate investment trust, or other entity (with the sponsor retaining the management contract) to free cash for future projects. Others have financed their building programs with the proceeds of a public stock offering or the cash generated from existing facilities.

Not-for-profits typically follow the ten steps outlined above. Some start with land and supplement their equity with fund-raising. A limited number have endowments that fund part of or the entire project. Some enter into partnerships with for-profit companies to develop and/or operate the facility.

2. Skilled-Nursing Facilities

New or renovated skilled-nursing facilities are often assumed to operate at almost full occupancy. Their revenue is typically a mixture of Medicare reimbursement, Medicaid reimbursement, and private pay, though Medicaid reimbursement is usually the predominant source of revenue. The feasibility of a skilled-nursing building program is usually gauged from detailed projections of these income sources and the expenses. Lending sources usually consider Medicaid reimbursement to be a risky source of revenue because of the possibility of states reducing their Medicaid budgets. Some nursing facilities have philanthropic support or endowment income to improve their operating statements.

3. Independent Living

The federal government has the HUD 202 program, which funds low-income housing units for seniors. HUD also provides public housing subsidies and Section 8 funding for low-income seniors. In addition, some states have subsidized housing programs for seniors with limited incomes or joint programs with HUD.

Middle- and upper-income independent living projects are typically financed using the same conventional sources as other multifamily housing developments. These projects depend largely on the financial strength of the sponsor supported by positive market and financial feasibility studies.

4. Continuing Care Retirement Communities

The structure of financing for CCRCs depends on the structure of resident fees. The most common resident fee structure is an entry fee, which can be substantial, plus a monthly service fee. The entry fee may be fully refundable when a resident dies or leaves, be partially refundable, or decline in value each month. Many CCRCs offer several entry-fee refund options.

If the CCRC is a life-care community, the entry and monthly fees typically cover the costs of the residents' care regardless of where they reside in the community (independently, with assistance in assisted living, or in the nursing center) for the rest of their lives. In other CCRCs (non-life-care), there are limits on the number of days that can be spent in the CCRC nursing facility without additional charges to the resident, and services are provided on a purely fee-for-service basis. Some CCRCs require residents to have long-term health-care insurance.

Entry-fee CCRCs have frequently been financed with little equity from the sponsor when 60-70 percent of the independent living units have been reserved with 10 percent deposits before the closing of the financing. The pre-sales demonstrate the strength of the CCRC market, and the entry fees act as a form of equity and create reserves.

GLOSSARY

Accreditation A process whereby a program of study or an institution is recognized by an external body as meeting certain predetermined standards. For facilities, these standards are usually defined in terms of physical plant, governing body, administration, and medical or other staff. Organizations that grant accreditation are usually created for the purpose of assuring the public of the quality of the accredited institution or program. The state or federal governments can recognize accreditation in lieu of or as the basis for licensure or other mandatory approvals. Public or private payment programs often require accreditation as a condition of payment for covered services.

Active adult communities Resortlike residential communities geared to younger retirees (55 years +) who are physically active.

Activities of daily living (ADLs) Basic activities that are important to self-care, such as bathing, dressing, using the toilet, eating, and getting in and out of a chair. ADLs are used to measure how dependent a person is on assistance in performing any or all of these tasks.

Acute care Care that is generally provided for a short period of time to treat a certain illness or condition.

Adult care homes Residences for aged and disabled adults who may require 24-hour supervision and assistance with personal care needs. Previously called domiciliary homes. Differ from nursing homes in the level of care and the qualifications of staff.

Adult day care This is a senior care setting that provides social interaction, medical care, and/or Alzheimer's care for a limited number of hours per day to frail physically or cognitively impaired older persons who require some supervision and care during the day but are able to reside in the general community.

Age-associated memory impairment A decline in short-term memory that sometimes accompanies aging; also called benign senescent forgetfulness. This is distinguished from dementia and Alzheimer's disease in that it does not progress to further cognitive impairments.

Aging in place A process by which individuals remain in their living environment despite the physical and/or mental decline and increased need for supportive services that may occur in the course of aging. For aging in place to occur, services should be available to respond to the individual's changing needs including physical and/or mental decline.

Alcove A small recessed space opening directly into a larger room.

Alzheimer's disease A neurological disease named for the German physician who first described it, Alois Alzheimer. This disease is marked by the development of dense deposits of neuritic plaques around the nerve cells in the brain, as well as twisted strands of fiber called neurofibrillary tangles within the nerve cells. This degeneration of brain cells produces progressive irreversible declines in memory (especially in the ability to store new memories), performance of routine tasks, time and space orientation, language and communication skills, abstract thinking, and the ability to learn and carry out mathematical calculations. Other symptoms include personality changes and impairment of judgment. Alzheimer's is the most common cause of dementia among older people, and is currently incurable, though numerous treatments have been used with varying success.

American Society for Testing Materials (ASTM) Organized in 1898, ASTM International is one of the largest voluntary standards development organizations in the world. ASTM International is a not-for-profit organization that provides a forum for the development and publication of voluntary consensus standards for materials, products, systems, and services.

Americans with Disabilities Act (ADA) A civil rights law adopted by the U.S. Congress in 1990 intended "to establish a clear and comprehensive prohibition of discrimination on the basis of disability." This law has had extensive repercussions in terms of building codes.

Assisted living A coordinated array of supportive personal and health services, available 24 hours a day, to residents who need those services in a residential setting. Promotes self-direction and participation in decisions that emphasize independence, privacy, dignity, and homelike surroundings.

Assistive devices Tools that enable individuals with disabilities to perform essential functions. These include telephone headsets, adapted computer keyboards, enhanced computer monitors, etc.

Behavioral symptoms of Alzheimer's This category of symptoms of Alzheimer's disease is particularly troublesome for caregivers. It includes wandering, pacing, agitation, screaming, and aggressive reactions.

Building codes Regulations, ordinances, or statutory requirements of a government unit relating to building construction and occupancy, generally adopted and administered for the protection of public health, safety, and welfare.

Building envelope The exterior structure of a building that separates the interior environment from the exterior environment.

Building-related illness According to the Environmental Protection Agency, the term "building-related illness" (BRI) is used to describe situations in which building occupants experience symptoms of diagnosable illness that can be attributed directly to airborne building contaminants such as lead paint or asbestos. Also known as "sick-building syndrome."

Caregiver Anyone who provides support and assistance to a physically or cognitively impaired person. This may include family members, friends, neighbors, or professionals.

Carpet backing Fabrics and yarns that make up the back of the carpet as opposed to the carpet pile or face. In tufted carpet the primary backing is a woven or nonwoven fabric in which the yarn is inserted by the tufting needles. The secondary backing is a lamination that is applied to the back of the carpet to reinforce and increase dimensional stability.

Carpet pile The visible surface of carpet consisting of yarn tufts in loop and/or cut configuration. Sometimes called "face" or "nap."

Certificate of need A certificate issued by a government body to a health-care provider who is proposing to construct, modify, or expand facilities, or to offer new or different types of health services. CON is intended to prevent duplication of services and overbedding, and to provide quality assurance. Granting of the certificate indicates that the proposal has been approved.

Chronic care Care and treatment given to individuals whose health problems are of a long-term and continuing nature. Rehabilitation facilities, nursing homes, and mental hospitals may be considered chronic-care facilities.

Chronic organic brain syndrome An alternate term for dementia or dementing illness.

Cognitive functions The mental activity by which an individual is aware of his or her environment, including all aspects of thinking, perceiving, reasoning, and remembering.

Cognitive impairment Damage or loss of intellectual or mental functioning. This may include impairment of short- or long-term memory; orientation as to person, place, or time; and deductive or abstract reasoning skills. Alzheimer's disease is the most common cause of cognitive impairment in older adults.

Color-rendering index A scale used to measure the color-rendering capabilities of lamplight: how much of the color spectrum is represented in the light and in what amounts compared to the perfect reference lamp of the same color temperature. The color-rendering index, ranging from 1 to 100, measures how well a lamp will render colors and determines the suitability of light for any given purpose.

Community-based services Services designed to help older people remain independent and in their own homes; can include senior centers, transportation, delivered meals or congregate meals, visiting nurses or home health aides, adult day care, and homemaker services.

Congregate care The precursor to assisted living, congregate care was provided as the first alternative to the extremes of custodial care and complete self-sufficiency on the spectrum of care options. Congregate care provides supportive services to accommodate the changing needs and varied populations in a residential environment for the aging. There can be broad differences between facilities with regard to size, services, staffing, and social programs.

Continuing care retirement community (CCRC) A residential community setting offering housing and health-related services for life or for a period in excess of one year that includes access to coordinated social activities, transportation, dining services, and multiple levels of health care, when and if the course of aging raises the need. May also include full or efficiency units, villas or cluster homes as well as community dining and recreational areas. CCRCs usually offer independent living, assisted living, and skilled nursing care facilities so that residents may receive the level of care they require while still "aging in place." Also referred to as "life care."

Continuum of care The entire spectrum of specialized health, rehabilitative, and residential services available to the frail and chronically ill. The services focus on the social, residential, rehabilitative, and supportive needs of individuals as well as needs that are essentially medical in nature.

Contrast The difference in brightness between light and dark areas.

Dementia An organic mental disorder characterized by a decline in cognitive functioning severe enough to interfere with a person's normal daily activities and social relationships. May include loss of memory, impairment of judgment and abstract thinking, and changes in personality.

Design development The second phase of the design process, during which the architect prepares more detailed drawings and finalizes the design plans, showing correct sizes and shapes for rooms. Also included is an outline of the construction specifications, listing the major materials to be used.

Disability The limitation of normal physical, mental, and social activity of an individual. There are varying types (functional, occupational, learning, physical), degrees (partial, total), and durations (temporary, permanent) of disabilities. Benefits are often available only for specific levels of disability, such as total or permanent.

Elevation A two-dimensional scale drawing of the three-dimensional vertical face of a building.

Environmental psychology An area of psychology that studies the relationship between human behavior and the physical environment, for the purpose of designing work or living areas.

Feasibility Likelihood of success.

Fire retardant A chemical compound used on or in textiles to reduce flammability.

Fire-rated A part of a construction (such as a wall or door) that takes a certain number of minutes to burn; usually 20, 60, or 90 minutes. Fire-rated items are often required for specific uses by building codes.

First cost The initial investment required for construction of a facility.

Flammability A product's capacity for combustion with respect to flame spread, fuel contribution, smoke generation, and other factors.

Footcandle A measure of light falling onto an area and on to a given object.

For-profit Organization or company in which profits are distributed to shareholders or private owners.

Functionally disabled A person with a physical or mental impairment that limits the individual's capacity for independent living.

Geriatric medicine The branch of medicine that deals with the diagnosis and treatment of diseases and problems specific to the aged.

Gerontology The comprehensive study of aging and the problems of the aged. Unlike geriatrics, gerontology is not limited to biological studies but also includes psychological and sociological issues.

Glare An intensely bright, blinding light.

Green architecture Sustainable or environmentally friendly architecture. See "sustainable architecture."

Home health agency A public or private organization that provides home health services supervised by a licensed health professional in the patient's home either directly or through arrangements with other organizations.

Home health care Includes a wide range of health-related services such as assistance with medications, wound care, intravenous (IV) therapy, and help with basic needs such as bathing, dressing, mobility, etc., which are delivered at a person's home.

Hospice A philosophy of care that focuses on relief of symptoms, pain control, and providing personal, emotional, and spiritual support to dying patients and their families.

Hue Color: the property of colors by which they can be perceived as ranging from red through yellow, green, and blue, as determined by the dominant wavelength of the light.

HVAC Heating, ventilation, and air-conditioning.

Independent living facility Rental units in which services are not included as part of the rent, although services may be available on-site and may be purchased by residents for an additional fee.

Intermediate care facility A nursing home, recognized under the Medicaid program, which provides health-related care and services to individuals who do not require acute or skilled-nursing care but who require care and services above the level of room and board.

Level loop A carpet construction in which the yarn on the face of the carpet forms a loop with both ends anchored into the carpet back. The pile loops are of substantially the same height and uncut, making a smooth, level surface.

Level of care (LOC) Amount of assistance required by consumers, which may determine their eligibility for programs and services. Levels include protective, intermediate, and skilled.

License/licensure Permission granted to an individual or organization by a competent authority, usually public, to engage lawfully in a practice, occupation, or activity.

Life-cycle cost A complicated mathematical calculation of the cost of a design decision over the course of its lifetime. This calculation is usually used for decisions that involve complex cost analysis, such as an HVAC system that includes both heating and cooling, with overall costs varying with season and over time.

Life care A type of contract that guarantees that CCRC residents will receive the amount of health care appropriate to their needs as they age.

Long-term care A range of medical and/or social services designed to help people who have disabilities or chronic-care needs. Services may be short- or long-term and may be provided in a person's home, in the community, or in residential facilities (nursing homes or assisted living).

Low-e glazing/Low-emissivity glass A special type of glass that has a transparent material fused to its surface that acts as a thermal mirror, reflecting heat so as not to increase the internal temperature of a building. This saves energy in the cooling season.

Medicaid (Title XIX) A joint federal and state program that provides medical care to low-income individuals. Specifics vary between states.

Medicare (Title XVIII) Federal health insurance program for persons 65 and over and some people who are disabled regardless of age. Medicare pays for skilled care in certified skilled-nursing facilities for up to 100 days following hospitalization in a calendar year. Beneficiaries are required to pay part of the bill for care after the first 20 days.

Medicare does not provide benefits for intermediate or custodial care.

Mobile care A truck equipped to provide medical exams and minor treatments.

Nonprofit/Not-for-profit An organization that reinvests all profits back into that organization.

NORCs Naturally occurring retirement communities.

Nursing facility or home Facility licensed by the state to offer residents personal care as well as skilled-nursing care on a 24-hour basis. Provides nursing care, personal care, room and board, supervision, medication, therapies, and rehabilitation.

Occupational therapy Therapy designed to help participants improve their independence with activities of daily living through rehabilitation, exercise, and the use of assistive devices.

Operating cost The cost of operating a facility. This includes staffing, utilities, maintenance, upkeep, and other continuing expenses.

Orientation An awareness of the parameters of one's immediate physical environment including time, place, and other people present, achieved through cognitive and sensory input.

Personal care Also called custodial care. Assistance with activities of daily living as well as with self-administering medications and preparing special diets.

Perspective drawing A type of drawing that gives a 3-D view of a building or space using a specific viewpoint and vanishing points.

Photovoltaic cell A semiconductor device that converts the energy of sunlight into electric energy. Also called solar cell.

Physical therapy Therapy designed to restore/improve movement and strength in people whose mobility has been impaired by injury or disease. May include exercise, massage, water therapy, and assistive devices.

Porte-cochere A roofed structure extending from the side or front entry of a building over an adjacent driveway to protect and shelter persons getting in or out of vehicles.

Power-operated vehicles (POVs) Electrically powered personal mobility vehicles often used instead of a wheelchair by nonambulatory individuals who lack the ability or have a limited ability to move by their own power.

Programming The architect and sponsor first discuss the goals, needs, and functions of the project, design expectations and available budget, pertinent building codes, and zoning regulations. The architect prepares a written statement setting forth design objectives, constraints, and criteria for a project, including special requirements and systems and site requirements.

Rehabilitation The combined and coordinated use of medical, social, educational, and vocational measures for training or retraining individuals disabled by disease or injury to the highest possible level of functional ability. Several different types of rehabilitation are distinguished: occupational, physical, speech, and others.

Resident rights In certified nursing facilities, the rights of each resident are protected by law to safeguard and promote dignity, choice, and self-determination. The Omnibus Budget Reconciliation Act of 1987 requires each nursing facility "to care for its residents in such a manner and in such an environment as will promote maintenance or enhancement to the quality of life of each resident."

Residential care The provision of room, board, and personal care. Residential care falls between the nursing care delivered in skilled and intermediate care facilities and the assistance provided through social services. It can be broadly defined as the provision of 24-hour supervision of individuals who, because of old age or impairments, need assistance with the activities of daily living.

Respite care Temporary relief for primary caregiver from the burden of caring for individuals who cannot be left alone because of mental or physical problems. This relief is provided in the home, a nursing home, or elsewhere in the community.

Schematic design The first phase of the design process, during which the architect consults with the owner to determine the requirements of the project and prepares schematic studies consisting of drawings and other documents illustrating the scale and relationships of the project components for approval by the owner. The architect also submits to the owner a preliminary estimate of construction cost based on current area, volume, or other unit costs. By the end of this phase, architectural plans and specifications should be 15–20 percent complete and generally include: a site plan, floor plans with identification of rooms, exterior elevations and cross sections, and actual gross floor area.

Section A type of drawing that cuts vertically through a building to show its interior and construction.

Senile dementia An outdated term once used to refer to any form of dementia that occurred in older people.

Senility The generalized characterization of progressive decline in mental functioning as a condition of the aging process. Within geriatric medicine, this term has limited meaning and is often substituted for the diagnosis of senile dementia and/or senile psychosis.

Senior housing developments Multi-unit apartment buildings, condominiums, cooperatives, single-family home complexes, and mobile-home parks restricted by age. Not originally planned to include activities, supportive assistance, or personal/health care.

Shared occupancy A residential or health-care unit that is shared by more than one related or unrelated individual.

Sick-building syndrome According to the Environmental Protection Agency, the term "sick-building syndrome" (SBS) is used to describe situations in which building occupants experience acute health and comfort effects that appear to be linked to time spent in a building, but no specific illness or cause can be identified. The complaints may be localized in a particular room or zone, or may be widespread throughout the building. This is distinct from building-related illness.

Site plan A drawing that shows the layout of a site including topography, vegetation, and groundwater.

Skilled care The provision of a higher level of care, such as injections, catheterizations, and dressing changes by trained medical professionals.

Skilled-nursing care Daily nursing and/or rehabilitative care that can be performed only by or under the supervision of skilled medical personnel.

Special-care unit (SCU) A long-term care facility with environmental features and/or programs designed for people with dementia; these units may also provide care for persons with head injuries or other disorders. Also, a unit within a senior housing facility specially designed to meet the needs of residents suffering from Alzheimer's disease or other dementias.

Specialized nursing units Units in a health-care setting that are organized around the delivery of care for a specific population, including those with dementia, younger adults, and those with physical disabilities.

Subacute care Short-term care provided by many long-term care facilities and hospitals that may include rehabilitation services, specialized care for certain conditions and/or postsurgical care, and other services associated with the transition between the hospital and home. Residents on these units often have been hospitalized recently and typically have more complicated medical needs. The goal is to discharge residents to their homes or to a lower level of care. Also called transitional care or postacute care.

Sundowning The tendency for the behavioral symptoms of Alzheimer's disease to grow worse in the afternoon and the evening. While the source of this term is unclear, writers have linked it to the historical term "sundowner," a person who hopes to obtain food and lodging after it is too late to perform work.

Tea kitchen/ Pullman-style kitchen A small kitchen area equipped with a sink, refrigerator, and microwave.

Tuft bind Force required to pull a tuft from a carpet.

Tufted carpet Carpet manufactured by the insertion of tufts of yarn through a carpet-backing fabric, creating a pile surface of cut and/or loop ends.

Value engineering The act of seeking design options that achieve the desired goal at a lower cost. This is not the same as cost cutting, which may include making sacrifices to save money.

Wayfinding What people see, think about, and do to find their way from one place to another. Wayfinding systems may be signs, arrows, other environmental methods, or person-to-person assistance.

Wellness A dynamic state of physical, mental, and social well-being; a way of life that equips the individual to realize the full potential of his/her capabilities and to overcome and compensate for a weakness; a lifestyle that recognizes the importance of nutrition, physical fitness, stress reduction, and self-responsibility.

Years to payback When choosing among building systems such as HVAC options with differing energy efficiencies, it is often valuable to calculate the years to payback; that is, if a more energy-efficient system is chosen, how many years it will take for the savings in utility bills to make up for the additional first-cost investment.

Zoning The control by a municipality of the use of land and buildings.

BIBLIOGRAPHY AND REFERENCES

American Institute of Architects. 1985. *A.I.A Design for Aging: An Architect's Guide.* Washington, D.C.: AIA Press.

Barry, John R., and C. Ray Wilgrove, eds. 1977. *Let's Learn about Aging: A Book of Readings.* Cambridge, Mass.: Schenkman Publishing.

Bednar, M. J. 1977. *Barrier-Free Environments.* Stroudsburg, Pa.: Dowden, Hutchinson, Ross.

Bonifazi, W. L. 1999. "Bathing the Alzheimer's Patient in Long-Term Care." *Contemporary Long-Term Care*, March, p. 56.

Brawley, E. C. 1997. *Designing for Alzheimer's Disease.* New York: John Wiley & Sons. Pp. 67, 196–197.

Briller, S., and M. P. Calkins. 2000. "Conceptualizing Care Settings as Home, Resort, or Hospital." *Alzheimer's Care Quarterly* 1 (no.1): 17–23.

Burgio, L., K. Scilley, J. M. Hardin, et al. 1996. "Environmental 'White Noise': An Intervention for Verbally Agitated Nursing Home Residents." *Journals of Gerontology Series B: Psychological Sciences and Social Sciences* 51 (no. 6): 64–73.

Byerts, Thomas O. 1979. "Toward a Better Range of Housing and Environmental Choices for the Elderly." In *Back to Basics: Food and Shelter for the Elderly*, edited by Patricia A. Wagner and John M. McRae. Gainesville: University Presses of Florida.

Carstens, Diane. 1985. *Site Planning and Designing for the Elderly: Issues, Guidelines, and Alternatives.* New York: Van Nostrand Reinhold.

Cohen, Donna, and Carl Eisdorfer. 1986. *The Loss of Self: A Family Resource for the Care of Alzheimer's Disease and Related Disorders.* New York: W.W. Norton.

Crisp, B. 1998. "Introduction." In *Human Spaces: Life Enhancing Designs for Healing, Working, and Living.* Gloucester, Mass.: Rockport Publishers.

Fries, James F. 1980. "Aging, Natural Death, and the Compression of Morbidity." *New England Journal of Medicine*, July 17.

Garg, A., and B. Owen. 1991. "Ergonomics." *AAOHN Journal* 35 (no. 11): 1353–75.

Goldsmith, Selwyn. 1976. *Designing for the Disabled.* London: RIBA Publications.

Hanser, S. B. 1996. "Music Therapy to Reduce Anxiety, Agitation, and Depression." *Nursing Home Medicine* 4 (no. 10): 286–91.

Harkness, Sarah P., and James N. Groome, Jr. 1976. *Building Without Barriers for the Disabled.* New York: Watson-Guptill.

Hiatt, Lorraine G. 1991. *Nursing Home Renovation Designed for Reform.* Boston: Butterworth Architecture.

Hoglund, J. D. 1985. *Housing for the Elderly: Privacy and Independence in Environments for the Aging.* New York: Van Nostrand Reinhold.

Howell, Sandra C. 1978. *Private Space: Habitability of Apartments for the Elderly.* Cambridge, Mass.: MIT Press.

—————. 1980. *Designing for Aging: Patterns of Use.* Cambridge, Mass.: MIT Press.

Koncelick, Joseph. 1976. *Designing the Open Nursing Home.* Stroudsburg, Pa.: Dowden, Hutchinson, Ross.

Lawton, M. Powell. 1980. *Environment and Aging.* Monterey, Calif.: Brooks/Cole.

—————. 1989. "Environmental Approaches to Research and Treatment of Alzheimer's Disease." In *Alzheimer's Disease Treatment and Family Stress: Direction for Research*, edited by B. D. Lebowita. Rockville, Md.: National Institute of Mental Health, U.S. Dept of Health and Human Services, Public Health Service. Pp. 340–62.

Lifchez, Raymond, and Barbara Wilson. 1979. *Designing for Independent Living: The Environment and Physically Disabled People.* New York: Whitney Library of Design.

Malkin, Jain. 1992. *Hospital Interior Architecture.* New York: Van Nostrand Reinhold.

Marberry, Sara O., ed. 1997. *Healthcare Design.* New York: John Wiley & Sons.

Moore, K. D., and M. Verhoef. 1999. "Special-Care Units as Places for Social Interaction: Evaluating an SCU's Social Affordance." *American Journal of Alzheimer's Disease* 14 (no.4): 217–29.

National Institute on Adult Day Care. 1984. *Standards for Adult Day Care.* Washington, D.C.: National Institute on Adult Day Care.

Pile, John F. 1988. *Interior Design.* New York: Harry N. Abrams.

Pride Institute Journal of Long-Term Home Health Care. 1984. Entire issue, vol. 3, no. 4, dedicated to Alzheimer's disease.

Proshansky, H., A. Fabian, and R. Kaminoff. 1995. "Place-Identity: Physical World Socialization of the Self." In *Giving Places Meaning*, edited by L. Groat. London: Academic Press. P. 94.

Rashchko, Bettyann. 1982. *Housing Interiors for the Disabled and Elderly.* New York: Van Nostrand Reinhold.

Regnier, V. A., ed. 1979. *Planning for the Elderly.* Los Angeles: University of Southern California Press.

—————. 1994. *Assisted Living Housing for the Elderly: Design Innovations from the United States and Europe.* New York: Van Nostrand Reinhold.

—————. 2002. *Design for Assisted Living: Guidelines for Housing the Physically and Mentally Frail.* New York: John Wiley & Sons.

Regnier, Victor, Jennifer Hamiltoon, and Suzie Yatabe. 1991. *Best Practices in Assisted Living: Innovations in Design, Management, and Financing.* Los Angeles: National Eldercare Institute on Housing & Supportive Services.

Regnier, Victor, and Jon Pyrnos. 1987. *Housing the Aged: Design Directives and Policy Considerations.* New York: Elsevier Science.

Rowe, John W., and Robert L. Kahn. 1998. *Successful Aging*. New York: Pantheon.

Schultz, D. J. 1987. "Special Design Considerations for Alzheimer's Facilities." *Contemporary Long-Term Care*, November.

Secretariat, Council of American Building Officials. 1994. American National Standard: Accessible and Usable Buildings and Facilities. A117.1, Sect 4.22, p. 16.

Sloane, P. D., V. Honn, S. Dwyer, J. Wieselquist, C. Cain, and S. Meyers. 1995. "Bathing the Alzheimer's Patient in Long-Term Care: Results and Recommendations from Three Studies." *American Journal of Alzheimer's Disease* 10 (no. 4): 3–11.

Sloane, P. D., J. Rader, A. L. Barrick, B. Hoeffer, S. Dwyer, D. Mckenszie, M. Lavelle, K. Buckwalter, L. Arrington, and T. Pruitt. 1995. "Bathing Persons with Dementia." *The Gerontologist* 35 (no. 5): 672–78.

Suchman, Diane R. 2001. *Developing Active Adult Retirement Communities*. Washington, D.C.: Urban Land Institute.

Wayne, K. 2001. "Assisted Living Review: A New Era for Regulation." *Nursing Homes*, March, pp. 64–66.

Webster, R., D. Thompson, G. Bowman, and T. Sutton. "Patients' and Nurses' Opinions about Bathing." *Nursing Times* 84 (no. 37): 54–57.

Zeisel, John, Gayle Epp, and Stephen Demos. 1977. *Low Rise Housing for Older People: Behavioral Criteria for Design*. Washington, D.C.: U.S. Department of Housing and Urban Development.

INDEX

INDEX

BUILDING TYPE BASICS FOR SENIOR LIVING:

1. Program (predesign)
What are the principal programming requirements (space types and areas)?
Any special regulatory or jurisdictional concerns?
1–25, 27–39, 41–101, 107, 138, 176, 188, 246–47

2. Project process and management
What are the key components of the design and construction process?
Who is to be included on the project team?
103–20, 248

3. Unique design concerns
What distinctive design determinants must be met? Any special circulation requirements?
121–36, 176, 188, 246–47, 261–62

4. Site planning/parking/landscaping
What considerations determine external access and parking? Landscaping?
33, 42, 60, 64, 69, 87, 126, 137–45, 153, 160–61

5. Codes/ADA
Which building codes and regulations apply, and what are the main applicable provisions?
(Examples: egress; electrical; plumbing; ADA; seismic; asbestos; terrorism and other hazards)
147–54, 163, 172, 181, 184, 218

6. Energy/environmental challenges
What techniques in service of energy conservation and environmental sustainability
can be employed?
18, 133, 151, 155–62

7. Structure system
What classes of structural systems are appropriate?
163–69, 261

8. Mechanical systems
What are appropriate systems for heating, ventilating, and air-conditioning (HVAC) and plumbing?
Vertical transportation? Fire and smoke protection? What factors affect preliminary selection?
16, 18, 35, 48–50, 61–62, 157–58, 171–76, 197–99, 217, 262–63

9. Electrical/communications
What are appropriate systems for electrical service and voice and data communications?
What factors affect preliminary selection?
133, 172, 177–91, 193, 217, 263–64

10. Special equipment
What special equipment is required, and what are its space requirements? Is security a factor?
78, 90–91, 133, 152, 193–201